WITHDRAWAL

D1223575

Policy and Performance in American Higher Education

HARVARD UNIVERSITY
GRADUATE SCHOOL OF EDUCATION
MONROE C. GUTMAN LIBRARY

Policy and Performance in American Higher Education

An Examination of Cases across State Systems

❋   ❋   ❋

RICHARD RICHARDSON, JR.

AND

MARIO MARTINEZ

The Johns Hopkins University Press
Baltimore

HARVARD UNIVERSITY
GRADUATE SCHOOL OF EDUCATION
MONROE C. GUTMAN LIBRARY

X101649

LC
173
.R53
2009

© 2009 The Johns Hopkins University Press
All rights reserved. Published 2009
Printed in the United States of America on acid-free paper

2   4   6   8   9   7   5   3   1

The Johns Hopkins University Press
2715 North Charles Street
Baltimore, Maryland 21218-4363
www.press.jhu.edu

Library of Congress Cataloging-in-Publication Data

Richardson, Richard C.
Policy and performance in American higher education :
an examination of cases across state systems /
Richard Richardson, Jr., and Mario Martinez.
p. cm.
Includes bibliographical references and index.
ISBN-13: 978-0-8018-9161-8 (hardcover : alk. paper)
ISBN-10: 0-8018-9161-2 (hardcover : alk. paper)
1. Education, Higher—United States. 2. Higher education and state—
United States—States—Case studies. 3. Education, Higher—United
States—States—Case studies. I. Martinez, Mario, 1967– II. Title.
LC173.R53 2009
378.73—dc22   2008037852

A catalog record for this book is available from the British Library.

Special discounts are available for bulk purchases of this book.
For more information, please contact Special Sales at 410-516-6936 or
specialsales@press.jhu.edu.

The Johns Hopkins University Press uses environmentally friendly book
materials, including recycled text paper that is composed of at least
30 percent post-consumer waste, whenever possible. All of our book
papers are acid-free, and our jackets and covers are printed on paper
with recycled content.

May 22, 2009

Contents

Foreword

The knowledge-based global economy, demographic shifts, and intensified economic and educational competition have converged over the past decade to raise the salience of higher education performance as a public policy concern for state and national governments. The "flat" world economy rewards individuals, communities, states, and nations that succeed in developing human talent—particularly college-level knowledge and skills—and it relentlessly penalizes the undereducated. Postsecondary education and training are necessary for both individual opportunity and national economic competitiveness. As governments have come to understand the advantages of higher levels of educational attainment for larger proportions of their populations, college access and completion rates have increased dramatically in most market-economy countries.

For the United States, although higher education accountability is a perennial public policy issue, the emphasis on performance is relatively recent. The aftermath of World War II saw two critically important changes in state and federal higher education. The first was the continuation of federally supported research and development at major universities. Largely justified by the public priority of national defense, federal support broadened to cover advanced education in almost all disciplines. The second was the unprecedented growth of enrollments as returning veterans benefited from the GI Bill. For many years, public and institutional priorities were closely aligned within a consensus that the priorities for higher education policy were growth, expansion, capacity building, and, for the states, institutional support. In this context, accountability focused, appropriately I believe, on inputs and resources—dollars, students, faculty, and the like.

This alignment of goals, or consensus, through much of the second half of the twentieth century contributed to an approach to public accountability that was highly deferential to the academic community. Examples include the acceptance of input measures to act as proxies for quality, and governmental reliance on institutionally controlled accreditation instead of more direct measures of effectiveness. Most of the current state structures for higher education governance and decision making were established in the last half of the twentieth century, and many have not yet been adapted to the present one. The principal contemporary public policy concern is influencing the performance of colleges and universities, not building new capacity.

Although standard of living and economic competitiveness rely on postsecondary education participation and degree attainment, this vital dependence is less visible than university research and development. While public support for higher education access is consistently high, the most direct beneficiaries of increased opportunity—students and their families—are not an identifiable pressure group. However, many state and federal leaders, well aware of the challenges of the global marketplace, have focused energetically, if not always effectively, on higher education performance. This is reflected in the development, revision, and restructuring of many state accountability systems and in the recent National Commission on Higher Education that made performance and public accountability the centerpiece of its policy recommendations.

In developing performance-based approaches to public accountability, policy leaders have come to recognize that colleges and universities can perform at a high level in ways that compete with, or at least fail to effectively address, public priorities. In fact, there is a growing mismatch between institutional aspirations and public needs. Institutions often seek higher prestige rankings, enlarged levels of expenditures, and enhancement of their institutional missions (*mission creep*); the nation and the states need more Americans with greater levels of postsecondary knowledge and competence—the *public agenda* for increased rates of access and attainment. As this gap between institutional and public agendas has widened, it has led to divergent concepts of quality and institutional effectiveness that are sometimes masked as differences over performance indicators, measurement, and assessment. There is less consensus now among public policy leaders and the professional academic community than in the past on the outcomes and performance government expects of colleges and universities.

In this book, Richard Richardson, Mario Martinez, and their colleagues have addressed the central contemporary higher education policy issue: the influence of public policy on higher education performance. Their state case studies are a rich and rigorous basis for their analysis of the linkages and the disconnections between policy and performance. The comparative focus on the *rules in use* and the influence of these on key actors and on state higher education performance offers a powerful framework for interpreting the case studies. Their findings and conclusions will challenge practitioners seeking to improve state policy. This is a bold, innovative, and groundbreaking contribution to higher education policy, one that is certain to shape future research in this field.

Patrick M. Callan
President
National Center for Public Policy
and Higher Education
San Jose, California

Preface

This book grew out of a larger study involving research teams in Canada, the United States, and Mexico, which examined links between policy and performance over a seven-year period. While we focus on the U.S. experience, our insights and conclusions were informed by frequent exchanges with our colleagues in Canada and Mexico as well as by the challenges of trying to agree on how to conduct studies of this type across international boundaries. We owe a debt to the many policy leaders and advisors whose active contributions made the project possible.

In September 1999, the Ford Foundation funded the Alliance for International Higher Education Policy Studies (AIHEPS), a three-year collaboration between researchers at New York University and the Centro de Investigación y Estudios Avanzados in Mexico City to extend the ideas described in the book *Designing State Higher Education Systems for a New Century* (Richardson et al. 1999) and apply them in new settings. A central objective of the Alliance was to improve our understanding of how national and state policies are linked to the performance of higher education systems and to make this information available to policy audiences.

The AIHEPS project developed an initial framework based on previous studies of higher education systems in seven U.S. states (Richardson et al. 1999), systems theory (Easton 1953), and the institutional economics of Douglass North (1990). This framework was used to guide studies of the federal higher education enterprise in Mexico and the United States and to organize case studies of two states in each country. The first three years of the project produced federal reports for the United States and Mexico, two state case studies for each nation, and a conceptual framework. This phase of the U.S. project culminated in a roundtable that brought together researchers and policy leaders to discuss conclusions and implications. The resulting report, *Purposes, Policies, Performance: Higher Education and the Fulfillment of a*

State's Public Agenda, was published by the National Center for Public Policy and Higher Education (2003).

In 2002, the Ford Foundation agreed to fund AIHEPS for an additional three years. The Autonomous University of Puebla became the home for the Mexican team, and the collaboration was expanded to include a research team at the University of British Columbia, with responsibilities for replicating the Mexican and U.S. work within a Canadian context. This second phase of the project made use of the framework produced during the first three years while concurrently aiming to create a more refined and improved framework linking policy to performance.

During years four through six of the project, case studies were initiated in the states of California, New York, and South Dakota, and in the Canadian provinces of British Columbia, Ontario, and Quebec. The Mexican team initiated studies of the states of Nuevo León and Puebla while concurrently dedicating their efforts to developing more comprehensive and reliable indicators of higher education performance for that nation. Within the United States, the earlier studies of New Jersey and New Mexico were updated, and the U.S. federal report was revised and expanded. While we conducted the case studies, we also worked to further refine the conceptual framework, which in turn helped us think about how to understand and explain the available evidence.

Fostering dialogue between researchers and policy leaders has been an important objective of the project since its inception. Policy leaders in each of the case study states read products from the research team and met with them to provide feedback and corrections. A final project meeting brought together policy leaders, researchers, and experts from all three nations. The focus of the meeting was on combining research with perceptions that were based on the practitioners' experience, and distilling from them how *rules in use* (defined as both formal and informal policies and related constraints and incentives) influence performance. Throughout the project, "real-world" input was as important to the conclusions of the study as the formal, systematic analysis of policy and performance data. We also attempted to take into account historical events that influenced current policy or performance in the states.

This book owes a great deal to two related streams of policy effort. The first was the work of the National Center for Public Policy and Higher Education, formerly known as the California Higher Education Policy Center. In particular, the support and encouragement of Pat Callan and Joni Finney, coauthors of *Designing State Higher Education Systems for a New Century*, helped us as we wrote the book. The second stream involves our colleagues at NYU, Ann Marcus and Teboho Moja, who in 1998 with Claus Moser and others convened a Ford-sponsored meeting in Florence to consider how higher education systems could learn from one another across international boundaries. Out of that meeting came the proposal for our study.

This work was supported in part by a grant from the Ford Foundation. We wish to extend a special thanks to Jorge Balán who, as our Ford Foundation program officer, participated in a number of the project meetings, providing his valuable perspective as a scholar.

We are also indebted to the many state and institutional policy leaders who supported the effort by providing interviews and documents and by participating in project sessions. We are particularly appreciative of those who organized the gatherings, cajoled colleagues into meeting with us, critiqued drafts of case studies, and in other ways provided their expert insights. Included among this group are Selma Botman, Murray Haberman, Bruce Hamlett, Carlos Hernandez, Jeanne Oswald, Tad Perry, John Porter, and James Sulton. Paul Lingenfelter and David Longanecker provided a national perspective for both the first and second phases of our project.

No work of this scope can possibly be the product of just one or two persons. We were fortunate to be part of a research team whose individual efforts are recognized in many places in the book. In keeping with the interests of the Ford Foundation in funding the project, many were doctoral students who served as graduate assistants or affiliated themselves with our effort in less formal ways. Others were colleagues who helped with specific phases of the work. We acknowledge with gratitude the contributions of Tom Carton, Alicia Hurley, Michael Klein, Maria Martinez, Shaila Mulholland, Tara Parker, Anne Prisco, Anely Ramirez, Christine Shakespeare, Nancy Shulock, Robert Teranishi, and Tom Smalling. Tara Parker and Christine Shakespeare were instrumental in the collection of data for the New York report. Robert Teranishi and Shaila Mulholland contributed to an early version of the California case study. Shaila Mulholland and Christine Shakespeare also wrote a valuable synthesis of the policy research literature.

We are especially grateful to Rollin Kent of the Autonomous University of Puebla and to Don Fisher and Kjell Rubenson of the University of British Columbia for their insights, patience, good humor, and thoughtful comments throughout the study. The report of the Canadian study, *Canadian Federal Policy and Postsecondary Education*, was published in 2006 by the Centre for Policy Studies in Higher Education and Training at the University of British

Columbia. The book *Las Políticas de Educación Superior en México durante la Modernización: Un Análisis Regional* (Kent, 2009) reports the results of the Mexican study.

Finally, we are grateful to two anonymous readers who peer-reviewed the manuscript and offered valuable suggestions to streamline and strengthen our message.

Policy and Performance in American Higher Education

CHAPTER ONE

Strengthening the Policy–Performance Connection

❖

Contemporary higher education systems operate in a dynamic policy environment. The ongoing quest for equal opportunity must increasingly compete against initiatives aimed at improving quality, which is often defined by an institution's share of high-achieving students and internationally prominent faculty. The rise of market economies fuels state and national concerns about economic competitiveness in a global environment, while labor force preparation and research and development remain high on most policy agendas. Cutting across all of these priorities are persistent calls for improved performance and institutional accountability, all operating with the threat and often the reality of diminishing public support.

The call for responsive and high-performing institutions is not new. For the last several decades, state governments have implemented widely different strategies in efforts to shape the outcomes of their higher education systems. Merit aid for students, a relatively new approach, has found favor across many states in the past ten years. Accountability initiatives—in the form of required reporting and performance funding—have furnished other examples of state-led efforts to improve college and university performance. Although the diffusion and implementation of a given policy may vary by state, policymakers will continue to search for new ways of influencing public and private institutions of higher education to pursue priorities defined to be in the public interest.

Traditional solutions persist as well. A host of scholars have either described governance arrangements or chronicled the many attempts to change them, reflecting ongoing efforts to influence outcomes. For the latter part of the twentieth century, scholars mostly advocated organizational autonomy as a defense against political or bureaucratic intrusion. But despite the extensive rhetoric, the trend in the United States over the last fifty years has been toward increased state coordination and control. Still, governance changes across states remain contentious. In the 1990s, policymakers in states such as Minnesota and Illinois successfully changed their structures (Minnesota toward more centralization, Illinois toward greater decentralization), but as recently as 2005, policymakers in Arizona and Maine encountered insurmountable resistance to proposed governance changes and abandoned their efforts. The absence of evidence linking governance arrangements to specific outcomes may account for the inconsistent patterns of change across states.

Policy leaders hope that through the implementation of purposeful change, colleges and universities will achieve those positive outcomes most essential to the public interest. While few would argue against goals like improved access and lower costs, there are often preferences for competing goals, as well as differences of opinion about which policies best achieve specified ends. Often the prescriptions offered by policymakers differ from the judgments of professionals who work within higher education. Divergent beliefs about which policies produce desired outcomes arise in part because a given outcome is often attributable to multiple policies, acting and interacting over time across different actors.

Further complicating the connection between state higher education policies and outcomes is the impact of such contextual influences as demographics, economics, geography, and a state's history. Context obviously affects the outcomes achieved by a state's higher education system. In its inaugural report card of state-by-state higher education performance, the National Center for Public Policy and Higher Education (2000) indicated that about 25 percent of the distribution of its report card grades was associated with factors such as wealth and income, and about 10 percent with race and ethnicity. These figures are clues that contextual variables like demography and socioeconomic status influence outcomes, but policy also plays a role.

The lack of definitive evidence about the role and impact of policy acts as a deterrent to informed public debate about the levels of performance for which higher education institutions can reasonably be held accountable at given levels of public support. One of our major goals in this book is to remove some of that mystery. In this volume we use comparative case studies of California, New Jersey, New Mexico, New York, and South Dakota to identify rules in use that state policymakers can control and that influence performance in predictable directions. We define *rules in use* as the norms and behavior patterns adopted by professionals to achieve preferred goals within the constraints of changing and sometimes conflicting policies (North 1990).

The five case study states were not in any way chosen to represent U.S. higher education. But they do reflect the continuum of state differences in governance arrangements, size, use of the private sector, and performance. In combined populations they account for more than one-fifth of all U.S. higher education. The diversity and scope of the five states represent a reasonable starting point for identifying rules in use that influence performance.

We discuss how the rules in use at federal, state, and institutional levels shape performance outcomes, with a focus on state-level rules that are malleable. We suggest actions that states might take to influence higher education systems to pursue outcomes consistent with public priorities. Our argument is simple: if higher education systems are not achieving preferred goals, then policymakers should change the rules. In this book we identify rule changes that offer hope for improving performance on the indicators of undergraduate preparation, participation, and completion (i.e., persistence and degree attainment).

Below, we briefly review state higher education policy research and the more general policy literature that influenced our work. Next, we present the conceptual framework that emerged from the dynamic interplay between the literature and the case study work. This conceptual framework identifies federal, state, and institutional rules that bear on higher education performance. We identify trends in federal rules that influence state and institutional actions and then provide a synopsis of the state and institutional rules found in the study states. We conclude with an overview of the performance indicators used in our study, followed by a description of the organization of the remainder of the book.

STATE HIGHER EDUCATION POLICY RESEARCH

Policy research in higher education has largely concentrated on issues of governance and finance. The study of financial aid currently dominates the landscape, as scholars have taken a particular interest in examining need- and merit-based state aid programs (St. John, Musoba, and Simmons 2003); loans and grants (Hauptman 1997); and the effects of different types of aid on different populations (Heller 1999). Some efforts have examined state funding in general (Callan and Finney 1997), and a few have concentrated on the effects of state appropriations on enrollments (Hossler et al. 1997). Others, like Robst (2001), have looked at how reductions in state appropriations affected institutional efficiency. Burke's writings (Burke 2005; Burke and associates 2002; Burke and Modarresi 2000) concentrate on performance funding and primarily describe problems and promising prospects associated with this strategy.

The literature on governance has a long descriptive history, with conflicting opinions about the desirability of centralization and its impact on institutions. Glenny's (1959) groundbreaking work led to the establishment in Illinois of what was known as the "system of systems," a somewhat centralized version of a federal model. It also influenced efforts to bring greater cohesion to higher education in California through the creation of a coordinating commission, although this commission has yet to achieve the authority vested in the Illinois Board of Higher Education. Governance changes in the mid-1990s in Illinois preserved most aspects of Glenny's model but dismantled two systems in favor of individual governing boards for the institutions involved. Moos and Rourke (1959) spoke against regulation and its impact on institutional autonomy. Berdahl (1971) and Millet (1984) articulated the purpose of governance structures in studies of higher education autonomy and state regulation. McGuinness, Epper, and Arrendondo (1994) established a widely used classification scheme for identifying the various governance structures for all fifty states, which the Education Commission of the States continues to update periodically.

Some research on governance has charted reform efforts (Marcus 1997), but studies that have sought to explore the relationship between governance and performance have produced mixed results. Volkwein (1989) found the degree of state regulation unrelated to administrative expenditures. Lowry (2001) associated more centralization with higher tuition, while Hearn, Griswold, and Marine (1996) concluded just the opposite. In another study, Hearn and Griswold (1994) found that, in general, centralized governance structures were linked with more innovative policy, but a study by McLendon, Heller, and Young (2001) found no relationship between centralization and innovation in state financing. As the literature on state higher education policy has matured, its focus has been on investigating possible ties between governance structures and performance. The findings are mixed, but they establish a precedent for thinking about how policy influences performance.

The work by Richardson et al. (1999) is perhaps the most ambitious effort to develop a conceptual framework for state higher education policy and performance using research from the higher education domain. It really represents the starting point for our book. The researchers conducted intensive case studies in seven large states to examine the relationship between state-level policy, governance, and the performance of each state's higher education system. Comparative work is both rare and significant, especially in light of McLendon's assertion (2003, p. 93) that case studies of higher education governance and policy are largely single-case studies, with virtually no comparative designs.

Richardson et al. (1999) concluded that the performance of higher education systems is influenced significantly by environments and system designs, both of which are established through policy actions taken over time. *Policy environments* are determined by the roles states adopt in trying to find an appropriate balance between the values and preferences of those who lead and staff colleges and universities and the demands of other stakeholders who rely on higher education services. As providers, states build and maintain institutions under the assumption that the professionals who staff them will incorporate the interests of other stakeholders into the services they provide. As regulators, states determine the services institutions are expected to provide, specify those eligible to receive the services, control prices, and constrain the uses to which available resources can be put. As consumer advocates, states rely less on regulation and instead strengthen the role of market forces by redirecting some funding from institutions to students. As helmsmen, states steer by structuring the market for higher education services in ways that support public priorities. The policy environment in any state is the product of historical compromises that follow no single pattern, with the large number of incremental decisions taken by different actors over time producing more of a patchwork quilt. Colleges and universities experience the greatest degree of autonomy where the predominant state role is that of provider. This may also be the arrangement least likely to produce progress toward public priorities when higher education professionals have other preferences.

System design encompasses the number and type of colleges and universities; the missions assigned to each; the characteristics and powers of agencies in the interface between government and institutions; the number, capacity, and diversity of academic programs; and the use that was made of the private sector. Richardson et al. (1999) characterized system designs in U.S. states as segmented, unified, or federal. Colleges and universities in *segmented systems* experience the most autonomy. They have individual governing boards and typically work directly with state government on such issues as budgeting and program duplication. In *unified systems*, a consolidated governing board oversees all public colleges and universities and serves as the single focal point for interactions between higher education and state government. *Federal systems* incorporate an interface agency (commonly titled a coordinating board) with specific responsibilities for representing the public interest in college and university decision processes related to budgeting, program review and approval, mission assignments, and the collection and dissemination of information about performance.

Richardson and his colleagues attempted to connect components within their framework to the outcomes of a particular type of higher education system. Unified, bureaucratic higher education systems were more likely to engage in planning and less likely to provide information that supported such planning to those outside the system. In addition, high-cost systems (measured as appropriations per full-time-equivalent, or FTE, student) did not necessarily produce more access, but lower-cost systems tended to limit student choice by requiring a majority of first-time freshmen to enroll in a community college. Finally, affordability seemed to fare best in states where it was obvious that a public entity (other than a governing board or a branch of state government) took responsibility for addressing issues that affected the prices institutions charged.

APPROACHES TO STUDYING POLICY

Ostrom differentiates among frameworks, theories, and models (1999, pp. 39–41), and we use the following definitions throughout our book. A *framework* helps to identify both the elements and the relationships among elements that should guide the analysis of all types of institutional arrangements. Our work was conducted using a variant of the institutional analysis and development (IAD) framework, which we elaborate on below. A *theory* makes assumptions and identifies the elements of a framework that have particular relevance for answering questions that are focused on diagnosing phenomena, explaining processes, and predicting outcomes. Competing theories are typically compatible with any framework. Our study concludes with theoretical propositions about the rules in use that most strongly influence performance for the variables we examined. A *model* makes precise assumptions about the variables that are related to a limited set of outcomes. However, our data did not lend itself to the construction of models.

Among the various frameworks used to study the policy process for higher education (see, for example, Kingdon 1984; Schlager 1995; Heck 2004), four had particular relevance to our goals: policy stages, system frameworks, multiple streams, and institutional analysis and development. The *stages* approach to policy analysis focuses on the identification of an ordered sequence of stages, or steps, in a specific policy. Also called the *linear model*, it is one of the most influential frameworks for understanding the policy process, particularly among American scholars (Sabatier 1999). This framework identifies the initiation, examination, selection, implementation, and continuation or elimination of policy. The policy stages framework was helpful in our study because it disaggregates the policy process into digestible components. In some states in our study—most noticeably South Dakota, with its small system and unified governing board—the policy stages approach seemed quite applicable, in that policymakers and higher education leaders were very systematic in the initiation and eventual implementation of a given policy. Others, like New York and California, have large and complex systems, and the events leading to a given higher education policy are quite convoluted, or even intentionally opaque. The policy stages approach in states such as these had limited usefulness for our purposes.

Easton's (1953) *systems framework* focuses on political activity in describing the elements of a social system, the interactions that take place within the system (among both individuals and groups), and the environment in which the system is located. Environmental demands and stresses become policy inputs, which are converted within the political system into policy outputs, which are then fed back into the environment. Systems theory suggests that the system is distinguishable from the environment in which it exists, yet open to influences from it. Variations in the structures and processes within a system may be interpreted as positive, alternative efforts by members of a system to regulate or cope with environmental and internal stresses. The capacity of a system to persist under stress is a function of the presence and nature of the information and other influences that affect decision making—that is, *feedback*. Feedback, and constant input into the system, hold the potential to influence either the entire system or individual elements within it.

The inputs and feedback into a higher education system may be uniform across elements, but they are often interpreted and acted upon in very different ways. Federal loan, tax, and aid policies act as both input and feedback in varying ways across the fifty U.S. states. The same federal policies have differential impacts, because some states purposefully alter their policies to take maximum advantage of incentives and constraints while others, perhaps guided more by ideological than practical considerations, do not. Colorado, Vermont, Ohio, and Pennsylvania, for example, have captured a greater share of federal monies by raising tuition prices in response to federal policies (Alexander 2006).

The *multiple streams* (MS) framework places its main emphasis on the role of actors, particularly in the agenda-setting process. Departing from Easton's systems model (1953), MS focuses on the process of transforming inputs into outputs. MS examines policy choice under conditions of ambiguity and provides insight into three important questions (Zahariadis 1999, p. 73). First, how is the attention of policymakers rationed? Second, how are issues framed? And third, how and where is the search for solutions and problems conducted?

Central to the MS framework is the *garbage can model of choice* (Cohen, March, and Olsen 1972) and the idea of *streams*. The garbage can model of choice describes educational decision making as a "garbage can" with uncertain goals, fluid participation, unclear technology, and uncertain outcomes. Unlike rational models of organizational decision making, educational decision makers may not act on the basis of their preferences, but rather discover their preferences through acting (Heck 2004).

Kingdon (1984) identified three streams flowing through the system: problems, policies, and politics. Each stream has its own rules and makes dynamic contributions to the agenda-setting process. The problem stream recognizes that sometimes attention to a problem is influenced by a more-or-less systematic indicator of a problem, while at other times it is impacted by a dramatic event that focuses attention on or highlights feedback from the operation of an existing program. In the higher education community, for example, the *Measuring Up* report card is used by policymakers to assess and compare higher education performance on a state-by-state basis (NCPPHE 2006).

The MS framework brings the dynamic, fluid, and often unpredictable nature of policy to the fore. The problem, policy, and political streams in this framework aptly capture the complexity embedded in states like California and New York, where there are many competing actors (individuals, groups, and organizations) hoping to set or change the higher education policy agenda. The level of complexity in California and New York cannot be adequately presented in a linear model, where substantively autonomous higher education systems with different structures exist within a domain of active citizenry and high-profile leaders. Conclusions about causality are confounded when one considers the accurate depictions of policy and policymaking offered by the

MS framework. In deference to this framework, our analysis does not advance causal claims (or models) but instead offers theoretical propositions that stem from careful and systematic comparisons of the five case study states.

The *institutional analysis and development* (IAD) framework identifies multiple levels of policy decision making (Ostrom 1999). At each level, a nested structure of rules within rules guides the interactions and decisions of higher education actors through the use of incentives and constraints. The strength of the IAD, for our purposes, involves its capacity to integrate the work of researchers from different disciplinary and policy perspectives. The IAD framework also focuses on how the rules of the game influence the incentives confronting individuals and their subsequent behaviors (Ostrom, Gardner, and Walker 1994; Ostrom 1999).

At national, state, and institutional levels, different combinations of actors make decisions about higher education services, clients, and goals based in part on perceptions of the constraints, incentives, and resources flowing from decisions reached elsewhere in the system. The IAD framework stresses the notion that rules in use are the most important independent variables in institutional analysis, because these rules ultimately determine the behaviors of actors and, subsequently, the resulting performance. Performance, in turn, provides feedback for the entire system, at all levels. Information plays a key role in the timing of feedback and how it is communicated to the various actors.

The concept of multiple levels of analysis is particularly important to our study of higher education systems, given the analytical challenges posed by our decision to collect information from varying levels of government and different sets of higher education institutions. The IAD framework simplified our task of studying state rules in use while concurrently taking into account the influence of relevant federal and institutional factors, without addressing all of the variables that might be linked to performance.

CASE STUDIES

We chose to look in depth at five states—California, New Jersey, New Mexico, New York, and South Dakota—and interviewed higher education leaders at the institutional and system levels, as well as elected officials or their representatives. We also talked to city officials, state assembly and senate members or their staffs, representatives from the governor's office in each of the states, and representatives from other state agencies. In addition, we made extensive use of documents and websites. The narrative description of each state's higher education system follows a common design, derived from the conceptual framework reported in the next section of this chapter.

After the narratives were completed, we asked key actors in each state to review the descriptions for their state to identify errors or omissions. Suggestions from these readers were incorporated into revised case studies, and the results were shared with a representative group of policy leaders in each of the five states. We convened meetings of representative policy actors in each state to review the final case studies and determine whether our perceptions of the rules in use matched those of the internal actors.

CONCEPTUAL FRAMEWORK

Understanding how state policies and the related rules in use influence higher education performance poses daunting challenges for practitioners and researchers alike. There are multiple intervention strategies and complex contextual variations. The effectiveness of any specific strategy to improve such outcomes as student preparation, participation, or completion may require at least a decade to evaluate. The reporting timelines for performance indicators further extend the period required to assess policy impacts. In the meantime, governors and legislators are replaced by successors who may not share earlier commitments and priorities. New policies emerge without much consideration of their potential impact on continuing policies. The results are frustrating to policymakers, who want to see outcomes change in desired directions, and to researchers, who would like to be able to report with conviction whether or not meaningful change occurred because of a specific policy change.

A major challenge for this project was the development of a conceptual framework to guide our study in comparing relationships between rules in use and the performance of higher education systems. We began by defining policy decisions as efforts to alter "the written or unwritten rules of the game or, more formally . . . the humanly devised constraints that shape human interaction" (North 1990, p. 73). Rules are created and revised through a political process that brings together, depending on the issue, a shifting array of actors representing international agencies, federal and state governments, the higher education community, and special interest groups. Rules help define the ways in which higher education goods and services are developed and exchanged by altering the relative strength of market forces, state regulation, and institutional autonomy (B.S. Clark 1998; B.R. Clark 1983; Dill 1997; North 1990; Williams 1995). Rules in use can be observed in federal, state, and institutional contexts as actors engage in policy formation and implementation.

This way of thinking about policy influences relied heavily on insights from the IAD approach, as well as on our own previous work. Like the IAD framework, our conceptual lens, the Alliance for International Higher Education Policy Studies (AIHEPS) framework, utilizes the perspective of North (1990) and related writers in the new institutional economics tradition, such as B.S. Clark (1998). Both also subscribe to the notion of bounded rationality as the most appropriate way of conceptualizing the behaviors of actors. Ostrom contends that actors "are intentionally rational but only limitedly so . . . Information search is costly, and the information-processing capabilities of human beings limited" (1999, p. 46). She adds that actors make mistakes in choosing strategies, but over time they acquire greater understanding and make choices that improve returns, thus reflecting a concern for public well-being in addition to self-interest.

The power of the levels-of-analysis approach inherent in the IAD framework is its capacity to focus on the state level without ignoring the reality that performance is influenced by rules in use elsewhere in the system. To the extent that they are known, rules in use at these other levels become part of the larger context and are described in the case study narratives. Actors, rules, and performance all operate in a dynamic system, but one that is coherently organized under a modified lens of the IAD framework.

The IAD also conceptually clarifies the nature and function of rules in use as the most important and malleable independent variables in studying performance, because they ultimately determine the behaviors of actors, who can be either individuals or groups. Rules in use reflect informal norms and established patterns of responding to threats and opportunities, as well as formal policies such as statutes and agency regulations. They cannot be inferred from legislation or regulations alone; they must be determined by fieldwork, including interviews, observations, and the study of documents and artifacts. Linking operational decisions in *action situations*—such as planning, program review, and resource allocation—to rules in use and then to performance allowed us to make the critical connections between policies and performance that we sought in our project.

Figure 1.1 presents the conceptual framework that serves as the organizing structure for our five case studies. This framework proposes that rules in use are central to a higher education system and its performance. Policymakers and their associated administrative agencies establish, alter, or reinforce the rules of the game to accomplish given priorities. Differences in state effort (defined as the level of tax support for higher education) also influence performance. Professionals in colleges and universities adopt the behaviors they believe are most likely to further organizational goals (which may or may not coincide with state-level goals) under the prevailing rules of the game. Feedback from performance at both state and federal levels leads to rule changes as governments seek to achieve the performance outcomes they prefer. The capacity to change rules varies among state and federal governments and is an important factor in explaining differences in the performance of higher education systems (Grindle 1996). Institutional rules are bounded by state rules and both, in turn, nest in overarching federal rules. Because education is a state responsibility, states have a choice about the degree to which the rules they establish are coordinated with those of the federal government.

Our conceptual framework is a starting point to begin linking rules to performance. The interaction between rules, actors, behaviors, and performance certainly is dynamic and complex. However, the current absence of empirical tools connecting higher education policy to performance heightens the need to use this framework as a foundation for examining that relationship. In the sections that follow, first we look at the context for state and institutional rules established by federal policies. We then consider some differences in state and institutional rules among our case study states, as a way of elaborating the idea of the nesting effect of these differing policy levels. Finally, we provide and summarize the effort and performance variables, including how these terms were operationalized for the purposes of this study.

Federal Context and Rules in Use

Federal rules exert an influence on both individual institutions and entire state higher education systems. This influence takes many forms, ranging from structuring conditions to create higher education markets to the practice of using rules and regulations to encourage collaboration and behaviors that move institutions and systems toward national priorities. During the past thirty years, the most enduring federal initiatives have centered on access and equity, with a gradual shift in emphasis from providing opportunities for the victims of previous discrimination to a much broader focus on keeping the entire range of U.S. postsecondary institutions reasonably affordable for the middle class. The mechanism for pursuing these initiatives, need-based

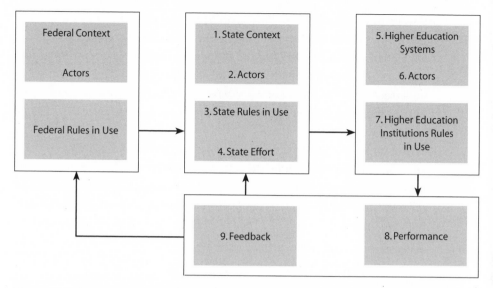

Figure 1.1. A framework for comparing state higher education systems. While this figure includes the federal context and actors, we have numbered only state contexts and actors to reflect their primary role in our analysis.

grants and loans targeted to individual students, has fostered a competitive market for higher education services open to any public or private, profit or nonprofit institution willing and able to play by federal rules. National concerns about a skilled workforce and school-to-work transitions have been an important aspect of this market.

Contributing to the emergence—and, many would argue, dominance—of the market mindset has been the federal role in funding an increasing proportion of all academic research, using competition as the basic mechanism for distributing funds. The Bayh-Dole Act—federal legislation encouraging universities to act as entrepreneurs through collaboration with commercial partners—has also emphasized market principles.

Globalization has been a significant thrust of the federal government since the late 1950s. The importance of federal influences in this arena became apparent following 9/11, when revisions to federal immigration policies impaired, for a time, the competitiveness of U.S. institutions in attracting students and scholars from other nations. Federally funded international programs meant to enhance global awareness have benefited the entire range of U.S. institutions, ranging from two-year colleges to four-year research universities. Federal efforts have enabled faculty, students, and entire institutions to become part of the global community through programs such as student and scholar exchanges, and the development of resource centers and language skills. Shrinking distances and expanding technologies continue to underscore the importance of the federal government's involvement in assuring that higher education contributes to and becomes a part of an increasingly global community.

Not all states have profited to the same degree from these discretionary and competitive federal initiatives. It remains unclear whether the variable impacts of federal policy are better explained by state policies or by inherent differences in the characteristics states bring to the competition. Probably both are influential.

State Context and Rules in Use

State rules in use are the focus of this volume. Because federal rules establish the context within which state rules operate, they directly and indirectly influence state policy, institutional behavior, and higher education performance. In our five case studies, we looked for evidence of state rules in what Ostrom (1999) calls *action arenas*. The eight common action arenas for state higher education systems include planning, program review and approval, information, academic preparation, student financial assistance, tuition and operational support, capital support, and economic development initiatives.

The structure that defines the action arenas for the five study states vary, providing an important basis for comparison. During most of our study, New Mexico was classified as a coordinating board state. Its higher education system seemed to give much greater attention to system inputs (students and funding) than outputs (retention and graduation). Its level of state effort (appropriations per capita) ranks consistently at or near the top of all fifty states. New Mexico's strong focus on access, its limited discussion of formal policy priorities, and the absence of specified performance criteria suggest that the state has yet to develop strategies for addressing quality and accountability. All of these characteristics, as well as the behaviors of actors described in the case study, provide clues to the rules in use in this state.

California has three largely autonomous public segments—essentially voluntary coordinating arrangements—and a private sector, which the state constitution bars from accepting direct public funding. Governance arrangements in California rely primarily on institutional processes to represent the public interest. Segmental goals consistently trump state priorities. In addition, accountability arrangements are loose enough so that segmental representatives can always interpret reported outcomes as evidence of satisfactory performance. Quality—measured by inputs (including enrollment)—is a core value. Access is celebrated, in spite of serious problems with completion, particularly in California's community colleges.

South Dakota has a consolidated governing board and a national reputation for getting its public institutions to pay attention to state priorities. Reporting, information, and funding are tied to these priorities. The entire process evolved through communication and collaboration between state policymakers and higher education leaders. Private institutions and technical institutes are slowly making inroads into broadening these state conversations about higher education. Most educational actors in the state recognize that South Dakota's priorities and accountability systems must be revised and adjusted with the times.

New York has (1) two largely autonomous public segments, (2) strong coordinating arrangements with respect to educational programs and mission changes for both the public and private sector, and (3) a private sector that receives direct public funding and is tightly integrated into the state design for providing higher education services. The state uses multiple, coordinated strategies to improve student preparation for college. There are informal networks that cut across all institutional boundaries, including ones that typically operate between basic and higher education, and those between education and other cultural organizations. The origins of many of these networks can be traced to the exceptionally broad mandate exercised by the statewide Board of Regents. Clearly, this mandate helps to explain the extensive collaboration between K–12 and higher education in such areas as student and teacher preparation.

For the most part, public higher education in New Jersey is a state-planned creation stemming from the last half of the twentieth century. Most of this development was guided by the firm hands of a strong Board of Higher Education and its chancellor, who served as a member of the governor's cabinet. Independent institutions function as full partners in providing state higher education services. New Jersey is heavily involved in *benchmarking*, a process used to track system performance by comparing national and state indicators. Public institutions publish annual accountability reports. The state's Commission on Higher Education prescribes the format for these reports and publishes its own accountability report for the system. In 1985 and again in 1994, legislation deregulated higher education, shifting the center of influence from the strong coordinating board in Trenton to individual governing boards and presidents. State budget cuts and very high debt levels for many of the state's public institutions are two less-favorable consequences of deregulation and increased reliance on market principles to reduce state costs.

Higher Education Systems and Rules in Use

While our study focused on state rules in use, we also looked at such institutional action arenas as planning, personnel administration, program review, enrollment management, information, budgeting and fiscal procedures, and facilities and technology management. In each of these areas, we found important differences in the rules that shaped the behaviors of professionals who influence performance.

Institutions in New Mexico are highly autonomous. State rules in use emphasize the importance of access over all other values. State fiscal procedures reward institutions for the number of students they enroll as well as for the types of programs in which they enroll, but not for the number who complete their degrees. State planning is not very much in evidence. Four-year public institutions developed campuses to serve as revenue centers, not necessarily as resources where state needs were and are the greatest. Four-year institutions also compete for students to maximize revenue flows. One result is that some public four-year campuses are significantly underutilized, while others seek state funding to accommodate a surplus of students. The two-year sector is a unique combination of (1) locally funded and controlled community colleges, (2) two-year branch campuses of universities, and (3) state-supported, free-standing institutions, each with its own board. Policy leaders are consistently disappointed in the state's overall performance in areas other than access.

The California Master Plan for Higher Education distributes responsibility for achieving state higher education goals among three segments: community colleges, state colleges and universities, and the University of California campuses. The governing board and a chief executive officer (CEO) for each of the latter two systems have the authority to manage the campuses and represent them as entities to state government. While there is a state board and a CEO for community colleges , there are also local governing boards and local chief executives, along with considerable legislation aimed at making these colleges behave more like a system. Most observers, however, see more evidence of anarchy than of a system. Institutional performance is often quite excellent on tasks that can be addressed by a single segment. Tasks that require cross-segmental collaboration tend to fall through the cracks.

South Dakota's six public universities have differentiated missions, with focused activities to realize their particular goals. However, common admission requirements and tuition charges, along with the absence of enrollment caps, blur some of these distinctions, especially in a state where a stable or declining admissions pool leaves regional universities with difficulties in maintaining enrollments. Institutions do not initiate new programs without meaningful consultation with other institutions and the state's unified governing board. New initiatives often involve collaboration across institutional boundaries, reflecting, in part, a pervasive concern with efficiency. Institutional leaders believe they have the flexibility to develop their own strategies for responding to state priorities. Aside from its role in academic issues, a faculty voice in decision making is muted by very weak collective bargaining arrangements.

During our study, the priorities of New York's governor were clearly reflected in the actions of the state's two large, public higher education systems. At the same time, a system of checks and balances prevented any single actor, including the governor, from intervening directly in internal decision processes. New York's two public systems are characterized by strategic planning and defined goals. While campuses have considerable independence in deciding how they will address system priorities, there are clear accountability arrangements to assess institutional performance. Campus presidents in both systems are evaluated in terms of their progress toward meeting system goals. Governance procedures allow faculty members to have an advisory influence. In addition, they are represented by a strong union that may have more access to elected state leaders than either system or campus executive officers. While faculty and administrators do not always agree, they are capable of considerable influence on the policy process when they do.

Through two major restructuring acts, New Jersey has moved steadily away from a tradition of central planning and close state regulation and toward a managed market approach. Institutional governing boards now determine programs, and the degrees each program will offer, that are consistent with their mission and strategic plan. A statewide council of institutional presidents makes the key judgment of whether further review is necessary. Institutional boards also set admission requirements and establish their own tuition and fee schedules. There are very few constraints on how the resources on individual campuses—including state appropriations (which have been decoupled from enrollments)—are spent in achieving institutionally devised strategies to meet state needs. Institutions may even pledge campus income as security for campus-backed bonds for capital construction. New Jersey has the best state information system among the five case study states. Requirements for annual institutional reports that address state priorities and concerns are intended to ensure an essential level of accountability. Despite a consistently high performance by national standards, some in state government are now voicing thoughts that New Jersey has gone too far in separating its public institutions from state oversight.

These thumbnail sketches introduce our contention that, across institutions of similar types in the case study states, differing rules in use shape the professional behaviors there. We provide a more extensive typology of these rules in chapter 2, and then present the details of how they operate in the five case study chapters.

ASSESSING EFFORT AND PERFORMANCE

Here we provide an overview of effort and performance, as these concepts are used in the framework shown in figure 1.1. Chapter 2 contains an extended discussion of how we assessed these variables. State effort is a measure of a state's direct support for higher education, either per capita or per $1,000 of personal income. Performance information for each state system was derived from data sets provided by the National Center for Public Policy and Higher Education (NCPPHE), National Center for Higher Education Management Systems (NCHEMS), and the National Center for Education Statistics and Postsecondary Education Opportunity. For our purposes, performance data consists of indicators related to preparation, participation, and completion. We purposely analyze individual indicators, as opposed to cumulative categories, in relation to rules in use to offer detailed insights into policy and performance linkages.

ORGANIZATION OF THE BOOK

Chapter 2 reports the rules in use developed from our five case studies and discusses definitions of performance. The goal of the chapter is to introduce the rules and the performance variables as tools for helping readers understand how these five states differ in the choices they make in structuring, funding, and regulating higher education services. We also show that these states differ in their performance indicators for undergraduate education.

In chapters 3 through 7, we present the case studies in comparative format, using the conceptual framework presented in figure 1.1 to organize the narratives. The individual cases are arranged in the general order of their performance on three measures—preparation, participation, and completion—beginning with New Mexico, which generally performed the least well, and ending with New Jersey, the overall top performer.

We used a guiding template for each state chapter.

- Introduction. A discussion of performance and key rules; the political, economic, and social context for the state; and state higher education issues that have emerged as important within this context.
- State actors. An overview of the individuals, groups, agencies, and organizations that are state-level actors who influence, or have the potential to influence, higher education performance at a state level. We also discuss how actors connect their positions, authority, and activities to the state higher education system.
- Rules in use at the state level. State actors come together in formal and informal arenas (action situations) to derive, utilize, or alter rules that govern planning, program review and approval, the use of information, academic preparation, student assistance, tuition and operating support, capital support, and economic development.
- Higher education institutional and system actors. An overview of individuals, groups, agencies, and organizations that are institutional or system-level actors who influence, or have the potential to influence, higher education performance at an institutional or system level. The overview connects the position, authority, and activities of each actor to the institution or system of institutions.
- Higher education system rules in use. Institutional and system actors come together in formal and informal arenas (action situations) to derive, utilize, or alter rules that govern planning, program initiatives, personnel and evaluation, enrollment planning, the use of information, budgeting and other fiscal policies, capital planning, and research and development.

The variation across cases is evident, as actors and rules that are important in one state may be only marginally visible in another. In addition, states like California and New York are characterized by multiple higher education systems, so several sections on institutional and system-level actors and rules appear in these cases. Despite this diversity, the five case study chapters adhere to the general guidelines above, with only minor differences. The standardization of our presentation, based on the conceptual framework we used, contributes to a systematic and comparative analysis of the policy and performance links for each state. All five of the case studies have been updated through 2007, along with selected information from 2008.

The states present contrasting approaches to managing higher education systems. The political, social, and economic backdrop in each state is quite fluid, and in some ways unpredictable, heightening the need for a common framework for analysis. We observed each of the states over time and have documented the changes that occurred in all of the states during the period of our study. These changes are important, because links between policy and performance require time to become visible. While we note changes, our discussion of the relationships between policy and performance is grounded in the arrangements that existed during most of our study.

Chapter 8 reports our analysis of the relationships between rules in use, effort, and performance. Our interpretations of these relationships mainly draw on literature and our analysis, but they are also informed by the many policy meetings we attended as the study progressed and by the feedback we received during the evolution of our work. Throughout our study, elected and appointed higher education policy leaders helped shape the conceptual framework we developed. Policymakers also suggested that a seven-year effort of such magnitude should offer ideas that might be promising as considerations for action in their states. The last chapter, therefore, is our best effort to interpret what our study means to policy practitioners and researchers concerned about higher education policy and the public interest. We also suggest that the locus of *where* changes to policy occur is an important contributor to a state's capacity to achieve improved performance on priority outcomes.

CHAPTER TWO

Rules in Use and Performance

✸

The conceptual framework from chapter 1 provides the foundation upon which each of the state case studies is built. The rules in use and performance indicators provide a basis by which to compare the case study states. Rules in use operate at the federal, state, and institutional levels. Our focus was state higher education systems, so state-level rules in use played the most prominent role in our study. This chapter describes the state rules in use (hereafter simply referred to as *rules*) and performance indicators derived from the five case study states. An initial overview of rules and performance provides the reader with notable highlights for and comparisons among the featured states prior to embarking on the more detailed narratives which appear in chapters 3–7.

The first section of this chapter identifies the rules and then presents six rule categories and their respective subthemes. The explanation and definition of each category is accompanied by a brief narrative that compares and contrasts the five case study states across the rules that comprise that category. The second section describes indicators related to preparation, participation, and completion, and includes data for each indicator across the study states. Again, a brief narrative summarizes similarities and differences among the states. The status of state effort across the five states concludes the chapter.

RULES IN USE

We used the empirical case study narratives as the primary source for deriving the rules that shape the behaviors of actors in state higher education systems. Rules include both formal policies—such as statutes and agency regulations— and informal norms and values that determine how actors make operational decisions in such action situations as planning, program review, and resource allocation. In each state, we interviewed higher education leaders at the institutional and system levels, as well as elected officials or their representatives. We also talked to city officials, assembly and senate members or their staffs, representatives from the governor's office, and representatives from other state agencies, and made extensive use of documents and websites. The five case study narratives flowed from this effort. For each narrative, we used qualitative data analysis software (QSR International 2006) to categorize the rules. Working across the five states, we identified and then wrote a composite list of rules, following seven guidelines:

1. Phrase rules in inclusive language to make them broadly applicable across the states
2. Focus on *what* is done rather than *how*
3. Avoid rules that require more than a single judgment about applicability.
4. Avoid rules that state the obvious or are characteristic of all five states
5. Avoid rules that express value judgments
6. Group rules that have thematic relationships
7. Limit the number of rules to those essential for describing the range of observed actions

Using both literature and contextual evidence from the narratives, we assigned each rule to one of six overarching categories, employing (1) a multistep iterative process involving members of the research team who worked in the different states and (2) several project meetings that included our international colleagues. The initial list of rules, by category, is shown in the appendix. The appendix includes all the rules that were observed in the study states, including those we later omitted because they were not associated with differences in performance. For each major category, we also identified *subthemes* reflecting different approaches to organizing or managing the comparable elements of higher education systems. Each subtheme contains one or more of the rules reported in the appendix. We defined the six major categories as follows:

1. *System design* includes rules about the relationship between state government and higher education, how authority is exercised, the number and location of public institutions, the degree to which there is coordination of distance education among the institutions, and the role assigned to private colleges and universities
2. *State leadership* reflects the direct authority states exercise, at least over their public institutions, and the rules they use to influence higher educa-

tion professionals to pursue goals and priorities that are defined by elected state officials as "in the public interest"

3. *Information* refers to rules about available data, including how states collect, analyze, report, and use this data

4. *Access and achievement* includes state initiatives and related regulations that influence college readiness and participation, and rules about the types of state financial assistance made available to students

5. *Fiscal policies* refer to the strategies that allocate and administer the financial support state governments provide directly to institutions, and the types of institutions that are eligible to receive this state aid

6. *Research and development* includes state strategies for improving research infrastructure and stimulating economic development

To validate the presence or absence of rules in each state, we developed a survey using a five-point, Likert-type scale (strongly agree to strongly disagree). The survey asked selected policy and higher education leaders to indicate which of the rules were in use in their state and whether any of them had changed significantly during the previous five-year period. A copy of the case study narrative was included with the survey. Response rates to the survey were very high (90% or higher, depending on the state) since those who received them were invited to a meeting convened by a key leader in each state. In addition to contributing to this substantial response rate, the meetings provided us with an opportunity to discuss the case study and survey responses for that state with our key informants.

Because participants in the state meetings—institutional presidents, state higher education executive officers and staff, legislative analysts, and elected officials—brought a variety of perspectives to the task, in some cases there were disagreements about the status of some of the rules. The seven rules at the bottom of the appendix were eliminated after the meetings, either because they were difficult to interpret or because respondents within a state often differed significantly on the status of the rules. The remaining rules made sense to meeting participants and were characterized as either "in effect" or "not in effect," based on the judgment of internal actors in each state.

In the following sections, we draw on this collective effort to highlight rule categories across the states. We describe each thematic category and its associated subthemes generally, and then provide an overview of how the five states compared across the rules. Chapter 8 will demonstrate the differences that were linked most powerfully to performance.

System Design

In some states, higher education systems and the institutional types that define them have developed either unintentionally or because of local need, while in other states they have been purposeful creations of intentional state-level planning. Table 2.1 summarizes the major subthemes found under the category of system design. The subthemes, in essence, define the differences in system design that readers will observe in reading the case studies.

States are free to design systems through statewide planning and coordination—as in New York, New Jersey, and South Dakota—or to let them evolve and self-govern—as in New Mexico and, to a degree, in California. South Dakota, through its consolidated governing board, has the strongest interface between state government and higher education. New York is a close second, with all of its public institutions reporting to two governing boards. Governing board oversight in this state is augmented by a strong statewide Board of Regents, which has planning and program approval authority. There is also a strong interface between the state and all of higher education in New Jersey, which has a mandated President's Council, with statutorily defined responsibilities, and a Commission on Higher Education. The latter, while much weaker than the department it replaced in 1994, nonetheless retains important capabilities, if the governor decides to use them.

Only California and New Mexico have constitutional constraints that limit the policy options of public officials. In California, these include the constitutional status of the University of California (UC) segment, twelve-year terms for trustees, a postsecondary education commission with advisory authority only, and a master plan that deflects rule changes not acceptable to the public segments. The famed California Master Plan for Higher Education had been described by its architect, Clark Kerr, as a compromise among these segments to achieve a system design acceptable to the state legislature (Richardson et al. 1999, p. 17). Until very recently, the political culture in New Mexico supported system design as essentially the sum of whatever the state's colleges and universities decided to undertake. Their interface with state government is lessened by the constitutional status of all four-year institutions, as well as by legislators' continuing actions that undermined a relatively weak higher education commission. The New Mexico Commission on Higher Education was replaced by a secretary of higher education during the late stages of our study, reflecting the dissatisfaction of policy leaders with prior arrangements.

TABLE 2.1
System Design

System design subthemes
Statewide planning
Statewide coordination and regulation
Self-governing public IHEs
Use of the private sector
Extensive two-year colleges

New York and New Jersey have significant private sectors, which they treat as an integral part of their planning in meeting state higher education needs. None of the other states consider the private sector explicitly in their higher education oversight processes. South Dakota, which enrolls as large a proportion of its students in private institutions as New Jersey, has only recently begun to consider the possible contributions of this sector to system performance and provide state financial assistance to state residents who attend such schools. Among the five states, California and New Mexico have the smallest proportions of undergraduate students attending private institutions. All of the states except South Dakota have comprehensive community colleges, strategically located to serve populations throughout the state. In California and New Jersey, a majority of all undergraduate students enroll in community colleges. However, South Dakota has a system of technical institutes, overseen by the same state board as the K–12 sector.

Design and governance rules also influence delivery strategies. The states with the strongest interface arrangements have been more likely to develop statewide programs to provide distance education, such as Empire State College in New York and Thomas Edison State College in New Jersey. South Dakota, through the centralized power of its governing board, is the only state with a coordinated statewide approach to distance education.

State Leadership

The state leadership rules reflect the many mechanisms that states use to influence higher education professionals to pursue specific goals and priorities. These rules also deal with accountability arrangements that assess institutional responsiveness to state priorities. Table 2.2 summarizes the major subthemes found under the category of state leadership.

State leadership rules refer to actions that occur on a statewide basis in

TABLE 2.2
State Leadership

State leadership subthemes
Defined goals and priorities
Use of market forces and accountability
Incentives, deregulation, and operational flexibility

an arena to which elected policymakers have ready access. New Jersey has made the strongest effort to combine the use of market forces with deregulation, strengthening the authority of institutional boards and encouraging competition between segments and sectors. New York has also undertaken deregulation and encouraged competition, but its legislature retains regulatory authority that limits the ability of the public segments to compete with each other. Neither California nor New Mexico use competition as a strategy for encouraging efficiency or responsiveness to public priorities. The California Master Plan actually discourages the use of market forces by tightly circumscribing missions within the public segments.

New York, South Dakota, and New Jersey have procedures for identifying higher education goals and priorities on a statewide basis. Only New Mexico and South Dakota have arrangements for achieving accountability, although New Mexico's legislation on accountability has not been implemented in any practical sense. New Jersey had some accountability mechanisms, including a performance funding program, before the latter was terminated by Governor McGreevey during a budget crisis that continued under a new governor.

In New York and California, most arrangements for defining goals and demonstrating accountability are situated within the higher education segments. Leaders within the UC system believe that the goals established by the UC board are the de facto goals for the state of California. In New York, a statewide Board of Regents also plays an important role in the planning process, particularly in terms of its authority to approve changes in the institutional plans of both public and private institutions.

Information

The rules that relate to information have to do first with whether states gather data, and second with whether that data is formally used in the policy decision-making process. For example, it is possible for states to gather informa-

TABLE 2.3
Information

Information subthemes
Data gathering
Data for decision making

tion, yet limit its dissemination and use to specified audiences and purposes. Table 2.3 summarizes the major subthemes found under the category of information.

Among the five states, only New Jersey (at the time of our study) possessed the type of state information system that was able to quickly and credibly respond to requests from elected officials. New Jersey also has arrangements for making institution-specific performance data available to the general public, and it does so routinely. In South Dakota, where data systems are generally managed by the institutions, the central governing board's staff organizes and publishes such reports for public officials. New Mexico has a less-developed information system that provides some reports, but limited staff, as well as incompatibilities between state and institutional information systems, hamper its state-level agency from providing data that are useful in decision-making processes. Until very recently, the public segments in New York and California carefully guarded information and resisted a state-level expansion of their information capabilities. The New York State Board of Regents had access to data reported by the segments and produced some useful reports, as did the California Postsecondary Education Commission (CPEC). Thanks to a legal decision, the CPEC now also has access to unit record data, which was previously under segmental control. The New York Board of Regents is currently working with institutional research offices in the State University of New York (SUNY) and the City University of New York (CUNY) to develop a similar capability. Nonetheless, during the period of our study, officials in New York and California clearly did not use state-furnished information in their decision-making processes to the extent of those in South Dakota and New Jersey.

It was not at all apparent from our case studies that elected officials regarded the absence of data from other than federal and segmental sources as a disadvantage. In both California and New York, governors cut statewide agency staffing and, like legislators, used their own sources of information to judge the amount of spin on the reports they received from institutions. In smaller South Dakota, a single governing board, responsible for all four-year institutions, developed information and shared it directly with elected officials through roundtables and other sessions where board members and elected officials worked together to define priorities and assess performance. Here, as in New Jersey, elected officials were quite satisfied with the quality and quantity of information, even though South Dakota's system was less formalized and the written reports were fewer in number.

Access and Achievement

The access and achievement category includes state initiatives and related regulations that influence college readiness and participation. Many of these rules have to do with collaboration between the K–12 sector and higher education and with coordinated efforts to improve access and success for economically and educationally disadvantaged students. The rules also identify the various types of state financial assistance made available to students. Table 2.4 summarizes the major subthemes listed under the category of access and achievement.

New Jersey and New York have the largest number of rules designed to promote access and achievement. In South Dakota, students who attend public higher education are less likely to be from disadvantaged backgrounds, and the state accepts little responsibility for its relatively large Native American population, who mostly attend tribal colleges supported by the federal government. Tribal colleges are also important in New Mexico. Because of the way its system is designed, California relies heavily on community colleges to provide access for disadvantaged students. New Mexico, too, makes significant use of community colleges for access, but it does so more because of geographic considerations than as an element of intentional state design. Both California and New Mexico depend more heavily on segmental or institutional strategies for serving disadvantaged students than on state-initiated or even coordinated activities.

While all five of the states have at least some student assistance awarded on the basis of merit, only New Mexico and South Dakota used this approach as a primary strategy during the period of our study. The South Dakota program is relatively new, with funding for merit aid dating from 2004. The merit-based programs in the three other states are quite small and heavily restricted. All five of the states provide at least some financial assistance to state residents attending private institutions, but the major initiatives were in California, New Jersey, and New York. These three states also have major need-based student

TABLE 2.4
Access and Achievement

Access and achievement subthemes

Open-access community colleges
Need-based student aid
Merit-based rewards and assistance
State-coordinated access programs
High school graduation exam
Measuring college learning outcomes
Convening K–16 actors

TABLE 2.5
Fiscal Policies

Fiscal policies subthemes

State budget submission procedures
State fiscal support for private colleges
Authority to set tuition and fees
Basis for determining state appropriations
Reliance on low-tuition two-year colleges

aid programs and require public institutions to set aside part of their revenues for student aid, in order to moderate the impact of tuition increases on low-income students. New Jersey and New York make the most extensive efforts to coordinate their programs with those offered by the federal government.

Fiscal Policies

We differentiate between fiscal and financial aid policies. *Financial aid policies* appear under the rules associated with access and achievement, and they primarily address the strategy of providing support directly to the student, regardless of the nature of that support. *Fiscal policy* deals both with the kinds of financial support state governments provide directly to institutions and with the types of institutions eligible to receive this aid. State support to institutions may be predicated on enrollments, performance, or direct requests and used either for capital projects or operating expenses. In addition, fiscal policies cover state rules that influence tuition levels. Table 2.5 summarizes the major subthemes found under the category of fiscal policies.

The formality of higher education budget submissions varies by state. New

Jersey, New Mexico, and South Dakota either had or currently have statewide boards or commissions that directly supply information and analysis on the relationship between budget requests and state needs or priorities. In South Dakota and New Mexico (until 2005), the board or commission provided a consolidated budget request for all higher education institutions. In the remaining three states, segments or individual institutions submit budget requests directly to an agency of state government.

California and New Mexico use enrollments as a major factor in determining state appropriations for higher education operating expenses. The other three states rely primarily on some combination of historical patterns and negotiations. In California, operating appropriations and tuition increases are negotiated directly between the governor and the executive officers of the two public four-year segments. Governing boards have considerably more freedom to increase tuition and fees in New Jersey, New Mexico, and South Dakota than in California or New York. In the latter two states, both access concerns and the impact of tuition increases on state obligations for funding large, need-based student aid programs promote tighter legislative and/or gubernatorial controls. New Jersey, in fiscal crisis and under a new governor during the latter stages of our study, moved to limit some of its previously granted institutional flexibility in raising tuitions.

New Jersey and South Dakota have experimented with performance funding. In California, the agreements negotiated by the governor and executives of the four-year segments set out some general performance and funding expectations, but this does not have the formality of a budgeting arrangement based on performance. California attempted to include a performance component in the budgeting process for community colleges, but the effort was never successful and did not survive. The central administrations of both SUNY and CUNY include performance criteria in their fiscal allocation processes, but these criteria are subject to change, depending on the level of state funding. In addition, these arrangements are not well documented in ways that permit comparisons across institutions by outsiders.

Maintaining lower tuition and fees in community colleges has been an explicit access strategy in California, New Jersey, and New Mexico. Historically, New Mexico has also been a low-tuition, low-aid state for four-year institutions, but the advent of a large merit aid program has changed the rules for student access. Community college tuition in New Mexico remains less than half the cost of that at public four-year institutions. However, the many governance and funding arrangements among community colleges in the state produce sharp differences in the prices they charge and the resources they eventually obtain.

Both New Jersey and New York provide operating and capital subsidies directly to private institutions. The remaining three states provide neither. The California constitution prohibits direct state financial support to private entities, although private institutions are eligible to participate in state bonding for capital improvements.

Research and Development

Policymakers in every case study state believe that higher education is intricately tied to economic development through research and institutional activity that relates to state industries and workforce preparation. Rules in this arena include state strategies for improving research infrastructure and stimulating economic development. Table 2.6 summarizes the major subthemes found under the category of research and development.

All five of the states have authorized their public institutions to establish independent foundation or development boards, both to assist in fundraising and to ensure that these monies are not used to supplant state appropriations. California, New York, and South Dakota either use or have used state funding to encourage enrollment or stimulate research activity in programs considered important for economic development. New Jersey, New Mexico, and New York have also used incentive funding to improve the training of their labor forces. In South Dakota, labor force training is more a responsibility of the technical institutes, which are oriented to the K–12 sector, than of baccalaureate-granting institutions. Most economic development strategies in California and New Mexico reside at the institutional or segmental level and are not coordinated statewide.

TABLE 2.6
Research and Development

Research and development subthemes

State incentive grants for research and labor force training
State funds for research facilities in private institutions
Public institution endowment and development boards

Except for New Mexico, all of the case study states use incentive funds as part of their statewide strategy to improve research infrastructure. Since private higher education in New Jersey and New York is an integral part of the state higher education system, private research universities compete for research funding on an equal footing with their public counterparts. In California and New Mexico, funds for improving research infrastructure may be appropriated in response to institutional or segmental budget requests.

PERFORMANCE

The conceptual framework in chapter 1 proposes that state higher education performance is influenced by the rules of the game. For the purposes of our study, performance data are organized in three categories: preparation, participation, and degree completion. While we are indebted conceptually to the National Center for Public Policy and Higher Education (NCPPHE) for these categories, we use different indicators for some of them, and we do not employ two of their categories, affordability and benefits. In one study (Martinez, Farias, Arellano, 2002), affordability was not intuitively linked to the other report card categories, and the authors suggested that several subcategories of benefits could not be attributed to the quality of higher education's service delivery. In addition, given the fact that more than half of the states received a failing grade in affordability on NCPPHE's 2006 report card, linking policy to performance, and distinguishing potentially helpful policies from harmful ones, is problematic for this particular measurement.

The standardized measures of preparation, participation, and completion have a long history of use across the states, and thus are less susceptible to validity challenges than affordability or benefits. For these reasons, we chose preparation, participation, and completion as the major categories by which to evaluate performance in the case study states. Although our study focuses on individual indicators of performance, these categories are also referenced for organizational purposes and because they adhere to familiar convention for most policymakers. The three major categories, along with the indicator descriptions that comprise them, are listed below.

1. Preparation
   - high school completion
   - K–12 student achievement

2. Participation
   - chance for college by age 19
   - college participation rate for dependent undergraduates from low-income families
   - percentage of 18- to 24-year-olds enrolled in college
   - percentage of 25- to 49-year-olds enrolled part-time in some type of postsecondary education in 1999–2000
3. Completion
   - freshman-to-sophomore retention rates for first-time college freshmen at two-year institutions
   - freshman-to-sophomore retention rates for first-time college freshmen at four-year institutions
   - three-year associate's degree graduation rates for first-time, full-time students entering two-year colleges
   - six-year bachelor's degree graduation rates for first-time, full-time students entering four-year colleges
   - the ratio of bachelor's degrees per 100 undergraduates

In the next sections, we document how the five states fare across the various performance indicators. A brief description highlights points of interest for performance for the different states. Since the case studies are concerned with both past and recent events that have given shape to state higher education systems, whenever data availability allows, performance for each state is given over a period of time. After discussing the three major categories and their associated indicators, we turn to a special discussion on state effort.

Preparation

Table 2.7 reports the performance of the five states in 1994 and 2004 on five preparation indicators. In general, New Jersey, New York, and South Dakota perform better on these indicators than California and New Mexico. However, California is the only state that recorded a substantial increase in high school completion over the ten-year period shown in the table. Where data from both 1994 and 2004 are available for the four achievement measures, most of the states show improvements over time.

TABLE 2.7
A Comparison of Performance on Five Preparation Indicators,
1994/2004 (in percentages)

	California	New Jersey	New Mexico	New York	South Dakota
High School Completion 18- to 24-year-olds with a high school credential	78/87	91/90	84/85	89/87	89/90
K–12 Student Achievement 8th graders scoring at or above "proficient" on the national assessment exam in math	16/22	24/33	11/15	20/32	—/35
Low-income 8th graders scoring at or above "proficient" on the national assessment exam in math	5/9	—/10	7/9	10/16	—/22
8th graders scoring at or above "proficient" on the national assessment exam in reading	22/22	—/37	24/20	34/35	—/39
7th to 12th graders taught by teachers with a major in their subject	51/68	65/85	45/55	73/80	47/68

Source: NCPPHE, *Measuring Up 2004* and *2006*.

Participation

Table 2.8 shows the performance of the five states on four participation indicators, covering various years. The data for participation came from a variety of sources, so information across time is not available for all measures. However, the inclusion of multiple indicators from different sources does allow a more comprehensive look at participation across the states. For example, residents in New Jersey and South Dakota have a better chance of attending college by the time they are 19 than is true in other states. Relative to the other three states, California and New Mexico have noticeably higher enrollments among the adult student population but lower participation among both the traditional student population and undergraduate students from low-income families.

TABLE 2.8
A Comparison of Performance on Four Participation Indicators (in percentages)

	California	New Jersey	New Mexico	New York	South Dakota	Nation
			2002			
Chance for college by age 19	35.0	52.8	35.0	36.9	48.1	38.0
			2003			
College participation rate for dependent undergraduates from low-income families	22.6	43.7	17.1	37.8	26.0	24.7
			1994/2004			
18- to 24-year-olds enrolled in college	32/38	37/37	31/33	35/38	34/35	—/40
			1999/2004			
25- to 49-year-olds enrolled part time in any type of post-secondary education	5.3/5.8	4.1/3.1	6.2/5.4	4.2/3.4	3.0/3.5	—/5.4

Sources: Chance for college: National Information Center for Higher Education
Policymaking and Analysis, www.HigherEdInfo.org;
College participation: *Postsecondary Education OPPORTUNITY* 149 (November 2004);
Enrollment by age: NCPPHE, *Measuring Up 2004*.

Completion

Table 2.9 reports the performance of the five states on five participation indicators over various years. New York, New Jersey, and South Dakota do better than California and New Mexico on retention for two-year students, while New Mexico and South Dakota lag behind the other states on completion indicators for four-year students. A peculiar characteristic of the South Dakota system is that the state's two-year postsecondary needs are met exclusively by technical institutes, rather than traditional community colleges, which may have bearing on the completion indicators for the state.

STATE EFFORT

State effort is a measure of a state's direct support for higher education, either per capita or per $1,000 of personal income. The level of effort in a particular

TABLE 2.9
A Comparison of Performance on Five Completion Indicators (in percentages)

	California	New Jersey	New Mexico	New York	South Dakota	Nation
			1999/2002			
Fall, first-time, full-time freshmen returning the following fall semester (4-yr.)	83.0/83.7	83.5/81.8	68.5/70.9	77.5/80.9	68.4/69.7	74.1/73.6
Fall, full-time freshmen returning the following fall semester (2-yr.)	48.4/47.7	58.0/61.0	51.5/51.6	62.3/60.7	—/57.8	55.1/54.8
			1998/2003			
3-year graduation rates for associate students[a]	46.2/43.6	15.3/14.8	30.2/19.3	24.3/26.9	65.4/65.9	29.5/30.6
6-year graduation rates for bachelor's degree students[b]	59.8/50.1	57.8/60.8	35.2/39	54.1/55.9	43.4/46.1	52/54.3
No. of bachelor's degrees awarded per 100 undergraduates	6.5/6.1	9.1/9.7	7.0/6.6	11.2/11.9	12.3/10.5	9.6/9.5

Sources: NCPPHE, *Measuring Up 2004* for 6-year bachelor's degree graduation rates; all other data are from the National Information Center for Higher Education Policymaking and Analysis.
[a]Graduation rates for first-time, full-time, associate's-degree-seeking students earning an associate's degree within 3 years
[b]Graduation rates for first-time, full-time bachelor's-degree-seeking students entering four-year colleges earning a bachelor's degree within 6 years.

state may erect boundaries, enable action, or provide incentives for institutions to behave in desired and undesired ways. The conceptual framework from chapter 1 accommodates this reality and suggests that state effort influences institutional behavior and, subsequently, performance. In this sense, state effort is an input, rather than a rule or a performance indicator.

State effort is a commonly understood measure across higher education policy and research domains, because it can be represented in a ratio that makes state-by-state comparisons meaningful and convenient. Effort is not the same as cost—which includes tuition and fees, income from auxiliary en-

TABLE 2.10
A Comparison of State Effort

	California	New Jersey	New Mexico	New York	South Dakota	Nation
			FY 2004			
State tax appropriations (in $1,000s)	8,451,851	1,740,829	644,996	3,752,758	153,281	60,694,185
Local tax appropriations (in $1,000s)	2,122,805	185,935	61,719	536,678	0	6,723,679
Total tax appropriations (in $1,000s)	10,574,656	1,926,764	706,715	4,289,436	153,281	67,417,864

			FY 2005			
			Dollars/Rank			U.S. average
Appropriations per $1,000 in personal income	7.3/19	5.26/42	13.42/1	5.54/39	7.16/22	6.59
Appropriations per capita	253.29/14	217.82/23	356.19/2	210.58/28	210.55/ 29	214.96

Sources: State tax appropriations: Palmer (ed.), Grapevine, revised FY 04 data reported by states in survey for FY 05;
Local tax appropriations: State Higher Education Executive Officers (SHEEO), *State Higher Education Finance 2004;*
Personal income appropriations: Personal income data are for the 2nd quarter of 2004. They are preliminary estimates retrieved from the Bureau of Economic Analysis, U.S. Department of Commerce, www.bea.doc.gov/newsrelarchive/2004/spi0904.xls (accessed December 4, 2004; this item is no longer available from the website);
Per capita appropriations: Population data are July 2004 estimates retrieved from the U.S. Census Bureau, www.census.gov/popest/states/tables/NST-EST-01.xls (accessed December 27, 2004; this item is no longer available from the website).

terprises and endowments, and federal appropriations, as well as a variety of other miscellaneous sources. State effort for higher education, as discussed in this volume, includes state and local appropriations for operating expenses for colleges, universities, and vocational-technical institutes; funding for statewide coordinating and governing boards; state financial aid; and other monies destined for higher education but appropriated initially to some other state agency. However, effort excludes funds for capital outlays and debt service and monies received from other sources, such as student tuition and fees (Palmer 2005). Table 2.10 provides a comparison of state and local appropriations (top of table) and state effort (bottom two indicators) across the five study states.

California and New Mexico make the greatest state effort, but they also generally do less well on the performance categories considered in our study. Some respondents, especially in California and New York, argued that the indicators we used did not include outcomes important to research and its impact on economic development. They pointed to the number of distinguished public universities in California and their success in attracting research funding from the federal government and other sponsors. University administrators in New York indicated inadequate state funding was a barrier to developing flagship public universities there, especially in the City University of New York. Indeed, one possible explanation for the discrepancy between state effort and performance is that the indicators in our study did not adequately capture measurements such as research support. We consider this argument in chapter 8.

A second argument for California and New Mexico's combination of low performance and high state effort concerns the exclusion of affordability as a category in our study. States that spend more per capita possibly attach greater priority to keeping their higher education systems affordable. This rationale helps explain why California received a B, and New Jersey a D, on the NCPPHE's affordability category in 2004. It does not, however, explain why the other three case study states, including New Mexico, were awarded Fs.

State higher education systems are complex organizational structures whose behavior and performance are the result of multiple rules in use—interacting over time, across different contexts, and through different actors. Both the conceptual framework in chapter 1 and the rules and performance data in this chapter provide a systematic starting point for researchers and policymakers to examine broad similarities and differences across the five case study states. Chapters 3 through 7 dig deeper by providing the details surrounding the rules and performance information. Combining the more generalized look across states that is highlighted in this chapter with the details of the case study chapters then leads to questions of whether patterns exist that link certain rules to certain performance outcomes, which is the subject of chapter 8.

CHAPTER THREE

New Mexico

✤

with contributions by Maria Emilia Martinez

New Mexico is a high-effort, low-performing state. In reading this case study, consider the informal rules that govern system coordination. Elected policy leaders have consistently voted to increase the authority of the state's Commission on Higher Education, but they have just as consistently worked directly with the administrative leadership of the constitutionally autonomous institutions—thereby weakening the commission's effectiveness. The New Mexico system of higher education was never planned from a state perspective. Rather, it has evolved as the sum of institutional aspirations and community desires. There are no formal goals or priorities, although a commitment to access seems palpable across a range of stakeholders throughout the state. Access programs are, however, managed by each institution, and student assistance is merit based. State appropriations for operating purposes are distributed on the basis of enrollments. These rules help to explain performance in ways that we discuss in more detail in chapter 8.

✤

The state of New Mexico provides an interesting demographic, geographic, and economic mixture against which to examine state higher education. On the demographic front, New Mexico has no ethnic or racial majority. Hispanics constitute 43.4 percent of the state's population, and non-Hispanic whites 43.1 percent. By population segment indicators, New Mexico is also younger than the average U.S. state, with a larger percentage of the population under eighteen and a smaller percentage over sixty-five (QuickFacts). The population in New Mexico is geographically dispersed, as the state is quite rural relative to other states. The few population centers in the state do have major enterprise operations within their proximity. Los Alamos National Laboratories in the north part of the state, and White Sands Missile Range in the south, conduct extensive research and development work for the government. Despite these examples of major employment and economic activity centers,

New Mexico's citizens consistently have a lower median income and a higher poverty rate than the national average. Higher education operates within this context, as policymakers and higher education leaders work to meet the needs of industry and an expanding, diverse population.

By almost any measure, New Mexico's support of higher education can be described as generous. Direct institutional appropriations in real and constant dollars have consistently increased over the last ten years, and appropriations per capita for higher education funding are routinely among the highest in the nation. The state also started a state merit aid program in the late 1990s. This funding history may well be attributed to a widespread belief in access across the state. Admittedly, the major source of proof for the existence of a "culture of belief" in access comes from the fact that this theme regularly emerges when one interviews the various actors who influence or are a part of higher education.

Higher education policy in New Mexico includes more than just funding. Its state-level higher education governance arrangements have recently undergone substantial change. Still, there is little question that the legal arrangements that initially granted universities constitutional autonomy have had a clear effect on the direction of state policy. Various individuals and organizations, inside and outside of higher education, also influence policy and performance in the state.

STATE ACTORS
The Governor

Bill Richardson was elected to his first term as governor of New Mexico in November 2003. Governor Richardson entered office with a Reform Agenda, part of which was meant to address higher education issues and instigate changes as necessary. Under the auspices of his reform agenda, Governor Richardson created the Governor's Task Force on Higher Education to review and analyze the state of higher education in New Mexico. The governor gave the task force a strict deadline; they were to formulate policy recommendations within a six-month period. Around the same time, the legislature passed a resolution mandating that the Commission on Higher Education conduct a study, called the New Mexico Student Success Study, to determine the standing of student success in New Mexico and compose a set of recommendations for its improvement. Both projects concluded simultaneously and contributed to the creation of a new state governance arrangement and to legislation for a need-based state aid program.

Most observers recognize that previous governors Toney Anaya and Garrey Caruthers raised issues in the 1970s and 1980s that created the conversation about governance changes in the state. More importantly, both former governors continue to serve in leadership roles within the present higher education structure. Former governor Caruthers, for example, was an executive in the health care industry after his term in office, yet he continued to be a vocal advocate for state-level governance change over the years. His fondness for and belief in higher education remains, as he is a board member for a national policy organization and currently serves as the business dean for a state research university.

Despite recent state-level interest in higher education, the historical extent of gubernatorial interest should not be overemphasized. Higher education has been a marginal concern for many policymakers, including Gary Johnson, who preceded Richardson. As governor, the extent of Johnson's interest in higher education concerned tuition. He was a proponent of prepaid tuition plans, and the legislature introduced a bill establishing such plans in 1999. By most accounts, Johnson also believed that tuition in New Mexico should be allowed to rise. One policymaker said the governor's office wanted to see tuition increase—with a long-term strategy, incrementally and thoughtfully— along with a rise in the amount of student aid. Aside from periodic commentary on the subject, Johnson remained largely silent on higher education issues.

Budget Division and Legislative Finance Committee

The state budget process involves two primary agencies: the Budget Division of the Department of Administration (representing the executive branch) and the Legislative Finance Committee (representing the agenda of the legislature). Both agencies assign an analyst to oversee the higher education formula and budget. Each entity presents its version of the individual agency budgets to a joint committee of representatives from the House Appropriations Committee and Senate Finance Committee. The joint committee members review and vote upon acceptance of the higher education budget in a lengthy process that occurs prior to each legislative session. The committee accepts either the executive or the legislative version of the budget, which later becomes part of the state's General Appropriation Act. Although possible, it is rare that the committee combines elements of each budget to create a hybrid of the two.

Board of Finance

The Board of Finance, within the Department of Finance and Administration, has oversight and final approval authority over capital funding for higher education projects. Institutions and their boards may obtain state funding for capital requests and finalize their plans, but the Board of Finance's role really occurs before actual spending or construction starts on any particular project.

The Legislature

New Mexico's 112-member legislature is controlled by its Democratic membership. The legislature has long been concerned with access-related issues. Some legislators believe access is really a function of affordability. Indeed, different respondents used different terms—such as *access, affordability,* and *opportunity*—although all seemed to be addressing the issue of making participation a reality for New Mexico citizens. In terms of affordability, some respondents made a distinction between the affordable operations of an institution versus affordability with respect to the price students are charged. An institutional board member for a two-year institution said the legislature looks kindly on her college because "affordability is a big thing, and people believe we do our job well and at much less cost than a university." A state representative tied several notions of affordability and access together when he recalled a legislative committee in the mid-1990s trying to improve efficiency so the state could have quality opportunities for students at an affordable price. He concluded that the tie between affordability and opportunity exists because a state "can't maintain affordability if it is inefficient."

At the onset of this project, most legislators appeared to be concerned about access, although few had really delved into higher education issues. One senior state senator suggested that from a legislative perspective, K–12 is a much bigger priority than higher education, because it consumes almost half the state budget. In addition, those legislators who tried to address higher education issues largely described their efforts as unsuccessful and usurped by higher education institutions. In 1995, an interim committee called Excellence in Higher Education was established to address, according to the former committee chair's perspective, issues related to the state higher education funding formula. According to the chair, however, different people had different ideas about what the committee should address, and no matter what draft legislation was offered, it was always rejected by higher education institutions. A higher education president, on the other hand, said that it was not the institutions that unraveled the committee's work and that higher education has gone far beyond any ideas generated in the committee.

In the end, the fact remains that previous attempts at passing significant legislation or restructuring governance arrangements were a difficult proposition because of the constitutional autonomy that the state's six universities enjoy. The legislature as a whole has been concerned with access, but only a few individual legislators have taken on the task of pursuing substantive change in some area of higher education policy. Several respondents believe that both the legislature and the governor need to play a complementary and cooperative role if a coherent list of policy priorities is ever to emerge. Respondents also stated that the legislature and the governor must cooperate with one another in order to get anything done. Until recently, the dynamics between state lawmakers and elected officials held little promise toward real change in higher education. Today, changes have taken place, but a brief history of state-level governance provides the appropriate backdrop by which to assess the potential effectiveness of these changes.

Board of Educational Finance and Commission on Higher Education

In 1951, the Board of Educational Finance (BEF) was established to deal with problems of funding higher education institutions in the state. Several policymakers said the BEF unified the budget-making process for higher education. Prior to the BEF's existence, institutions had approached the legislature individually, and state-level officials wanted to minimize the need for individual institutions to present their requests directly to the legislature. One college president said the BEF's purpose was to stop end runs (by the institutions) to the legislature and to keep relationships between higher education institutions within some type of structure. Many believe that the BEF was quite effective at achieving its intended objectives. One state-level official said that the BEF was able to accomplish its goals, while another college president described the BEF as effective because "it had a strong focus."

Over the years, the legislature continued to use statutes to define and identify a number of additional responsibilities for the BEF. In 1986, the BEF was renamed the New Mexico Commission on Higher Education (NMCHE, hereafter referred to as CHE) to acknowledge its expanded obligations. These supplemental duties more clearly detailed the CHE's role in institutional finance. Statutes specifically addressed areas concerning student financial aid, the coordination of new technologies, the expansion of new campuses and learning facilities, and the CHE's role in educational programs and operations (NMCHE 1999a, b).

The now-defunct CHE was a statutory coordinating body that worked to offer a statewide perspective in recommending and establishing policy direction for New Mexico higher education. The CHE had thirteen commissioners, appointed by the governor for six-year terms. The commissioners were charged with addressing policy and governance issues related to the CHE. The executive director for the CHE served as the state higher education executive officer and managed a staff that addressed issues ranging from articulation and transfer to higher education's role in teacher quality. Various respondents said that some of the commissioners and the executive director did not see eye-to-eye on many issues, which led to internal problems. One former commissioner also added that the number of commissioners on the board was simply too large, so there was never a chance to move in a particular direction. Another former commissioner agreed with this assessment and added that disagreements among commission members plagued its ability to get anything done.

The CHE was described by many as understaffed. In the late 1990s, the CHE itself commissioned an independent consultant to assess its activity and effectiveness. An important finding in the report was that the CHE had a capable staff, but that it was trying to "fight a hundred fires with a hundred buckets of water" (NCHEMS 1999b). One former CHE staffer summarized the situation by saying that much of what the CHE produced was statutory, since legislative requests and requirements had to be fulfilled, but there were no resources to respond to additional needs. Several policymakers acknowledged that during its time, the CHE played an important role but faced resource challenges. Many people remember the BEF as effective because of its focus, and part of the difficulty for the CHE staff was the constant added responsibilities.

Respondents also spoke directly about statewide policy priorities. Most believe that the CHE had difficulty in establishing statewide policy directions for New Mexico higher education. Many consider that what is true for the legislature-governor relationship was also true for the CHE—the constitutional autonomy of the six state universities makes it extremely difficult to establish an audience for any policy framework built on consensus. Some used terms such as "the culture" and "the environment" in describing an atmosphere that was not conducive to instituting a statewide agenda for higher education policy priorities.

It is likely that recent higher educational changes will require the alignment and forward momentum of several forces, including the governor, the legislature, and all education-related agencies. A number of interviewees described the lack of previous gubernatorial and legislative interest in developing a statewide higher education policy agenda as a major impediment for the CHE's worthy but unsuccessful efforts at trying to develop widely accepted priorities. A policy advisor said that it would take more alignment and force to move higher education than it would to reform K–12, but even if this cohesion did happen, he would remain skeptical. The advisor recalled an earlier time when "momentum from a few different directions" existed that could have influenced higher education. For instance, an ad hoc legislative group called the Interim Committee on Excellence in Education operated during the same period that the CHE was conducting statewide roundtables to address higher education issues. "Still, nothing happened," the advisor concluded.

Policy officials and higher education administrators believe that there is a role a higher education agency could play. One former CHE commissioner said that the CHE clearly controlled graduate programs, made principal funding recommendations, and outlined capital outlay suggestions that were relied upon by the governor. An administrator from a comprehensive university confirmed that graduate programs were very much subject to approval by the CHE, but noted that because of this it was extremely difficult to respond to market needs.

The CHE's review of institutional budgets was one mechanism by which priorities or messages were sent to the institutions. Because funding recommendations are about money, the CHE was a legitimate vehicle to influence institutions. Some interviewees said that even though budget recommendations went through the CHE, institutions circumvented the system, much as they did before the establishment of the BEF. One legislator said the CHE's role in budgeting was simply one of consolidating the budgets.

Today, institutions continue to approach the legislature independently for special projects and additional funding. Oftentimes they are successful in getting their requests fulfilled. A university administrator, reflecting on his university's lobbyist, said, "Lobbying overall isn't beneficial to accomplishing state priorities, but it is an institutional necessity." There is little doubt that the CHE was, as one state legislator described it, "stronger on paper" than in reality. There are pockets of optimism that concomitant events and interests may be producing an opportunity to set the stage for a serious statewide higher education discussion that would lead to policy priorities. Legislators are interested in accountability, and they have passed legislation that requires all New Mexico public agencies to address this issue. Institutional presidents meet on a regular basis. And the CHE has given way to a new, more centralized governance form, called the New Mexico Higher Education Department.

New Mexico Higher Education Department

In 2005, the legislature passed and the governor signed Chapter 289 (House Bill 745), creating the New Mexico Higher Education Department (NMHED, hereafter referred to as HED), a cabinet-level agency. The new agency replaced the CHE, and the new statute expanded some of the authority of the department, although much of its operational functions remain the same as the CHE. The new law also created the Higher Education Advisory Board to advise the department and the governor on policy matters. The board is administratively attached to the department and replaces the former commission. The former commissioners were all appointed by the governor; the fourteen members on the advisory board are essentially assigned or appointed by the cabinet secretary. Any board seat which requires representation of a group or a number of institutions is an appointed seat. The fourteen board members consist of the following:

- the presidents of the three research universities (permanent representation)
- the president of one of the regional universities
- three two-year college representatives
- one accredited private postsecondary institution representative
- one business representative
- one representative of the tribal colleges in New Mexico
- one representative of the Indian nations, tribes, and pueblos
- one student representative
- one faculty representative
- one nonfaculty representative

Several respondents had interesting reactions to the new advisory board. Some said that board members often sent surrogates to the meetings because they did not believe the work of the board would be taken seriously. However, Governor Richardson's intent, by many accounts, was to centralize decision making and create a more powerful state entity by making the HED a cabinet-level agency. Given that the new HED board is advisory, it is understandable how past players equate the new board with a weakened version of the old board, which was viewed by many as ineffectual.

Ad Hoc Advisory Committees and Task Forces

Under the statutory authority provided to the new department, the HED has the ability to create additional advisory committees or task forces to advise and make policy recommendations. Many of the following current task forces are continuations from previous CHE activities:

- articulation
- alignment
- college affordability
- formula enhancement
- geographic service areas
- nursing enhancement
- data sharing

In prior years, the CHE relied heavily on institutional participation, due to a lack of staff resources. Ironically, the HED does not have enough staff resources to help run the task forces and logistically support its policy responsibility. It is still too early to tell if the new task forces will be anything different from the old CHE advisory committees. Since some of the same resource challenges that the CHE struggled with still exist for the HED, difficulties are probable if the task forces attempt to implement any new initiatives.

ARTICULATION TASK FORCE

Articulation, or the ability to align the courses or requirements at one institution with those at another, has been a concern in New Mexico for some time. As far back as the 1980s, some legislators were engaged in discussion with the Association of Students of New Mexico, a college student lobbying organization involved with the need for improvements in articulation. In 1993, legislation required universities to report the number of accepted or denied transfer credits from community colleges. Universities submitted data and at times had to explain cases where credits were denied. This groundwork, along with the work of faculty groups defining transfer modules, paved the way for better articulation and transfer.

The Articulation Task Force exists in response to a more recent statute mandating higher education articulation. The first priority of the task force is to analyze the current articulation structures within institutions and diagnose the status of articulation throughout the New Mexico system. The task force has already assessed articulation models in existence for early childhood development and general business programs. The task force's second priority is to develop the policies and structure of a statewide general education core for automatic transfer between all New Mexico institutions, as well as to initiate specific procedures for institutions to submit courses for consideration as part of this general education core. The Articulation Task Force continues with significant momentum as it strives to create an effective articulation model.

ALIGNMENT TASK FORCE

A large problem in the New Mexico education system is the increasing need for remedial education. Often, students who assumed they had followed a college-preparatory curriculum throughout high school are surprised to have to take some type of remedial courses when they arrive at a New Mexico higher education institution. One university provost stated that 50 percent of the students attending research universities in New Mexico need remedial education. He stated that better alignment is critical, and that New Mexico high school students need math beyond Algebra II.

In an attempt to address remediation problems, the HED recently developed the Alignment Task Force. This task force is a collaborative effort between the New Mexico Higher Education Department and the New Mexico Public Education Department, which is responsible for the K–12 system in New Mexico. The eventual goal of the task force is to provide recommendations to align the high school curriculum and proficiency with college placement requirements, in order to decrease remediation at the higher education level. The responsibilities of this task force support Governor Richardson's education reform agenda "to develop seamless transition between secondary and postsecondary levels of education."

According to the HED, the major goal of the Alignment Task Force is to create a uniform policy to help high school students prepare for college. The task force will begin the development of a pilot phase, utilizing tests and test scores to track effectiveness. It also plans to identify intervention strategies and support services for middle school education.

COLLEGE AFFORDABILITY TASK FORCE

New Mexico has never had a substantial statewide, need-based aid program for college students. In 2003, when the Governor's Task Force undertook its work to examine higher education in the state, the former CHE also completed a project called the Student Success Study. Largely as a result of this study and the work of the Governor's Task Force, the College Affordability Financial Aid Act was passed into law in 2005. The intent of the act is to "encourage New Mexico students with financial need to attend and complete educational programs at public, postsecondary educational institutions in New Mexico." This new, needs-based student financial aid program will follow the federal eligibility criteria for awarding Pell grants. The initial legislation did not include an appropriation; however, in a recent legislative session, the HED received a special appropriation for an endowment fund of $49 million. The intent of the original legislation was to create an endowment of up to $250 million from nonrecurring state funds. The corpus of the endowment will remain intact, and interest revenues will provide funds for the financial aid program. Under current conditions, more than 40,000 New Mexico students could qualify for the state's new, need-based aid program (New Mexico Higher Education Department 2006a). According to one community college administrator, this program could also have a positive affect on the adult basic education population, and even eventually help raise the income levels of this demographic by providing access to additional education. The College Affordability Task Force will design the distribution and allocation structure of the need-based program.

FORMULA ENHANCEMENT TASK FORCE

The Formula Enhancement Task Force is an extension of a previous CHE committee called the Blue Ribbon Task Force. The Blue Ribbon Task Force studied the higher education funding formula, and the Formula Enhancement Task Force will further develop and implement portions of performance-based funding tied to the current formula-funding structure. The task force will also recommend additional potential performance measurements.

GEOGRAPHIC SERVICE AREAS TASK FORCE

The HED has statutory authority over the development of two-year, four-year, and graduate-level degrees. The Geographic Service Area Task Force will review higher education geographic service areas for these degree programs throughout the state. The task force will also recommend policy and rule changes determining the governance of new academic programs. New policies are expected to reduce duplicative services and minimize the high cost of continuing or expanding existing programs. Not surprisingly, the formulation of the task force occurred after the recent and somewhat controversial addition of a four-year program at a two-year institution and the shift of one small learning center into a full branch campus.

NURSING ENHANCEMENT TASK FORCE

New Mexico continues to suffer from a nursing shortage. In 2005, the Legislative Finance Committee conducted a performance audit aimed at deciphering the total amount of state and federal dollars spent toward improving this issue. Focus was placed on the effectiveness and accountability of nursing enhancement programs. The Nursing Enhancement Task Force will review and develop performance measures for nursing programs in New Mexico. This task force will also make performance recommendations pertaining to nursing funds within the higher education funding formula to the Formula Enhancement Task Force.

DATA SHARE TASK FORCE

The Data Share Task Force also evolved from a previous CHE data and reporting committee. However, recent legislation mandated that overarching state education agencies "establish a common, shared student data system from pre-kindergarten to postsecondary levels of education, including adult basic education and training." The focus of the new Data Share Task Force is to develop a statewide plan for student data sharing, including the implementation of a uniform student identifier throughout the education pipeline, from pre-kindergarten through college. The previous CHE data committee primarily served in an informational capacity to higher educational institutions, and it was not as successful at developing new systems and information. It is difficult to tell if the new Data Share Task Force will be effective in accomplishing the full scope of the new legislation, especially because of apparent resource constraints.

Summing Up HED

The college and university administrators we surveyed indicated that it is too soon to know where the HED is going. They commented that the transition from a commission to a cabinet-level agency occurred because the CHE lacked political clout and synergy with the legislature. One respondent anticipates that cabinet-level status could result in a strong higher education policy agency, yet the shortfall may be that higher education will become too dependent on the executive level of government. Judging from some interview comments, it seems that the new structure limits institutional input and leaves all decision making in the hands of the HED's central staff. From a state viewpoint, that is precisely what previous policymakers and Governor Richardson seem to have pushed for. Yet, despite the recent successes New Mexico has had in creating a change in educational structure exemplified by the HED, there are plenty of observers who believe that continuing staff constraints and a substantial turnover in staff will hamstring the ability of the HED to fully exercise the influence the law intended it to have.

College and University Policy Associations

In the early 1990s, the New Mexico Association of Community Colleges was formed to represent the community college sector. The executive director's charge is twofold: to provide a link with and keep the community colleges visible to the state. The association is also an avenue through which stakeholders and constituents can communicate with the community college sector. By almost every account, the association has been a great success and has enjoyed stable leadership.

Partly because of this success, the state's public universities formed the Council of University Presidents. The council employs an executive director and is comprised of the presidents of New Mexico's six public institutions. The council adopted three areas that topped its priority list in the late 1990s and into the new decade: (1) accountability, (2) teacher quality, and (3) the economic impact universities have on the state. Its executive director believes that it is important to define priorities and address them; however, what is equally important in the council's dealings with the legislature and higher education stakeholders is "educating, reporting, and trust-building." A university president said that the role of the council is critical because policymakers, from his perspective, seem to support community colleges more than universities, perhaps because these individuals have a better understanding of the missions of two-year institutions. Part of the council's purpose is to help policymakers understand the universities and the role they play in educating New Mexico residents.

The state's three private, nonprofit, four-year institutions—all comprehensive liberal arts universities—are represented by the Council of Independent Colleges and Universities of New Mexico. The private nonprofits have low enrollments relative to the public sector. The for-profit sector also has a presence in the state, most prominently represented by the University of Phoenix, Webster University, and National American University. A representative for the nonprofit area said the for-profit arena and its institutions are competitors, but "this type of institution is fine for that sector of the market that benefits from what they offer."

STATE RULES

Communication and collaboration among state actors and institutional leaders in New Mexico may best be described as a work in progress. The state's six public universities are constitutionally autonomous, and this independence has, by most policymakers' accounts, hampered the state's ability to define a common set of state policy priorities. Recent developments within New Mexico—one of which is the creation of the HED—have laid groundwork that may improve planning and the state's ability to move, through increased central control, toward a coherent higher education policy agenda. The results from the opposing forces of more centralized state power (if it is realized through the HED) and constitutional autonomy have not yet played out, but it is clear that the state rules are dynamic and evolving in New Mexico. Recent history and current events are chronicled below, revealing how the rules are changing and how they operated in the past.

Planning

Historically, New Mexico has been unable to produce a common set of policy goals for higher education. In 2005, legislation was passed mandating that the HED "cooperate with colleges and universities to create a statewide public agenda to meet higher education needs and goals." Performance planning and measurement is also in the nascent stages throughout the New Mexico higher education system. Laws were passed in 2003 to enforce accountability for the state's public agencies, including higher education. Yet even today, many questions remain, since the legislation does not specify exact guidelines for performance indicators or for program review and evaluation. Likewise, there has been no indication from the state as to which priority or problem areas must be addressed by any given agency. Thus implementation of the 2003 accountability legislation in New Mexico is slow moving.

The executive director for the Association of Community Colleges said that two-year institutions have been working on understanding their own performance for some time, and he sees no problems with satisfying state requirements. One of the top three priorities for the Council of University Presidents is accountability. The executive director for the council said that when he was hired, he believed that providing accurate and relevant information demonstrating accountability was absolutely essential from a policymaker's perspective, and that universities needed to make it a central issue.

While a few policymakers are skeptical about the work that the community colleges and universities have completed regarding accountability, most acknowledge that higher education is further along than most state agencies. One community college administrator said that the universities have made more progress than his sector, because they have the resources and the personnel to focus on accountability. All higher education representatives said they were making important strides in accountability, because they felt it was an area of importance. Several also noted that it is better to lead the way in this effort, rather than have something imposed on them when state performance measures are developed at a legislative level.

The exact impact of the state's performance and planning legislation is yet to be determined. Over time, many are hopeful that institutional strengths and weaknesses will emerge. One administrator said that if the universities provide information only on how well they are doing, then policymakers will not trust the comprehensiveness of their reporting. The real test of this performance legislation on higher education will be whether it leads to improved information that helps inform policymakers' decisions. A subsequent test would be whether legislation tying funding to performance provides real incentives or instead creates negative consequences for actual performance.

Program Review and Approval

Historically, undergraduate programs would emerge due to competitive offerings at other institutions, since there was no statewide coordination of such programs. "If UNM offers it, then NMSU has to offer it, too," said one policymaker. One administrator said the former CHE promoted collaboration, but the system didn't reward it. When asked about duplication, another university administrator said that graduate programs had to be approved by the CHE, but he viewed this as constraining his university's ability to be competitive. When asked about undergraduate programs, the administrator admitted that the CHE only needed to be informed of additions or revisions, and that his institution could act as it wished in this area. The HED will continue to approve graduate programs, and a new provision in the statutes gives the HED review authority over all new undergraduate programs. On paper, the HED has more control over undergraduate program review than the former CHE, but most of the study respondents said it is unclear what "review authority" means under the new structure. The HED has not provided a definition of or process for review, and the institutions have been content to operate as they have in the past. One could easily see the institutions challenging the HED, perhaps in a legal arena, if they feel any definition for review authority for undergraduate programs presses against constitutional status or historical practice.

Information

There has been no change within the higher education information system as a result of the transition from the CHE to the HED. Institutions are required to provide enrollment information to the HED, as they were to the CHE, on a semester basis. The information is entered into the Data Editing and Reporting (DEAR) system. In the past, the CHE hired data staff to provide raw data from DEAR to the CHE analysts. The analysts would then formulate research methodology to support state policy and program development. DEAR is the only state higher education data repository; thus the HED, like the CHE before it, is essentially the sole interface to state-related higher education data. According to one former employee familiar with the CHE and the DEAR system, for the last five years of the CHE's existence, there was only one staff member with an adequate level of expertise who could deftly provide information and reports. Now, the same staff member is the only resource within the HED, again continuing the staff limitations that long plagued the CHE. Respondents also cited the extraordinary turnover of other staff members as the CHE gave way to the HED. Support staff who may have had expertise with information systems were lost. Moreover, turnover meant that individuals with the institutional memory and knowledge to help steer the central agency through its duties had also left.

In addition to constraints on staff who might otherwise have provided information and fulfilled legislative requests, the DEAR system does not include (and never did) data sufficient for analysis and evaluation of specific initiatives. The state does not have a unit record system to track students by social security number. The original design of the system was to support funding, so it is not particularly useful for reporting outcomes for such areas as program review. Furthermore, the universities may use some informational sources and databases other than DEAR, such as the Integrated Postsecondary Education Data System (IPEDS). This means that information and outcome data are not centralized or standardized, which further reinforces institutional autonomy.

The former CHE created an annual report that profiles the conditions and characteristics of higher education in New Mexico, and the HED has continued to produce it. The report is descriptive only and includes information on enrollment, student aid, tuition, faculty salaries, capital outlay, and other highlights of New Mexico's postsecondary industry. Lawmakers had different reactions to the annual report. One representative said she knows whom to call when she needs information and appreciates anything that helps her understand higher education. Others simply said the annual report was "necessary" or "helpful." One state official said that no matter what a central higher education organization does, "it can't be a strong voice without gubernatorial and legislative support and interest." One thing seems certain about the information available in New Mexico—policymakers trust data from a central state agency more than they do that from institutional sources.

There have been instances where reports and information have attempted to raise an issue, such as in the area of completion. The challenge of improving completion rates for associate's and bachelor's degrees in New Mexico is documented by both state and national sources. Although not frequently mentioned in our interviews, some policymakers and administrators did acknowledge issues related to this area. In its 1999 annual report, the CHE noted that the likelihood of a New Mexico student completing a bachelor's degree remains lower than desirable, and added, "Comparing older to more recent cohorts of students being tracked in these analyses failed to reveal any evidence of significant improvement in degree completion rates for the more recent cohorts." The National Center for Higher Education Management Systems (NCHEMS) stated that New Mexico's institutions produce relatively fewer graduates than institutions in surrounding states, particularly at the baccalaureate level. NCHEMS also commented that New Mexico did much better on graduate education completion, believing that the state's higher education system is effective in fulfilling graduate and research functions and is best suited to serve the wealthiest and most populous counties in the state (NCHEMS 1999b).

Completion rates within six years for first-time students continue to be especially low, significantly depressing the state's performance on this measure. In several of its reports, the CHE indicated that the time to completion for those who do persist also needs attention. Although there was no numerical evidence, one former CHE source said New Mexico's lottery scholarship program seems to be increasing the time to graduation, since the required courseload is only twelve credit hours per semester. One state senator said that when the state is footing the bill, graduation is a problem if it is taking the universities seven to eight years to graduate some students. But, he said, in the past many issues in New Mexico that seemed important within higher education were nonissues at the state policy level.

Academic Preparation

In the past, the CHE and the state Board of Education, now the Public Education Department (PED) for K–12, held roundtable discussions and statewide meetings on issues related to preparation. Today, a more formal alliance between the HED and the PED exists within the structure of the new Alignment Task Force. If academic preparation is to be addressed, it will be through this task force.

Student Assistance

The Lottery Success Scholarship Program dominates state financial aid policy in New Mexico. The need-based aid that will eventually be part of the state's financial aid picture is not yet at the point of implementation, because the endowment that will provide student awards is still not fully funded. The lottery program was started in 1996, largely at the behest of a powerful state legislator. The acceptance and implementation of the lottery scholarship program was undoubtedly helped by its perceived relationship to access and its political appeal. Through the lottery program, every New Mexico high school graduate (or GED recipient), regardless of income, who meets relatively modest criteria can get 100 percent of his or her tuition paid at a New Mexico public college or university. However, this program excludes private-sector institutions.

The lottery scholarship program is widely considered to be the policy mechanism that has increased access to higher education, although no definitive empirical reports exist to substantiate this claim. Many public higher education administrators believe that this increased access has led to greater student choice and increased affordability. Other respondents said that the most significant aspect of the lottery is that it allows more New Mexico students to participate in postsecondary education than ever before. The perceived effectiveness of the Lottery Success Scholarship Program in promoting choice, affordability, and participation has probably been amplified by its political popularity, which has taken the state to a point of no return. There is no way of knowing how many of the lottery recipients would have participated if the program did not exist, or how many did participate because of the program. Nor is there any way of telling exactly how many students would have chosen to attend a two-year institution instead of a four-year institution if the lottery scholarship hadn't been available. Policymakers and higher education administrators all seem to agree on one thing—the lottery scholarship has been a positive development for higher education in New Mexico.

Both the strength and the weakness of the lottery program is its popularity. As enrollment increases and tuition rates rise, projections for the lottery tuition scholarship fund cause serious concern. The HED projects annual expenditures to rise from $34 million in 2006 to as high as $58.8 million by fiscal year (FY) 2010–11 . Projected revenues are predicted to constantly decrease. The expected net effect will result in a negative fund balance of $16 million by midyear 2010 (New Mexico Higher Education Department 2006b).

Many proposals to expand or change the criteria for the lottery have been introduced in the legislature within the past few years, all with no success. In 2005, the Senate mandated that the Legislative Council Service analyze the lottery tuition scholarship program. The interim committee to conduct this study has yet to release findings or recommendations from the project. A summary of state financial aid does show that many of the concerns regarding the lottery program's financial viability should be taken seriously. In 1998, the lottery program accounted for 20.9 percent of all New Mexico state financial assistance for higher education students, whereas in 2004 the program accounted for 42 percent. In addition, 12 percent of the total resident undergraduate enrollment in FY 2005 received a lottery scholarship, compared to 4.9 percent in 1998 (NMCHE 1999a, b, 2000, 2001, 2002, 2003, 2004, 2005; NMHED 2006b).

These NMCHE reports show that, despite the increase in lottery scholarships, state financial aid increases in New Mexico were outpaced by growth in federal and private sources in 1998. Even private dollars surpassed state contributions to student aid in 1998, although the number of state aid recipients still exceeded private aid recipients. Data from the more recent reports suggest that funds from federal sources were more than three times the amount of both private and state dollars available to students in 2004–5. This information indicates that most students receive some combination of both state and federal assistance.

While the lottery program excludes the private sector, there is a program in the state that awards need-based scholarships to students attending private institutions. The Student Choice Scholarship Program is funded by state appropriations and is based on a formula that takes public tuition into account. However, the program furnishes monies for just a small proportion of students in relation to the lottery. A private sector respondent, discussing the Student Choice Scholarship, said, "The state subsidy for students in the public sector is so tremendous that the state actually saves money by diverting students to the private sector. By giving us $3,000, they do not have to give the University of New Mexico $8,000."

Fiscal Policies

State appropriations and capital funding processes have been in place for some time, and institutions play by a set of explicit and implicit common rules. The process of institutional budgeting is relatively straightforward. Institutions submit operating budget requests to the HED, and this department then reviews the budgets and makes a recommendation to the legislature and the governor's office. The recommendations are taken seriously, providing the basic input for formulating the state's higher education budget.

The higher education appropriations process in New Mexico has essentially followed along the same lines ever since the inception of the CHE. The formula, which is enrollment driven, was legislatively initiated in 1978. The state's then governor, Jerry Apodaca, was under pressure from the legislature to formalize the funding process, since it was essentially a free-for-all with each institution approaching the legislature individually with its requests. According to one source, "the creation of the enrollment-driven model in New Mexico was very much an accomplishment at the time. This was because the state had and continues to have a very progressive attitude toward equity and access that is a cultural attitude of the state." The enrollment-driven formula was intended to provide a rational, systematic approach to funding higher education. "Having a formula, whatever its weaknesses," said one respondent, "has the advantage of lessening political game playing."

The New Mexico higher education funding formula uses current-year appropriations as the base appropriation figure for the following year, and instructional funding calculations are based upon prior-year student credit hours. The net result is a two-year lag between the student-component credit hours and the funding year. Increases in fixed costs allow for inflationary-type additions for utility payments and rising insurance premiums. An enrollment increase of 3 percent, or a decrease of 5 percent or more, determines applicable workload adjustments. All credit hours, including those for summer school and extended learning, are considered to be equal throughout the formula.

The structure of the funding formula supporting higher education also includes five incentive funds. These funds have yet to receive general fund appropriations—or have received very little—so they are not yet established as true incentives. The incentive monies include a faculty endowment (to improve faculty quality), a performance fund, a program development enhancement fund, a workforce development fund, and a technology enhancement fund.

There are slight differences of opinion about which actors influence the process of adjusting or revising the funding formula and about who drives conversations about incentive funds. A former CHE administrator said there was no formal process for revisions and that all adjustments have been minor. She added, "CHE had to approve any change, and if institutions even would want a change, they must present a united front." The former administrator's sense was that institutional agreement would not mean an automatic change. An institutional administrator concurred about the absence of a formal process but emphasized institutional influence, noting that "it is difficult to make changes that do not have institutional support." The CHE was widely viewed as interested in feedback from the institutions. One former staffer noted, "CHE did not revise the formula in isolation, nor did it wish to. Our intention was not to surprise anyone. We took a collaborative approach to our work." Over the last several years of its life, the CHE had an informal funding formula task force, comprised of two-year and four-year representatives, to discuss possible modifications to the formula. The Formula Enhancement Task Force is the formal entity of the newly created HED, and only time will tell if performance-based funding gets off the ground, or if the formula will ever change in a significant way.

One prominent factor in the appropriations process concerns tuition increases. Each year the legislature determines a "reasonable" amount by which tuition might or will increase. The amount that the legislature stipulates can be thought of as a *tuition credit*. There is no way that the legislature can hold institutions to any guideline, though, since institutions are free to determine their own tuition levels. Nonetheless, institutional appropriations are not reduced for raising tuition, as long as increases do not exceed the tuition credit. If an institution boosts its tuition beyond the legislatively determined tuition credit, however, the subsequent year's appropriation for that institution is reduced, because their tuition credit has gone past the acceptable limit. The penalty assessed for exceeding this acceptable limit cannot occur within the same year as the tuition hike, since the legislature typically appropriates funds before institutions make decisions about tuition prices.

Some higher education institutions consistently increase tuition beyond the level that the legislature allows. For example, for the four-year schools, the average tuition increase of 11.5 percent in 2005 was above the legislatively approved 3 percent rise. According to the Legislative Finance Committee, "universities on average have consistently imposed resident undergraduate tuition rates greater than the tuition credit." In contrast, in the mid-1990s, two-year institutions imposed resident undergraduate tuition rates lower than the assumed tuition credit. Most legislators we interviewed believe that four-year institutions disproportionately raise tuition as a result of the lottery scholarship program. This has caused some to feel that higher education is raising prices because it is being subsidized. One president said that the lottery scholarship amount is actually quite small compared to total tuition and revenues, so the lottery's effect on institutional action is negligible. According to another administrator, "there has not been an impact on tuition and fees as some speculate. We don't make pricing decisions based on the lottery scholarship. That funding is much too small to make an impact on our decisions."

Although tuition has risen in New Mexico, levels remain low compared to national averages. A likely factor contributing to these low tuition rates is the state's generous funding for higher education institutions. Mortenson (1999) concluded that on a funding-per-student basis, New Mexico's efforts to invest in higher education are extraordinary.

From policymakers to administrators, there is a strong sense that low tuition is an important part of New Mexico's higher education culture, because it enables access. Institutional presidents said they were committed to access because it is crucial to the mission of their institutions. One president stated that while there is a strong message from the legislature to keep tuition affordable, as far as his institution was concerned, "that's singing to the choir, because that's what we are trying to do anyway." One community college president described access as his institution's top priority, and that realizing that commitment meant keeping tuition low.

The process of submitting higher education capital funding requests is similar to that for operating budget requests. Institutions present a list of priority projects to the HED. The HED reviews all the capital funding lists and then prioritizes projects from a statewide perspective, which makes it possible that one institution's top two requests may be ranked higher than another institution's top request. The HED's recommendation is then passed on to the legislature and the governor's office.

Despite these rational procedures, the universities approach the legislature individually for capital funds and special projects, employing lobbyists to communicate their priorities and advocate for additional funds, in addition to working together through the Council of University Presidents. The community colleges lobby the legislature as one body, through the New Mexico Association of Community Colleges. The community colleges, of course, also have another way to fund capital projects. According to a state higher education analyst, pending voter approval, all the community colleges with taxing districts and a governing board could implement debt-service mill levies. Based on these criteria, all two-year institutions in New Mexico, with the exception of Northern New Mexico College, could issue bonds.

In 2001, the CHE hired a company to produce an assessment of the facilities on state higher education campuses. The scope of the project was to analyze the condition of these buildings and present repair and remodel costs to the state. Findings from this study identified a backlog of $820.7 million in maintenance and update remodeling projects (NMCHE 2001). In 2006, the legislature appropriated $60 million toward this backlog, but the governor vetoed this line item, due to the lack of a recent assessment and a prioritized schedule of projects. The HED then hired the same company to update the original assessment, which subsequently reported a backlog of $1.5 billion for these projects (NMHED 2006c).

Research and Development

Higher education administrators and state officials alike believe that economic development is one of the benefits of higher education. The existing evidence regarding higher education's contributions in this area is somewhat impressionistic, but this issue has attracted increased attention in New Mexico. Policymakers and community college administrators agree that two-year institutions are collaborating to a great extent with business and industry. One board president for a community college said that the success of her institution is largely predicated on its ability to do so, and the state knows this institution does a good job of interfacing with the business community. The board president noted that this collaboration happens because every program has a committee that communicates with business and industry constituents.

State officials seem a bit more skeptical when they are asked to connect universities with both state and local economic development. In fairness, little is understood about the precise linkages between university activity and economic development. Thus far, the universities have produced reports to highlight what they are doing in this regard. A report from the University of New Mexico, for example, outlines several areas it believes demonstrate the institution's contribution to economic development:

- information on graduates, in terms of the numbers and types of degrees
- workforce training and development, which includes descriptions of programs and the numbers of individuals receiving this training
- research and other activities, in terms of the out-of-state revenues, jobs, and expenditures related to such activities
- support of business development and the ability to attract new business, which include descriptions of programs and efforts

Administrators agreed that these reports were the result of both state interest in economic development and the accountability statutes. Increased state-level attention to performance has stimulated some institutional response addressing the question of economic development, but that response has been to document current activity rather than to change it. However, university officials do feel that higher education is contributing to economic development, and the reports are a way to begin highlighting that contribution.

HIGHER EDUCATION SYSTEMS

New Mexico's higher education system is, by most accounts, expansive for a state with a population under two million. The state's six public universities and nineteen community colleges are a testament to the culture of access that has long been a part of its history. The state is also home to three private, non-profit, liberal arts universities. According to population estimates and institutional data (Chronicle of Higher Education Almanac 2002), in New Mexico there is one postsecondary institution available for every 38,600 residents. The national average is 63,726, placing New Mexico seventh by this measure.

The University of New Mexico (UNM), New Mexico State University (NMSU), and Eastern New Mexico University (ENMU) all have two-year branch campuses that function as community colleges but operate under the governance of their respective universities. UNM and NMSU each have four branch campuses, and ENMU has three (Bowes 1997). Interestingly, all of these branch campuses decided to remove themselves from the New Mexico Association of Community Colleges. This move was triggered by the branch campus leaders, who feel that their structure and needs are very different from those of the other nine community colleges around the state. Some discussions suggest that the branch campuses may become a subgroup of the Council of University Presidents, since their requisites are more intertwined with their parent universities.

From several perspectives, New Mexico's higher education system design encourages participation in a college education and provides a choice of public institutions. A university or community college is within a reasonable distance of virtually every rural and urban area. A representative from the Council of Independent Colleges and Universities of New Mexico agreed that there are plenty of public institutions, but he also noted that private institutions have been left out of the picture and that New Mexicans have less choice because of it. The representative said that the specific effect of limiting lottery scholarships to public universities has "hurt the private sector in terms of recruiting students" and "distorted where people want to attend college."

The belief that New Mexico's public institutions maximize the opportunity for participation has raised challenges in the debate on the need for distance education. When asked about distance education as a means to increase access, one president noted: "There is no state with as many institutions within reach of its population as in New Mexico. With the number of institutions we have in this state that are accessible and within proximity to our population, don't you have to ask, How much of a need is there for distance education?" For some regional universities that are not located in populated areas of the state, however, distance education is another avenue to increase enrollment and take education beyond the immediate service area. Still, one gets the sense that universities using distance education struggle not only with the lack of state incentives to promote such offerings, but with actual enrollments that would justify the cost of delivery.

System Actors

Trustees

A summary document by the former CHE states that the ten public university branch campuses have locally elected advisory boards, but major policy and budgetary matters are within the domain of the university governing boards under which these branch campuses operate. The ten branch campuses have statutory authority to tax districts in their areas. The remaining nine community colleges are governed under various arrangements. The state constitution established two additional institutions, both of which are overseen by a board appointed by the governor. The New Mexico Military Institution has a dual focus: high school education and a general curriculum content that is geared toward transfer programs. Northern New Mexico Community College was originally established to prepare bilingual educators. Both of these institutions receive their support from the state, and they cannot receive operational expenses through local support.

Locally elected boards govern four of the nine independent public community colleges. These institutions receive state funding, but they also are able to draw on local support and issue bonds for capital outlay. San Juan College and Clovis Community College actually started out as branch campuses, but they both became independent and locally governed in the 1980s. The final three community colleges started out as vocational institutions. In 1986, technical institutes were authorized to grant associate's degrees (Bowes 1997). Today, Mesa Technical College, Luna Vocational-Technical, and Albuquerque Technical Vocational Institute (ATVI) all offer associate's degrees and are community colleges. ATVI has evolved into the state's largest comprehensive community college, and in 2006 changed its name to Central New Mexico Community College to more accurately convey its purpose and mission. All three technical institutions that metamorphosed into community colleges are independent and governed by locally elected boards.

Each of the constitutionally autonomous universities has its own governing board. The governor may appoint no more than three of the five members for each board from the same political party. The governing boards for the universities continue to have great freedoms in all matters related to their institutions. The appointment process offers the biggest potential for a governor to influence a board, although the restriction on party affiliation somewhat tempers the governor's influence.

Administration and Faculty

Prior to the existence of the Council of University Presidents, there was no formal mechanism by which these institutional leaders shared ideas, searched for areas of commonality, or found opportunities for collaboration. One president from a research university said there was no structure or coherence to any conversations he had with his colleagues prior to the council's existence, whereas "the council provides a great opportunity for us to work together to serve the state." Community college leaders conveyed a similar sentiment in reference to the New Mexico Association of Community Colleges. A byproduct of the establishment of the university council and the community college association is that it created a forum for these two sectors to communicate and meet with each other and with state-level officials. However, even with the existence of the council and the association, most university and community college executives continue to carry out their work in what may be described as a decentralized environment. The result is little standardization either in the information institutions choose to report or in how they carry out certain administrative tasks, such as strategic planning.

Faculty members, like their administrative counterparts, operate quite autonomously. According to interviews, the one formal avenue through which faculty across campuses communicate is when faculty senate leaders from different campuses occasionally meet. One respondent said the meetings are not very purposeful and rarely lead to any action items. In New Mexico, faculty members are not unionized.

System Rules

Planning

Most community colleges and universities have formalized their strategic planning processes and made progress toward defining performance measurements. The impetus to improve planning and publicize its progress was, of course, the accountability legislation. This legislation does not prescribe parameters for planning and for performance measurement, so the institutions have taken the initiative to define their own processes and measures.

Therefore, from a state perspective, the evolution of institutional planning continues to lack a standardized component.

Program Initiatives

Few, if any, program initiatives exist at the system level. The new task forces may produce some that focus on policy priorities, but that seems years in the making. Still, there are areas that need attention. The issue of completion was raised in the past and continues to be a concern around the state, although no initiative exists to improve performance in this area. The production of teacher graduates has been another very important issue of concern in the state. Teacher quality is not a statutory charge, but there has been a growing collaboration between the HED and the Public Education Department for K–12 (PED) to address the issue. According to a state report, New Mexico institutions produce approximately 1,300 new teachers each year. Projected retirement and attrition rates, coupled with out-of-state recruitment efforts, leave the state with an estimated annual shortage of approximately 1,500 teachers (NMCHE & NMPED 2000). The teacher shortage issue is something many states are struggling with, but the problem is magnified in a rapidly growing state like New Mexico. A well-known state legislator said that teacher education has been a priority for the legislature since the early 1990s, but there was no formal mechanism to hold institutions accountable and determine whether they were doing their part. If there is any one area where policymakers seem eager to create initiatives, the most promising seems to be that of teacher recruitment and teacher quality.

In the past, initiatives involving incentives were even harder to steer in a particular direction. A legislative aide gave an example that demonstrates why there are still obstacles to overcome, even when money is used as an enticement for collaboration. The aide recalled one initiative for state-funded grants targeting distance technology. Colleges were asked to forward proposals outlining how the monies they received would be used. The primary criteria in the guidelines called for collaboration but, according to the legislative contact, just about every proposal ignored this issue.

Enrollment Planning

Institutions do not strategically engage in enrollment planning in New Mexico. Their basic, unconscious strategy is to enroll as many students as possible, because the state funding formula provides more money as enrollment increases. The proportion of state appropriations for community colleges continues to increase relative to that for four year institutions. Community college enrollment has been growing strongly since the early 1990s. Between 1990 and 1998, community college enrollment grew 42 percent, while enrollment in the four-year sector remained flat. Between fall 1999 and fall 2002, community college enrollment grew another 12.5 percent; university enrollment also increased slightly during this period (NMCHE 1999a, b, 2000, 2001, 2002, 2003, 2004, 2005; the following enrollment figures are also from these sources). The strongest enrollment growth occurred in the state's largest comprehensive community college, the newly named New Mexico Central Community College. Central's growth rate from 1990 to 1998 was 48 percent, an impressive figure considering that it was already the state's largest two-year postsecondary institute in 1990. From 1999 to 2002, Central experienced another 24.6 percent increase in enrollment.

The state's two largest research universities also recorded enrollment growth during the last half of the 1990s (coinciding with the initiation of the state's lottery scholarship program), but the regional comprehensive universities had trouble maintaining their enrollments, effectively canceling out the enrollment gains made in the research universities. From 1999 to 2002, two regional comprehensives experienced minimal growth, while one institution suffered a 5.6 percent decline. Eastern New Mexico University, considered by many to be an innovative institution guided by strong leadership, is one example of an institution struggling with the enrollment issue. ENMU is located in the eastern part of New Mexico, far from the state's three major population centers. One state respondent, commenting on ENMU's leadership role in distance education, said it was probably true that ENMU was innovative and cutting-edge relative to other institutions, but that perhaps the geographic challenges it faces contribute to that innovation. An ENMU administrator said that distance education has been important, but that equipment and technology are fast becoming outmoded and updates are needed. The administrator also wondered about the expense of such a delivery mode for the modest numbers currently being served.

Clearly, there is variation in enrollment trends among the many institutions in New Mexico. On the whole, statewide enrollment in public colleges and universities has increased every year since 1990, not just since the lottery program was implemented in 1996. Given this upswing, it is difficult to gauge the lottery's exact impact on participation levels, but almost everyone in the state believes that the lottery program has made a university education a viable option for those who otherwise would not have even considered it a possibility. One university president said that after the lottery took effect, freshman enrollment increased by nearly 25 percent at his campus. Some state-level officials believe increasing enrollment at public four-year universities is an undesirable and unintended consequence of lottery scholarships, because it encourages students to begin their postsecondary careers at these more expensive four-year institutions.

Higher education has been a steady growth industry in New Mexico. Two predictive factors for higher education enrollment lead to conflicting conclusions about future trends. On the positive side, overall population increases continue. The U.S. Census Bureau estimates New Mexico's total population growth at 15.4 percent for the time period between 2000 and 2030. On the negative side, estimates from the Western Interstate Commission for Higher Education (WICHE), project an overall 7.9 percent decline in New Mexico high school graduates between 2006 and 2018. The growth that does occur in subpopulations of high school graduates will be in groups having a higher risk of not attending a postsecondary institution immediately after graduation. For example, Latino projections are expected to comprise up to 52 percent of New Mexico's total number of high school graduates by 2014 (WICHE 2004).

There is little doubt that the rules of the game in New Mexico influence the extent to which higher education policies and priorities are established, pursued, and implemented. For example, the evidence suggests that the autonomy and structure of New Mexico's higher education institutions, combined with the state's fiscal policy, have been particularly influential. The autonomy of institutions and the governance structure that existed over the majority of our study period largely constrained any ability policymakers had to forward a coherent set of policy priorities. Despite policymakers' somewhat limited ability to directly influence higher education, New Mexico institutions have experienced a very reasonable funding climate relative to other states.

In many respects, New Mexico higher education represents a system that gives precedence to what goes into the system (students and funding), rather than what comes out of it (retention and graduation). Burke (2004) charts the maturation of a system: first it focuses on growth, then efficiency, followed by quality, and finally by responsiveness. New Mexico's attention to access and its somewhat absent discussion on formal policy priorities suggest that the state has not yet fully engaged in strategies to address quality and responsiveness. Although funding measurements, such as appropriations per capita, might indicate a state's commitment to higher education, high values on such measures might just as easily point to an expensive system that is somewhat inefficient.

When addressing issues of performance, several of the higher education administrators represented in our study spoke of an inherent tradeoff between access and categories such as completion. One president said he is increasingly hearing that his institution doesn't retain and graduate enough students, yet the most accessible institutions across the nation always have lower retention and graduation rates. Another president said his institution could simply raise admissions criteria if they wanted to increase graduation rates, but his university was committed to modest entrance requirements. Indeed, the message of access resonates with policymakers and higher education officials alike. The number of institutions across the state, coupled with the funding they have received over the years, is a testament to this philosophy.

The longstanding rules of the game in New Mexico may be on the verge of changing. Several policymakers in the state say that public priorities are needed, and perhaps the relationship between state officials and higher education leaders will shift with the newly created Higher Education Department . This cabinet-level state higher education agency has a direct line to the executive branch and a wider range of tools from which to create state-level policies than was previously true for the now-defunct Commission on Higher Education. The next five years will be particularly interesting in New Mexico, as the HED works to establish itself as a legitimate actor on the higher education scene.

CHAPTER FOUR

California

❖

with contributions by Nancy Shulock

*California is close to the median in effort, and its performance is mixed.
On some measures it does very well; on others, it ranks among the lower-
performing states. This seems unusual for a state with good economic resources,
a fine past reputation (stemming from the 1960 California Master Plan for
Higher Education), and high-performing research universities. One possible
answer might rest with the rules for distributing state funds in California,
which clearly favor the University of California at the expense of low-tuition
community colleges. California's state constitution prohibits the direct
appropriation of public funds to private institutions. The vaunted Master Plan
(later described by its author as a treaty among the segments) discourages
the use of market forces by tightly circumscribing the missions and enrollment
pools for each of the three public sectors. A lack of consistent and effective
statewide coordination has produced concurrent conditions where goals and
priorities that can be established and implemented by a single segment can
achieve very high levels of excellence, while those that require collaboration
across the segments fall through the cracks. Shared governance, along with
other regulations mandated by the legislature, and taxpayer initiatives aimed
at lowering property taxes have so muddied the waters for community colleges
that distinguishing either their mission or their priorities can be a serious
challenge.*

❖

California, with 36 million residents, has the largest population of any U.S.
state. Over the next twenty-five years, California will be the fastest-growing
state, adding 12 million residents, or one-third of its current population. The
demographics are also changing. Between 1980 and 2000, the proportion of
the population that was white decreased from 67 percent to 47 percent, while
the Latino, Asian Pacific American, and black populations increased from 33
percent to 50 percent. By 2030, owing to high rates of immigration, the Latino

and Asian Pacific American populations will grow to represent approximately 60 percent of the total population.

California's economy is the largest of all fifty U.S. states, and by this measure would be the fifth largest country in the world. The manufacturing and agricultural industries in this state are the largest in the nation. California is also home to some of the newest and fastest-growing companies in the rapidly changing technology industry. Despite its impressive economy, during our study California faced a massive budget deficit, caused by a decrease in stock-market-related income and legislative inability to raise revenues and/or cut spending.

The deficit for the 2004–5 budget year was $15 billion. Between 2001 and 2003, nearly 300,000 Californians lost jobs, representing more than 10 percent of all jobs lost in the nation. In October 2003, through a special recall election, Governor Gray Davis was replaced by Arnold Schwarzenegger. Much of the public discontent with Governor Davis involved the state's continuing budget deficits. In 2008, California faced one of the two largest state budget deficits in the nation.

More than half of California's General Fund budget of $87 billion goes to education, with $36 billion going to the K–12 sector and $12.9 billion going to higher education, including community colleges. California is notorious for tying up the majority of its state budget in statutory commitments (i.e., *autopilot spending*). As the single largest discretionary item in the state budget, higher education is particularly vulnerable to budget cycles. Any downturn in revenue has significant implications for state-funded higher education programs and student fees. After decades of low fees in all segments, relative to their national counterparts, California colleges have significantly increased their student fees in recent years as a corollary to the budget crisis. In spite of state deficits, however, the new governor kept his commitment to fund enrollment growth in higher education in his budget for 2005–6 and his proposed budget for 2006–7.

Partly because of its size, the state has many economic development initiatives, but the role of higher education is shaped largely as a result of individual institutional or segmental strategies. While policy leaders support regional initiatives, they tend to view statewide efforts as undesirable or impossible in a state this large. Such efforts would also be difficult because of the way California has designed its system of higher education.

A common discussion is whether California is governable. The sheer size, diversity, and complexity of the state present severe obstacles to forming consensus around public policy goals. Voter disaffection with elected officials has led to a heavy use of the initiative process, which, ironically, has hamstrung elected officials and led to greater voter discontent. Partisan-driven reapportionment has eroded the political center, causing more gridlock and still more dependence on initiatives. *Ballot box* budgeting, where voter-approved propositions install spending requirements in the state constitution and statutes, has taken the place of the traditional public budgeting mechanism where elected officials set public priorities for funding from a general fund. Term limits have decreased legislators' experience in dealing with complex policy and increased their preoccupation with campaigning for the next office.

California's flagging policy capacity is mirrored in the character of the discussions surrounding higher education. The state seems unable to move beyond old problem definitions and failed "solutions." Higher education policies continue to be focused on managing and regulating institutions more than on governing across educational sectors to promote student success and state economic development. The state's many pressing problems also divert attention away from higher education issues. Budget deficits, immigration, housing, K–12 performance, flood risks, a crumbling transportation infrastructure, health care, and more take precedence over higher education issues. Most policymakers do not see any major problems with higher education, in large part because they focus on individual institutions and not on the longer-term challenges of educating Californians into the next decades. The state has recently committed $3 billion to fund infrastructure improvements for higher education.

STATE ACTORS

State-level actors with major impact on higher education include elected officials, executive branch agencies, and stakeholder interest groups. The state actors we discuss are the governor, the secretary of education, the Department of Finance, the California Postsecondary Education Commission (CPEC), the legislature, the Legislative Analyst's Office, the Student Aid Commission, and the K–12 sector. We also look at three nongovernmental groups who influence policy discussions in the state: (1) private postsecondary institutions; (2) a recently formed nonprofit group that represents the interests of the CEOs of California's seventy-two community college districts; and (3) the California Business Roundtable. We then consider governing boards for the state's three public higher education segments, along with their executive staffs, in the institutional governance section. Rather than offer a complete description of each entity's duties, we focus on those aspects of their roles (both formal and informal) that most influence higher education policy and practice.

The Governor

The role of California's governor has been shaped by the 1960 California Master Plan for Higher Education, which formalized the organization of the state's public higher education system into three component parts, called *segments*. The three segments are the University of California (UC), the California State University (CSU), and the California Community Colleges (CCC). This strict division has led governors to deal individually (and differently) with each segment, rather than address state priorities for higher education as a whole. In addition, the governor typically interacts only with the central system leadership and not with individual campuses. In recent decades there has been little centralized gubernatorial leadership exercised over higher education. In part because of this segmented structure, and in part because of the constitutional autonomy of UC, higher education does not generally emerge as a central focus of any governor's attention.

The budget process allows the governor considerable formal power over higher education. The governor proposes a budget to the legislature, holds line-item veto power to modify legislative adjustments to that proposal, and can blue-pencil amounts in the final budget. The legislature, however, can have a major impact on the outcome, as evidenced by the 2004–5 budget process, when the legislature reversed the governor's proposal, which would not have funded enrollment growth at UC and CSU.

Another source of gubernatorial power is in the appointment of members to the segmental governing boards. The governor appoints the majority of the members of the UC Board of Regents (to twelve-year terms) and the CSU Board of Trustees (to eight-year terms), and all of the members of the CCC Board of Governors (to terms of variable length). These appointments are subject to Senate confirmation—somewhat limiting the governor's power to shape higher education policy via board composition. In February 2008, for example, senate Republicans blocked the confirmation of three appointments to the Board of Governors because the nominees had expressed support for the California Dream Act, which would provide financial aid for undocumented students.

The heads of UC and CSU believe their relationships with the governor are critical to getting needed support for their priorities. Beginning with the Wilson administration in 1991, the two four-year segments have negotiated individual agreements with the governor, variously called *partnerships* and *compacts*. In order to provide budget stability, these compacts laid out multiyear expectations for state funding. While these agreements have also included expectations for segmental priorities and performance, they have not been designed as accountability mechanisms, nor have they been used to assess performance for purposes of budget development or reallocation. Nevertheless, the governor retains substantial influence over the segments through the budget negotiation process, and the segments devote considerable energy to maintaining good relationships and obtaining support for their internal priorities.

The governor's influence over CCC is potentially greater, because CCC does not enjoy the autonomy of UC or the regulatory flexibility of CSU. There is also much greater legislative intervention and oversight for CCC than for UC and CSU, as well as many more statutory constraints against governor-led changes. The central issue here is local autonomy. To exercise power over community colleges, the governor must risk political battles with the legislature. This is in contrast to the partnerships with UC and CSU, which are negotiated completely independently of the legislature. The governor does exercise appointment authority over vice-chancellors for CCC, a level of management intervention that would be unthinkable in the four-year segments.

Despite political constraints, Governor Schwarzenegger has not been reluctant to exercise executive leadership. His California Performance Review, now discarded, proposed consolidating the responsibilities of the Student Aid Commission, the California Postsecondary Education Commission, and the CCC Board of Governors within the Office of the Secretary of Education. More recently, the governor has fully funded Proposition 98 (which earmarks a part of the state budget for K–12 education and community colleges) and has made a strong commitment to community colleges. Many observers believe, however, that the state has little executive leadership for higher education policy.

Secretary of Education

Former governor Wilson created the position of secretary of education as his principal advisor for all education issues, but this position has never been formally established by statute or constitutional provision. Its responsibilities are vague and its role in guiding state policy, especially in higher education, is negligible. It is much more heavily involved in K–12 issues, and even in that arena faces an ambiguous set of roles. In higher education, the office remains only a potential source of executive power and influence. There is no higher education staff to speak of, and no one to whom the governor routinely turns for policy advice. The office could have become a major player if the recommendations of the California Performance Review had been enacted into law. But, as noted previously, these recommendations have been withdrawn. The secretary's higher education focus is primarily limited to community colleges, because of their interface with K–12 over vocational education and workforce issues.

Department of Finance

The Department of Finance (DOF) serves as the governor's chief fiscal policy advisor and is charged with ensuring the financial integrity of the state. It is the one influential part of the executive team in higher education policy, but its focus is almost exclusively short term—on preparing the annual budget. The DOF has not typically been a leader in higher education policy planning. This short-term focus helps to account for the observation that the DOF currently dominates budget discussions to such an extent that it limits the linkage between budget policy and longer-term state higher education priorities. Within the governor's guidelines, the DOF largely determines the outlines of the budget. Details are negotiated during the budget process.

With so much of the state higher education budget driven by the governor's decisions on funding enrollment growth, the influence of the DOF over funding levels is somewhat limited. Nevertheless, its positions can have a substantial impact on segmental budgets. For example, its support for the Partnership for Excellence for CCC helped increase funding for that segment, albeit temporarily. Conversely, its opposition to CSU's long-standing request to have funding formulas calculate full-time equivalencies at a financially greater rate for graduate education has inhibited growth of the graduate mission in that segment. In short, the DOF functions as a *control agency* with the primary role of restraining growth in spending.

California Postsecondary Education Commission

The California Postsecondary Education Commission (CPEC), the state's co-ordinating body for public higher education, is almost entirely an advisory agency. The CPEC website lists its three primary statutory functions as state-wide planning, policy recommendations, and advice to the governor and leg-islature on budget priorities. Although CPEC has never developed or main-tained a comprehensive statewide plan, at times it has played an important role in recommending state policy and advising the legislature and governor on policy and budget priorities. Among its most important functions is the maintenance of data on the three segments covering enrollment, degrees, the transfer of students from community colleges, faculty salaries, eligibility, and facilities. It produces an array of reports, some regularly and some upon re-quest.

Current CPEC goals and priorities include accountability, access and aca-demic preparation, and the nexus between the workforce and postsecondary education. CPEC oversees a technical advisory committee on accountability, composed of members from each segment, that is working on a statewide framework for informing policymakers of progress toward postsecondary goals. CPEC is also refining an online data system for students, parents, and policymakers to use in determining how systems and institutions are per-forming. The work CPEC has done over the past several years in analyzing a variety of indicators related to growth and access provides a foundation for this undertaking. A series of briefs that focus on how California's postsecond-ary education system contributes to the needs of the state's economy and its future is also in progress, under the guidance of an advisory committee that includes participants from the labor and workforce communities as well as segmental representatives.

CPEC consists of sixteen members: nine come from the general public, two are students, and the remaining five represent the three public segments, the independent colleges and universities, and the State Board of Education. Authority to appoint the public members is shared evenly among the gover-nor, the Senate, and the Assembly. A statutory advisory committee to CPEC includes the chief executive officer (or designee) of the three public segments. This split-appointment authority and segmental influence necessitate a deli-cate balancing act for CPEC between a legislature that wants a stronger com-mission and the segments that generally favor a weak agency. This conflict, which has dogged the agency since its founding, is well summarized in a report by the Legislative Analyst's Office (2003) which focuses on the tension between the roles of coordination and independent analysis. When the agency achieves an acceptable balance between these conflicting pressures, CPEC's role as an independent voice in the development of state policy is strengthened. Absent such a balance, the default is more political consensus-seeking than the provision of independent policy advice to the legislature and governor.

CPEC was most effective in the years immediately after 1978, when an executive director who had a hand in its creation teamed with a sympathetic and supportive governor. The 1990s saw a decline in CPEC's effectiveness and standing, culminating in sharp budget cuts that reduced the agency from its 1990–91 staffing figure of fifty-two to eighteen positions in 2003. Governor Schwarzenegger advanced two separate proposals to eliminate CPEC as a freestanding commission and move it under the control of the governor. Both proposals have now been discarded, but concern remains that the state needs more effective coordination. Legislation proposing reorganization of CPEC has been introduced in each of the last two legislative sessions.

The Legislature

Probably no other legislature in the country labors under a greater number of voter-imposed restraints than California. Assembly members are limited to three two-year terms in their lifetime. Senators may serve a maximum of two four-year terms. By most accounts this has reduced the policy capacity of the legislature. Authority to raise taxes and allocate resources has been constrained by voter initiatives. Governor Schwarzenegger has continued the practice of negotiating budget appropriations directly with UC and CSU.

Term limits seem to have both advantages and disadvantages. One positive aspect is that there are more people with local government experience and closer links with their districts, including ties to local colleges. Legislators as a group are also more diverse. On the negative side, familiarity with institutional history is largely missing, and incumbents are said to be constantly looking for their next office. Term limits have clearly changed the level at which legislators engage in discussions of higher education issues. One staff member said, "We just get them elected and they are gone." Another added, "There is little leadership from elected leaders, most of whom have trouble thinking beyond next Friday." The true impact of term limits on higher education is just being felt, with the "terming out" of some long-time legislators who were leaders in the field.

Despite these constraints, the legislature wields influence through the budget-adoption process and the inclusion of "supplemental" language that specifies legislative intent around certain issues and requires the submission of particular information. Apart from the budget process, the legislature often adopts statutes and resolutions setting forth goals for higher education. One example is the resolution endorsing the joint educational doctorate (EdD) programs between UC and CSU. Another is periodic legislation aimed at improving the community college transfer process. The legislature also has a long history of intervening in such community college issues as faculty governance. In general, the legislature oversees CCC much more closely than it does the other two segments.

The periodic Master Plan reviews, which occur with legislative leadership and oversight about every ten years, have been more noteworthy for leaving the plan's original tenets in place than for changes of any significance. Very recently, the legislature has also concerned itself with higher education accountability, although its first attempt at devising a state accountability plan was vetoed by the governor.

Legislative Analyst's Office

This nonpartisan fiscal advisory office of the California legislature plays a significant role in framing issues for legislative consideration and in helping the legislature respond to the governor's annual budget recommendations. The Legislative Analyst's Office provides basic data to support such recommendations as setting comprehensive fees for higher education at a fixed percentage of instructional costs. It has also recommended that the legislature disregard the newly negotiated compact between the governor and UC/CSU, arguing that established funding targets for six years remove legislative discretion in making annual budget policy. Most recently, in its analysis of the governor's proposed budget for 2006–7, it questioned the proposed funding increases and advised that financial commitments toward enrollment and for additional funds should be made with more explicit reference to the needs of the state. Recommendations are generally aimed at identifying cost savings for the legislature and at increasing the legislature's authority and oversight.

Student Aid Commission

The California Student Aid Commission (CSAC) provides financial aid to students through a variety of grant and loan programs. About half of the money awarded is from the state's General Fund—all of which is used for direct student aid for students in the public, independent, and proprietary segments. A special fund covers CSAC's operating costs. The agency's loan auxiliary administers federal student loan programs. CSAC also provides some financial-aid policy analysis and leadership, but none that is integrated with other aspects of finance policy, such as student fees and appropriations. CSAC is overseen by fifteen board members—eleven of whom are appointed by the governor and four by the legislature—representing the higher education community, students, and the general public.

CSAC's main policy role revolves around the large Cal Grant program, which has both entitlement and competitive components. In addition to administering the Cal Grant programs and a small loan program for prospective K–12 teachers, CSAC awards early academic outreach grants to consortia of educational institutions in seventeen areas of the state, oversees a state work-study program, and offers a general program for teacher interns and a range of smaller specialized programs. CSAC also sponsors financial-aid assistance preparation programs and publishes a range of analytical reports that detail its activities and their consequences.

The governor's California Performance Review Commission (CPR), as well as the reorganization plan based on the CPR report, recommended merging CSAC with other state agencies (including CPEC) and lodging these functions in a unified higher education division in the executive branch. The CPR report also argued for the elimination of Cal Grants in favor of tuition waivers administered by each campus. CSAC saw the report as "dismantling" its operations and, in two strongly worded press releases, pointed out the problems the proposal would create for college access and affordability. CPEC has recommended consolidating all General Fund student aid centrally, through the Cal Grant program. The segments believe that they can more effectively meet the needs of their students by using campus-based aid programs (funded through a combination of general funds and student fees), so as to tailor aid packages more individually to student needs. As of the writing of this chapter, none of the proposed changes seemed probable.

K–12 Education Sector

The governance structure for K–12 education is notoriously fragmented and ambiguous, contributing to the state's inability to develop any coordinated K–16 policies. The California Department of Education is led by the elected, nonpartisan state superintendent of public instruction. Department employees serve as staff to the superintendent. The State Board of Education consists of eleven members appointed by the governor and has its own small staff. Finally, there is a secretary of education, reporting to the governor, with a very limited staff and no formal authority over programs. The respective roles and responsibilities of these various offices are competing, overlapping, and vague.

Responsibility for K–16 initiatives is widely dispersed in California, with no apparent center for coordination. The California Education Round Table, on which both the superintendent and higher education leaders sit, and the associated Intersegmental Coordinating Committee provide forums for discussion and for such action as fits the priorities of a voluntary membership. Various programs aimed at improving K–12 and higher education preparation and articulation are housed in each segment. The absence of clear mechanisms for coordination between the K–12 sector and higher education led those involved in the 2002 review of the Master Plan to recommend a Master Plan for *Education* (instead of "Higher Education"). In spite of the rhetoric around the creation of a seamless K–16 education system, the 255-page report focused mostly on recommendations internal to the K–12 sector. The Master Plan did recommend the creation of a California Education Commission, but this new commission was to be an add-on to an already complex and confused governance and planning structure, which would continue to include the California Postsecondary Education Commission. The recommendations were presented to the legislature in January 2003, but no changes have been implemented and the governance problems remain.

In the meantime, the CPR advanced a different solution to the same issues, leading to a stalemate between the governor and the legislature. Without effective coordination, progress must come from individual efforts, such as the widely acclaimed reform negotiated between CSU and the K–12 sector to align eleventh-grade standards testing with CSU proficiency standards and the Cal-PASS Project6, which brings high school and college faculty together regionally to align standards and curriculum as a means of enhancing student success.

Private Higher Education

There are 254 private degree-granting institutions recognized by the state. Of these, 104 are nonprofit and about 75 belong to the Association of Independent California Colleges and Universities (AICCU). There are approximately 2,500 non-degree-granting vocational schools and programs leading to licensure. Authority for approving for-profit institutions is vested in the Department of Consumer Affairs and is divorced from other higher education policy and planning activities. The 104 nonprofit institutions enroll about 23 percent of the state's students but award nearly half of all master's degrees and over half of the doctorates, largely because the Master Plan has confined doctoral production in the public sector to UC. Applied doctorates, such as the EdD, have provided fertile ground for many private institutions, because these fields are not central to UC's mission. This has now changed somewhat with recent authorization for CSU to offer this degree.

The state constitution prohibits direct support to private entities, but the AICCU works with the governor's office, the legislature, and CPEC in support of priorities which affect the private higher education sector, of which the Cal Grant program has long been the most important. Some legislators believe that eligibility for state scholarship monies should trigger accountability arrangements that, at present, seem as lacking for this sector as for the public segments. Independent institutions are also eligible to use the state's facilities-bonding authority, and a representative from the sector is a member of the Education Round Table and of CPEC.

Despite a 1987 revision to the Master Plan calling for the state to consider the capacity of the private sector in its planning, California does not view private institutions as part of the solution to state capacity needs. This is symptomatic of its general lack of formal mechanisms for looking across sectors. The Master Plan provides only limited recognition of private higher education. Through the Cal Grant program, however, the state does financially assist students who choose to attend a private institution.

STATE RULES

California's seven rule categories—planning, program review and approval, information, academic preparation, student assistance, fiscal policies, and research and development—are characterized by two broad themes. First, there are huge differences in rules across the three public segments of higher education—making it critical not to overgeneralize about rules in California. The range of regulation extends from the constitutional autonomy of UC to the highly regulated community college segment, which the state treats more like the K–12 sector from which it evolved. Second, there is a strong and historical tendency to share power in California. Institutions have seemingly been designed to be weak or dependent. Shared-power arrangements—such as split appointment authority over board and commission members; local and statewide governance of the community college segment; fragmented authority for the K–12 area; statutory shared governance, which grants faculty near-veto-power in community colleges; and the existence of both a faculty senate and a faculty union in CSU, which have overlapping roles and membership— are all part of the political and cultural landscape that shapes how business is conducted and how higher education goods and services are delivered.

Planning

Other than those general goals and values contained in the original Master Plan, the state lacks a strategic plan or a set of statewide goals for higher education. More importantly, there is no accountability plan. Depending on whom you talk to, the 1960 Master Plan for Higher Education is either a great achievement—because of the stability it gives to the system—or a significant challenge—because of the degree of insulation it provides against change. Many contextual factors have altered significantly since 1960, but the Master Plan remains the guiding force for higher education in the state. It is impossible to discuss planning for higher education without reference, or deference, to the Master Plan. The Master Plan's chief contributions to planning were (1) the mission differentiation by which each of the three multicampus segments was granted authority to offer certain kinds of degrees and set different eligibility standards, and (2) the core values of access, affordability, and quality that continue to guide all planning discussions. The Master Plan also established a mechanism to coordinate planning across all segments—a coordinating council charged with reviewing program and capital development with respect to statewide needs.

Clearly, the Master Plan reduced both the politicization of campus development and resource allocation and the mission conflict that occurred elsewhere during the high-growth decades of the 1960s and 1970s. In addition, it has enabled the state to develop several top-tier research universities while maintaining open access to a university education via the community colleges and the transfer process. But a growing proportion of the policy community believes the plan is a major barrier to addressing statewide higher education issues. One report, for example, spoke of the "Master Plan culture of complacency" and suggested that differentiation of missions and segments discourages a statewide perspective on planning, evaluation, and accountability (Shulock and Moore 2002, p. 33).

There are also varied opinions on the extent to which planning today can effectively be guided by the original Master Plan's broad framework and tenets. UC is the most supportive of the original plan because it secured, for forty-five years, UC's exclusive authority among public institutions to offer doctorates and first professional degrees; enhanced its prospects of competing nationally and internationally in research and graduate education; and protected quality by limiting freshman eligibility to the top one-eighth of high school graduates. CSU is generally supportive of the Master Plan, but it has sought authority to offer professional doctorates in fields where it views UC as having given such degrees a lower priority than is justified by the current labor market. In a major breakthrough that has been carefully framed as an "exception to" rather than a "change to" the Master Plan, the legislature recently authorized CSU to offer an independent doctorate in education. CSU is also more vocal about shortcomings in the community college transfer function, probably because accommodating transfer students is a much larger part of its mission than for UC. CCC is mostly concerned with the mismatch between the resources it receives and the missions assigned to it under the Master Plan.

Critics of the Master Plan note that much has changed in the years since its enactment. Supporters counter that it has been reviewed and updated approximately every decade. All would agree, however, that the plan offers only a broad framework. It is probably more effective as a guide to what cannot happen than as a blueprint for what should. One example of how the Master Plan constrains alternatives is the new UC campus in Merced, which opened in fall 2005. The state's need for additional capacity to accommodate undergraduates is clear. By contrast, there has been no compelling case put forth for California needing additional research university capacity. Yet as growth in both population and political power occurred in the heavily Latino Central Valley, the choices available under the Master Plan were for a research university (a new UC campus) or a less-prestigious CSU campus that would focus on undergraduate education. Political rather than educational priorities drove the decision, something the Master Plan was designed to prevent.

With the Master Plan providing only broad guidance, California does not have either a strategic plan with specific state goals and priorities or a state-wide planning process. It has no long-term financing plan, which is particularly troublesome to many in view of the huge enrollment growth the state is experiencing and will continue to encounter for some time. There is no accountability plan that monitors outcomes and progress with respect to state goals, in large part because there is no goal-setting by an authoritative statewide agency.

The absence of a statewide planning process and CPEC's advisory status mean that segmental priorities prevail, or at least set the framework around which policy discussions occur. A recent comparison with seven high-growth states described California as "dead last" in its ability to identify urgent issues, communicate them, and establish a statewide agenda for meeting them, adding that there was no reason to expect independent segmental efforts to collectively meet state needs (Shulock and Moore 2004, p. 37). The major planning tools, under these circumstances, are the annual budget and the individual compacts with the governor.

The need for more centralized planning and for incorporating the K–12 sector was addressed in the most recent review of the Master Plan, undertaken by a joint committee of both legislative chambers. The final report, published in 2003, included some fifty-six recommendations, many of which called for more centralized attention to state needs. As of this writing, none had been adopted and the governor's proposed centralizing reforms have been withdrawn. Even if more policymakers were convinced of the need for statewide planning, there is no working consensus about how such planning should be undertaken, or by whom.

Program Review and Approval

CPEC has statutory responsibility for reviewing and commenting on new degree and certificate programs proposed by the segments. The process is intended to promote efficiency in the use of state resources and assure that programs meet student and societal needs. Recent changes to the review process call for CPEC staff to comment on proposals in the context of long-range plans, so that segments are alerted to concerns before proposals are actually submitted. Seven criteria are used in the review process: student demand, societal needs, appropriateness to mission, number of similar existing and proposed programs, cost, quality, and advancement of knowledge. During the 2004–5 academic year, the commission conducted twenty-four independent reviews of new academic and vocational programs proposed by the segments: eleven from community colleges, nine from UC, and four jointly submitted by UC and CSU.

CSU is not required to submit proposals for baccalaureate or master's degree programs that have been through their campus's and the system's review and approval processes unless the programs will require significant additional operating resources or a major capital outlay project. UC is only required to submit proposals for new graduate programs or for joint graduate programs with CSU.

The most difficult recent program review issues for CPEC involved evaluation practices for UC and CSU's joint doctoral programs in educational leadership, and a legislative initiative opposed by UC and the independent sector that would allow CSU to offer its own doctoral degrees in selected fields. (As noted, legislative approval was recently granted for independent CSU doctorates in education; however, the issue will continue to pose challenges for CPEC if CSU pushes for independent doctorates in additional professional fields.) With respect to evaluation, CPEC has proposed a path analysis approach that requires demonstrating the indirect effect of a doctoral program in educational leadership on student learning. On one level, the approach seems laudable. From a practical perspective, it could also be viewed as a delaying tactic, as it submits new joint programs to a level of scrutiny that few if any existing programs would be able to withstand. On the matter of independent doctoral degrees for CSU, CPEC advances a fence-straddling argument that reflects the difficulties of an advisory agency taking an independent position on an issue where there is strong disagreement among key higher education actors.

Information

California has vast amounts of data but, during our study, lacked a coordinated data system useful for planning and assessment purposes. Each of the segments uses its own highly sophisticated system to produce extensive data about its operations. Such information provides good support for internal management and planning and for external reports of the type required by the governor and legislature. But a serious lack of standardized data definitions across the segments prevents accurate statewide planning and analysis of basic factors such as enrollment, costs, and fee revenue.

CCC has the most comprehensive segmental data systems, probably because the strong regulatory environment in which it operates has placed a premium on providing detailed, campus-based information. However, there is some variability in its quality, because the system relies on 110 colleges to submit data to the central office. The CCC data system includes both student-level and course enrollment statistics, i.e., information on the individual courses and course outcomes for students. Neither UC nor CSU has centralized data on course enrollments with respect to classes taken by individual students, but they do collect and report vast amounts of information on aggregate enrollment by various categories.

CPEC plays an important role in central data collection and reporting. It maintains a website that provides detailed and easily accessible demographic information by county as well as extensive student outcome data on enrollments, transfers, and degrees. Currently, CPEC's staff is able to report on retention rates, graduation rates, time-to-degree, the proportion of minority enrollment to state minority populations, the part-time to full-time student ratio, and other enrollment trends. Thanks to 1998 legislation, a subsequent favorable legal decision, and six years of wrangling, CPEC is now receiving student-specific data from UC and CSU. An accountability framework proposed by CPEC relates these statistics to two of five identified goals (student success and efficiency in student progress, and diversity and access). Data to address the other three goals (efficiency in administration, educational quality, and public benefit) is not currently available. The student-level information now available to CPEC does not include course-level data, so the agency is better positioned to use it to identify overall progress and trends than to have it as a base for recommending specific policy solutions.

The delays in developing a statewide student tracking system for California, even after the passage of enabling legislation, illustrates the larger issues of balance of power and a lack of trust among key players. They also complicate CPEC's announced goal of creating an interactive accountability prototype on its website for use by legislative staff, higher education analysts, students, and parents.

Heightened legislative interest in shaping a statewide accountability plan could be the catalyst for change. In 2004, the legislature passed accountability legislation (Senate Bill 1331) addressing three of the goals in the current proposed accountability framework (educational opportunity, participation, and student success). The bill was vetoed by the governor, in part because of his pending (at the time) recommendations to consolidate agencies and strengthen the role of the secretary of education. Subsequently, the legislature enacted a detailed district-level accountability system for the community colleges, and new legislation, modeled on the vetoed SB 1331, is under consideration. If statewide accountability issues become a continuing legislative focus, there will be a need for better, more centralized data and standardized data definitions. This is not a concern for the governor, because he has a paragraph in each compact/partnership agreement with UC and CSU that requires data reporting.

Academic Preparation

California has a very extensive array of academic preparation programs that can be loosely grouped into three categories: segmental initiatives; voluntary collaborations that may cross segmental, sector, and K–12/higher education boundaries; and individual initiatives between institutions. No single state agency, however, has the authority to develop such initiatives. Over the past several years, CPEC has analyzed an array of indicators related to growth and access to higher education that have served as the basis for extensive work on these issues by CPEC.

Perhaps the most significant recent initiative by an individual segment is the collaboration between CSU and the California Department of Education. The Early Assessment Program (EAP) incorporates CSU placement standards for college English and mathematics into existing high school standards tests. This allows high schools and CSU to know the preparation status of individual students early enough so that the students' senior year can be used to address deficiencies that would otherwise have to be corrected following college matriculation. In spring 2004, the EAP became available on an optional basis to all high school juniors taking the English and mathematics courses required for admission to CSU.

Another example of a segmental initiative is the searchable website, maintained by UC, that lists courses for all regular California public high schools that fulfill requirements for admission to UC and CSU. By statute, all school districts must provide a full precollegiate program with adequate sections to serve all students. They also must actively advise students to enter these programs and must avoid discouraging students for cultural or linguistic reasons.

In addition, each segment offers many collaborative programs with school districts, all aimed at improving outreach to underrepresented student groups. Examples include early academic outreach (EAOP) and programs in engineering and the sciences for minorities. While centrally coordinated, such programs typically operate at the campus level. As an illustration of how short-term budget concerns, rather than statewide planning, drive issues such as academic preparation, the budgets for outreach programs have been reduced during lean times on the basis of there being little point in recruiting additional students with enrollments already straining the funding capacity of the state.

The federal GEAR UP program provides an example of voluntary collaboration. The U.S. Department of Education mandates participant collaboration across segmental, sector, and K–12 boundaries. In 1999, the state responded with a proposal involving seventeen partners, representing all of the educational sectors. But such voluntary approaches have their weaknesses, because the scope of the partners' activities is limited to the purposes for which the grant was sought, and continuation depends upon support from an external agency. In a second example highlighting the limits of voluntary coordination, the K–18 curricular issues subcommittee of the Intersegmental Coordinating Committee (ICC) is working to determine its role, "if any, in designing strategies to enrich the teaching profession." Outside of the ICC, the only mechanisms for addressing improvement strategies for K–12 teachers are in the hands of the various segments.

While the number and diversity of academic preparation efforts in California are impressive, the total impact does not seem to add up to an effective program. Some of the conclusions of the 2002 Master Plan review (Joint Committee to Develop a Master Plan for Education 2002) confirm a number of long-standing issues:

- course alignment and articulation remain problematic at the postsecondary level (p. 70)
- collaboration among K–12 and postsecondary institutions has not been sufficient to fully align curricula and academic content, admissions procedures, and expectations for students. As a result, many students who graduate from high school, including the top third, are not adequately prepared for higher education (p. 71)
- the lack of overall coordination among the state's multiple education agencies is one of the largest systemic governance problems in California (p. 105)

Student Assistance

California policymakers' strong commitment to the affordability goal of the Master Plan is reflected in the state's extensive, need-based student aid initiatives that are administered through CSAC. In 2000, the state expanded the Cal Grant program whereby all recent high school graduates and community college transfer students under twenty-four years of age who demonstrate need are entitled to a financial aid award. To create the entitlement provision, awards to older students were reduced. Older students may still apply for competitive grants, but funding for this type of assistance is limited by the available annual appropriation. Students who are eligible for financial aid are ranked according to a scoring system developed by CSAC. Overall, there is about an 80–20 split between need and merit, making California one of the top states in providing need-based aid. Segmental leaders perceive this division to be about right.

The principles reflected in the state's student aid programs are access, affordability, and choice. Award levels take into account tuition differentials across the segments and provide an amount close to the UC rate for students who choose private institutions. Grant award levels are generally linked to fee levels; as fees increase, the award levels increase accordingly. Cal Grants are used for fees as well as for indirect costs of college attendance, but there are different allowable uses and different eligibility conditions for different parts of the Cal Grant program. Financially needy students attending community colleges are eligible for fee waivers, which are administered by the Board of Governors. Therefore, Cal Grant funds are used in this segment more for indirect costs than for fees. Community college students do not need to complete a federal financial aid form for student assistance (FAFSA) to qualify for a fee waiver.

UC and CSU maintain large, campus-based aid programs. State policy requires them to redirect a portion of their fee revenue each year toward financial aid, which is then administered through these programs. Each university segment also receives an annual General Fund appropriation for their campus-based aid programs. There is ongoing tension between state-level actors and segment leaders about the relationship between the state Cal Grant program and campus-based aid programs. Segment leaders believe their campus-based programs provide a student-centered focus on individual needs; state-level actors, including the Legislative Analyst's Office, favor consolidating aid under the state Cal Grant program as a means of providing more coordinated policy direction. There is no campus-based aid program equivalent to those at UC and CSU for the community colleges. Consequently, community college students have fewer options for state-funded financial aid and traditionally do not apply for federal aid at rates commensurate with their financial need. Affordability, therefore, is a major concern in the community college arena, in spite of the low fees and the fee waivers.

The governor proposed significant reductions to student aid awards for the 2004–5 budget, most of which were rejected by the legislature. This signaled a strong consensus across the state that access and affordability should continue to be honored through state policy and budgets. Student aid thus appears to be one area where California's lack of centralized leadership and direction for higher education does not hamper coordinated policy development. This could be both because it is the expression of the state's strong cultural value in favor of access and because maintaining a centralized aid policy does not particularly bring the segments into conflict with one another.

Fiscal Policies

California's provision of higher education for its citizens is based on a long-standing commitment to access, one set out in the 1960 Master Plan and funded through fifty years of low-cost public institutions as well as by state funding for financial aid. Historically, the commitment to access was expressed by a combination of no tuition, low fees, and significant financial aid. Now, the average amount for undergraduate tuition, fees, and room and board charged to full-time students in public four-year institutions is well above the national average. Still, the net cost, thanks to student aid, has remained relatively stable (California Postsecondary Education Commission 2006). However, fees at CCC are by far the lowest in the nation for community colleges.

California is clearly grappling with a difficult transition to a new framework for tuition and fees. The state has yet to define or adopt a rational fee policy for all public institutions, although recent deliberations and agreements with the legislature and the administration are a start toward building more lasting frameworks in the UC and CSU segments. Still, no consensus has developed around a policy criterion for establishing base-fee levels for universities—only that fee increases should be gradual, moderate, predictable, and accompanied by appropriate increases in need-based financial aid. Consensus is further away in relation to the community colleges, where the governor rolled back fees from $26 to $20 per unit in 2006 while others argued for fees to be increased significantly. The policy discussions over CCC fees are complicated by state budgeting practices, which make it disputable whether the revenue from increased fees would augment college budgets.

Technically, the power to set university fees rests with the UC regents and the CSU trustees. In practice, however, the legislature holds this power, because of its ability to adjust budgets to negate anticipated fee revenues. If the segments were to raise fees higher than the legislature was willing to allow, the legislature could reduce appropriations by the same amount as the anticipated revenue, thus rendering the fee increase moot. Because of this power, there have been several years when budget negotiations—including the governor's 2006–7 budget—yielded increases in the General Fund appropriations for UC and CSU, for the sole purpose of avoiding a fee increase that these segments argued would otherwise be necessary to sustain quality and enrollment levels. Under the state's Education Code, fee levels for CCC are set by the legislature.

As is the case in most states, operating support for higher education in California has fluctuated with economic trends. There were major downturns in state funding during the recessions of the early 1990s and again in the first half of the following decade. Despite its students' extensive use of lower-cost two-year institutions, California is above the median in state effort, calculated on the basis of per capita dollars. There are some nascent attempts, spearheaded by the nonprofit Campaign for College Opportunity, to develop a long-term finance plan for higher education in the state, in view of anticipated enrollment growth. But absent any leadership from the governor or secretary of education on this front, finance policy will likely continue to be developed on a year-to-year, segment-by-segment basis.

Capital funding for UC, CSU, and CCC is provided by general obligation bond issues. After such bonds are approved by the governor, they are submitted to the voters every two to four years. Lease-revenue bonds, with the cost of amortization paid by the students, provide the monetary resources for residence halls and other revenue-producing facilities. State-funded plans are subject to detailed review by the DOF and the Legislative Analyst's Office. However, CSU and UC have considerable autonomy over their non-state-funded capital outlay plans. Capital outlay for CCC is financed by a combination of state bond revenues and local bonds, with the vast majority of these monies coming from local funds. Local districts have found strong popular support for this approach to financing capital needs, once the required majority vote was changed from two-thirds to 55 percent.

Research and Development

Economic development initiatives originate with each of the segments, since there is no agency with the authority or the capacity to coordinate cross-segmental efforts. On the recommendation of the president of UC, California has funded the Industry-University Cooperative Research Program (IUCRP), which awards grants in five fields of engineering and science, in addition to offering a microelectronics grant. Through this and related efforts, four major new institutes of science and innovation have been funded, as well as an Internet 2 initiative that includes a component to link with the K–12 segment.

According to a private-sector spokesman, the state has done relatively little in providing incentives for collaboration with business and industry, investing in research infrastructure, and using tax policy to foster economic development. There is widespread recognition that the state's lead in the areas of computers and biotechnology is closely linked to the number and quality of its educational institutions, but there may be less enthusiasm for special initiatives unless and until there is more evidence that the state's leading position in economic competitiveness is threatened. A recent report from the National Center for Higher Education Management Systems provides evidence that this may now be the case (Jones 2006).

The absence of coordinated measures to promote state economic development is consistent with California's overall tendency to focus on individual segments. In addition, devotion to the Master Plan's tenets, which do not include economic development, may have prevented concerted and separate attention to economic development as a statewide goal, an element present in other states' strategic plans.

PUBLIC HIGHER EDUCATION SYSTEMS

California's system of public higher education is internationally regarded as unparalleled. Its 110 community colleges and 33 public universities are impressive in both size and reputation, but the major investments in operating and capital budgets that occurred between 1950 and 1974 have not been sustained. California's public system of higher education is considered "universally accessible." Nearly 60 percent of the graduates from public high schools enroll in public higher education in California. Approximately 2.5 million students register in any given term, with about 74 percent in community colleges, 17 percent at CSU campuses, and 9 percent at UC campuses.

Over the next decade, the projected increase in demand for higher education at a time of severely constrained state resources will create tremendous challenges. Enrollment estimates by the DOF and CPEC show an additional 500,000 students in public higher education over the next eight years. There are serious questions about how well the state can respond to this within the prevailing resource and time constraints. When its population grew rapidly following World War II, California added 65 new CCC campuses, 11 new CSU campuses, and 5 new UC campuses between 1945 and 1975. Since then, however, there have been only an additional eight new campuses for CCC, three for CSU, and one for UC (opening in 2005 with about 1,000 students). While there is no clear plan for how public higher education will accommodate the growing enrollment demand in terms of both physical and budgetary capacity, efforts are underway to begin such planning. Options under consideration include the use of technology to offer off-campus courses and the conversion of off-campus community college centers into full-fledged campuses. Significantly, the initial planning was spearheaded by a nonprofit organization and several private foundations. Unlike some other states, in California there is no apparent trend toward privatization as a way to relieve taxpayers of growing obligations. This is a testament to the strong emphasis in the Master Plan on universal access to higher education.

University of California

The University of California is widely acknowledged as one of the country's finest research institutions. Several of its ten campuses routinely rank among the top universities in numerous fields. UC leaders attribute much of this success to the Master Plan, which limited eligibility to the top one-eighth of high school graduates and designated UC as the only segment authorized to offer doctorates as well as all professional degrees. Most observers acknowledge that this plan has concentrated research and graduate-level resources to achieve a degree of excellence that would not be possible with more widely dispersed authority for research and graduate programs.

The UC segment now includes more than 210,000 students, 160,000 faculty and staff, and more than 1.2 million alumni across its ten campuses. UC routinely leads all other states in federal research funding from the Department of Defense, the Department of Health and Human Services, NASA, and the National Science Foundation. The segment also leads all other states in research support from private industry, largely fueled by the technology industry. Of the 229 rated UC graduate programs, more than half are in the top twenty nationally.

UC has been a significant driving force for all education in the state. Because it has minimum course distribution requirements for admission (the "A through G" pattern), secondary schools have been mandated to align their curricula to these standards so that these required courses are available at all public schools. Policy debates continue, however, over the degree to which the A through G pattern should be the default curriculum and the standard expectation for all students.

UC Actors

The principal actors for the University of California segment include the Board of Regents, the Office of the President (which refers to the central administration for the entire segment), the faculty, the Academic Senate, and the campus chancellors and their staffs.

BOARD OF REGENTS

UC is governed by a twenty-six-member Board of Regents. Eighteen of the regents are appointed to twelve-year terms by the governor. A student member is appointed by the regents for a one-year term. Seven ex officio members include the governor, the lieutenant governor, the superintendent of public instruction, the Speaker of the Assembly, the president of the university, and the president and vice president of the alumni association. The board appoints the president of the university, campus chancellors (on the recommendation of the president), and the principal officers of the regents. The constitution gives the regents full authority for "organization and government" of the university. Some legal cases have referred to the regents as a "fourth branch" of state government.

OFFICE OF THE PRESIDENT

The UC Office of the President (UCOP) in Oakland is the headquarters for the entire UC segment. Eight divisions oversee academics, budgets, university affairs, business and financial activities, and the national research labs operated under contract with the U.S. Department of Energy. There is also a governmental relations office in Sacramento. UCOP plays a key role in negotiating the UC segment's budget with the legislature and governor. This process has been described as "enormously cumbersome" and involves developing a Regents Budget based on campus academic plans and priorities, gaining support from the regents, and negotiating at the state level, first with the executive branch and then with the legislature.

Another important role of UCOP is to maintain coordination and consistency across this segment. Keeping individual campuses from being too autonomous is a particular challenge, due to diverse missions, academic programs, and student characteristics and to differing levels of selectivity and their associated status. Campuses are becoming more restive toward central office constraints. An executive compensation scandal has also produced significant change in the way the Board of Regents operates, with the regents enlarging the number of staff members who report directly to them.

FACULTY AND ACADEMIC SENATE

UC's Academic Senate is an umbrella for faculty governance, providing the organizational framework that enables the faculty to exercise influence on university decisions. The senate consults with and advises the president, regents, and senior administrators through a number of avenues that include the senate chair and vice-chair, standing committees of the senate, the Academic Council, and the Academic Assembly. Parallel structures at the campus level foster consultation between campus senate chairs and their chancellors.

The senate is a powerful internal player, particularly on issues of academic planning and eligibility. One observer noted that the administration would never approve a new degree to which the senate had objected. In addition, the regents have delegated their constitutional authority to set admissions policy to the faculty, allowing the faculty to determine the minimum eligibility criteria that will be used to keep within the Master Plan's standard of 12.5 percent of California high school graduates being able to enroll in UC. The senate must be consulted on appointments, promotions, and tenure. According to one regent, tenure and curriculum decisions never get to the board; UCOP will only get involved on a policy level, but most decisions are made at the campus level. Faculty influence extends beyond the formal structure of the Academic Senate. Faculty members are the dominant group involved in the selection of presidents and chancellors, although some regents would like to have more board involvement in making these decisions. As powerful as the senate is internally, it has never been a powerful or visible actor in statewide politics, a reflection of UC success in presenting a united front in Sacramento.

CAMPUS CHANCELLORS

The degree to which the University of California functions as a single entity, as distinct from a system of individual campuses, is considerably less now than it was in 1960. While UC has rules that apply across the entire segment, chancellors have significant leeway in the operation of their campuses. Admissions standards represent one key area in which chancellors exercise autonomy. When campuses face more eligible applicants than they can accommodate within their budgetary and physical constraints, they can adopt higher admissions standards. This has long been the case at Berkeley and UCLA, but most campuses are now in this situation. Chancellors' roles are also changing as the state's share of funding declines and they are expected to engage in more fundraising.

Over the last ten to fifteen years, central administrators have relaxed line-item control over campus budgets and delegated more authority to the chancellors, allowing them to allocate campus resources in exchange for more accountability on how the funds are used. Even so, UCOP has nothing resembling a formal accountability system over its campuses, relying on negotiation and typically deferring to campus discretion. A major political firestorm erupted over revelations that chancellors had routinely approved large compensation supplements off the books, invisible to state overseers and not subject to the regents' approval. As a result, the regents implemented stronger oversight procedures over UCOP and the chancellors in the area of compensation.

Chancellors play very large roles in the development of capital outlay plans for their campuses—both for plans that request state funding and those developed with private resources. Beyond the increased level of autonomy chancellors enjoy on their individual campuses, they also exercise a growing influence on the direction and priorities of UC as a whole. The choice of the last two UC presidents from the ranks of sitting chancellors speaks volumes about that influence.

Rules for UC

Despite the level of autonomy among the UC campuses, there remains a strong common culture of central control—especially in state governmental relations—and a set of rules that guide the general mission of the institution. The unified budget helps reduce competition among campuses by making clear the common set of criteria that govern most budget allocations. In some instances, funds are allocated without regard to size or enrollment, such as to support growth at smaller campuses or to emphasize particular centers of excellence.

PLANNING

Planning for UC occurs on a segmental basis, through a range of councils and task forces. An Office of Planning and Analysis within the Division of Academic Affairs works with an academic planning council to raise issues, frame questions, and analyze alternatives. Its product is not a static plan, but rather a process that moves UC toward consensus on major issues. The topics it considers include long-range enrollment planning, student engagement in performance, academic institutional quality and accountability, and budgetary issues (from an academic perspective).

A new presidential long-range guidance team was formed in early 2005 to address the long-range strategic issues facing UC. Comprised of regents, campus chancellors, officers of the Academic Senate, and vice presidents, the guidance team will commission studies and discuss priorities arising from a recently completed strategic assessment exercise. The object for this team is to produce a strategic framework to direct future decisions.

The budget office provides long-range fiscal planning. Its website, available to regents and the general public, brings together historical and comparative data, fiscal projections, and university priorities. Along with all this information, the website delivers a message about resources and the trends they suggest. Current UC concerns include balancing the pressures for increased undergraduate enrollment with the need for maintaining strong graduate programs, facilities maintenance and expansion, and preserving UC's competitiveness on such indicators as faculty salaries and investments in research infrastructure.

PROGRAM INITIATIVES

Academic planning occurs both centrally and on individual campuses. At both levels, it is a coordinated effort between administration and faculty. Through its planning process, UC gives CPEC enough advanced notice on its programs to allow CPEC's staff to provide preliminary comments and suggestions. During 2005, UC submitted nine proposals for new campus graduate programs and four for new joint doctoral programs with CSU. University long-range plans project 168 graduate programs through 2010, predominantly in engineering and the computer sciences and, to a lesser extent, in the life sciences.

ENROLLMENT MANAGEMENT

The UC campuses are increasingly turning down students because of high demand and what are termed "impacted" programs and campuses. According to the Master Plan, every qualified student who is a resident of California is entitled to admission to a UC campus. Eligibility criteria, however, apply to the UC segment as a whole, not to individual campuses. A student who meets segment-wide criteria may not get into the campus of choice. Typically, such a student would be referred to one of the less-selective campuses, one to which that student may not have applied. To date, UC has been able to grant admission somewhere in this segment, but many students are now "redirected" to the two least selective campuses. The university also has the challenge of creating equitable access for students of color and low-income students.

CPEC performs periodic eligibility studies to determine how well UC and CSU are staying within the Master Plan's eligibility standards. The most recent *University Eligibility Study* (California Postsecondary Education Commission 2004) found that the proportion of high school graduates eligible for admission to UC has increased in recent years. According to the report, 14.4 percent of California public high school graduates met UC's eligibility requirements in 2003, up from 11.1 percent in 1996. Accordingly, UC changed its requirements to bring the proportion of high school graduates eligible for admission closer to the 12.5 percent figure recommended in the state's Master Plan.

More stringent admissions policies are a concern to some in the UC segment and to many in policy positions, because of their likely impact on access for students of color and low-income students. The 2004 *University Eligibility Study* analyzed the effects of stricter eligibility requirements. In three different scenarios, the report estimated a disproportionate reduction in overall eligibility among blacks and Latinos compared to whites and Asian Americans. In some cases, a change in policy would result in nearly a 20 percent reduction of eligible black and Latino high school graduates. These concerns about access are magnified at UC's most sought-after campuses.

INFORMATION

UC produces much data, but it is sometimes criticized for providing too little information. There is no central website for researchers or legislative staff to consult, as is the case for CSU and CCC. Information provided by UC typically comes in the form of major reports carefully crafted to convey the university's message, often in response to legislative requests. New attempts to develop a state accountability system are beginning to expose data problems, and the legislature has a precedent for intervening to provide CPEC with more authority over the kinds of data they receive.

BUDGETING

UCOP coordinates a unified budget for UC, which ultimately becomes the Regents Budget. The priorities in the Regents Budget are a result of meetings with chancellors and vice-chancellors. Campuses do not present campus budget requests to UCOP, but they are heavily involved in submitting ideas for new initiatives. The Regents Budget is a request. The governor's annual budget proposal in recent years has been influenced, in part, by multiyear funding plans negotiated between UC and the administration. The legislature is not a party to these agreements, or *compacts*, and considers the governor's proposal on the basis of a half-dozen cost factors, including enrollment, student fees, financial aid, and cost-of-living considerations. State funding of higher education is not "explicitly linked with the actual performance of the public higher education system" (Legislative Analyst's Office 2005, p. 45). The legislature also designates some special allocations for high-priority initiatives, such as teacher training institutes and research and technology initiatives.

Once the legislature has made its appropriation to the system, UC allocates funds among the campuses. Funds are distributed primarily based on enrollment, but there are other factors and special initiatives that influence final allocations. UCOP engages in some reallocation to meet unique campus needs.

There is no uniform budgeting process to guide the UC campuses. Each campus, therefore, must create its own process. In most cases, the budget is determined by institutional priorities, reflecting the recommendations of the vice-chancellors.

Each campus prepares a five-year capital program, based on an assessment of facility needs and the amount of capital funding expected. UCOP and the regents review these plans and adopt a segmental capital plan that is reviewed by the DOF and the legislature. According to a UCOP report, projects proposed for state funding in the current capital improvement budget year are based on intensive, detailed planning and predesign analysis that typically starts three years before initial state funding (University of California Office of the President 2006). This process supports effective internal decision making; ensures that commitments, once made, can be met; enables the university to explain the proposed projects effectively during state review; and improves project management during design and construction stages.

California State University

The California State University is the largest system of senior higher education in the country. Since 1995, CSU has added one campus and about 83,000 students. There are now twenty-three campuses with more than 420,000 students and 46,000 faculty and staff members. Sizes range from seven campuses near or above 30,000 students to the two newest campuses, with enrollments below 4,000. This segment faces enormous growth, with projections calling for more than 100,000 additional students over the next ten years. CSU plays a very large role in the transfer student pipeline. Students who transfer from community colleges earn about two out of every three of the baccalaureate degrees awarded by CSU.

Under the Master Plan, CSU is assigned the primary mission of undergraduate and graduate instruction through master's degree programs in the liberal arts, sciences, and professional education, including teacher education. CSU is also authorized to offer selected doctoral programs jointly with UC and private universities and to support research related to its instructional mission. In the 2005–6 legislative session, CSU won a hard-fought political battle with UC and received the authority to offer independent doctorates in education. The trustees have recently authorized ten campuses to begin to develop these doctorates. About 80 percent of all CSU students are undergraduates. Many of the campuses began decades ago as teacher training institutions, and teacher education remains a large part of the CSU mission. CSU trains about 60 percent of the state's K–12 teachers.

Unlike UC, CSU does not have constitutional status, a difference that leaves the latter segment vulnerable to periodic efforts by executive departments or the legislature to impose regulatory solutions to perceived problems. During the past two decades, the trend has been toward less state regulation, in part because the system has been seen as responsive to public priorities. While the CSU system has historically served primarily commuting students, the construction of residence halls has now become a priority, particularly at campuses with available space for additional students.

CSU Actors

The principal actors for the California State University segment include the Board of Trustees, the system chancellor and central administration, campus presidents, the statewide CSU Academic Senate, and the faculty union.

TRUSTEES

There are twenty-five trustees (twenty-four voting, one nonvoting). Five trustees are ex-officio members: the governor, the lieutenant governor, the Speaker of the Assembly, the state superintendent of public instruction, and the chancellor. The statewide CSU Alumni Council appoints an alumni trustee. The governor appoints a faculty trustee from nominees proposed by the statewide Academic Senate. The alumni and faculty trustees serve for two years. The governor appoints two student trustees from nominees proposed by the California State Student Association, one of whom has full voting powers. The student trustees serve staggered two-year terms. The sixteen remaining trustees are appointed to eight-year terms by the governor and confirmed by the California senate. Board meetings allow for communication among the trustees, the chancellor, campus presidents, executive committee members of the statewide Academic Senate, representatives of the California State Student Association, and officers of the statewide Alumni Council.

SEGMENTAL ADMINISTRATION

The character of the central administration has changed dramatically over the last several decades as the degree of external and internal regulation of CSU has been reduced. Unlike the civil servants that led this segment in its first few decades, recent leaders have been more entrepreneurial and more broadly experienced in statewide politics, both in California and in other states. Unlike UC, CSU leaders have not typically been drawn from within its academic ranks. The chancellor and his staff have a reputation for effective internal management, for representing the segment's interests and priorities effectively to state government, and, perhaps most importantly, for being responsive to state priorities on issues such as community college transfer and a K–16 alignment of proficiency standards.

CSU administrators generally support the Master Plan for its clear direction on institutional mission and the relative absence of legislative intervention. However, as noted above, they have been engaged in a battle to win authority to offer professional doctorates. It is not clear to what extent they will continue to press for doctorates in other professional fields, now that they have gained the ability to award an education doctorate.

Employees in the CSU segment are heavily organized with regard to collective bargaining, through eight separate unions and eleven separate bargaining units. Collective bargaining occurs centrally for this segment, but it involves considerable campus-level activity as well. Union priorities and tactics continue to be a challenge for segmental administrators, although they have made progress in instituting merit-based compensation and modernizing classification systems and procedures to give more flexibility to managers. Grievance procedures are a major part of campus and segmental activity. From the perspective of administrators, employee unions constrain the budget process through their expressed preference for returning to a line-item budget, which they see as a way of maximizing compensation and minimizing expenditures on central administration.

CAMPUS PRESIDENTS

Campus presidents wield considerable power at the segmental level via the Executive Council, on which they are all represented. Although CSU was known, decades ago, for its cookie-cutter nature across campuses, in recent decades the individual campuses have been encouraged to define their own niches and identities. As a result, individual campuses have become more closely connected with their regions and increasingly varied in character, including even their curricula and the nature of their student bodies. While individual campuses have developed close relationships with neighboring community colleges, this does not readily translate into intersegmental cooperation on a statewide basis. At the segmental level, there is a sense that California is simply too large to allow for many statewide agreements. Therefore, presidents are encouraged to pursue local and regional partnerships on issues such as data sharing, outreach, curriculum, and facilities.

FACULTY SENATE AND UNION

Faculty interests are represented through a segment-wide Academic Senate, as well as the faculty union and the collective bargaining process. The senate takes its shared governance responsibilities very seriously. It is also quite active on intersegmental issues, such as community college transfer. The Academic Senate is not as hostile as the union to segmental administration, but the two organizations hold many positions in common, because the same leaders rotate through both. Compared to UC, the CSU faculty senate is not as powerful internally, in terms of its influence on segmental decision making, but it is far more political and active in state politics than the UC faculty senate.

Rules for CSU

Prior to the 1990s, CSU was subject to extensive regulatory requirements, with many of its activities being closely overseen by state agencies. Since then, CSU has gradually obtained more flexibility, although it still is not comparable to UC in this arena. Budget, personnel, and procurement represent areas where more leeway now exists. Campuses are also much freer to use resources as they see fit, and they are allowed to retain year-end carryover funds.

Internally, CSU has a highly developed and influential accountability system. This provides the central administration with a means of monitoring campus performance on such key issues of segmental and statewide interest as graduation rates and units-to-degree. This system is not, however, well aligned with the information requirements of the governor's compact. As state actors continue work on a statewide accountability plan, the CSU internal accountability system may serve as a model for the other two segments.

PLANNING

Most planning in the CSU segment occurs at the campus level. Campuses develop both academic and capital plans for approval by the Board of Trustees. Planning at the segmental level tends to look at the big picture, as in the recent case of deliberations for a state-supported summer session. In 1998, the year in which the current chancellor arrived, the board adopted the Cornerstones Plan, which was heavily oriented toward the annual reporting of outcomes. Under the present chancellor, implementation strategies have been devised, and the direction for the CSU segment has moved away from outcome assessments based on measurable numbers and become more focused on how results are being used to make improvements.

Segmental administrators have been very interested in trying to anticipate California workforce needs and in identifying and assessing skills common across jobs. There are also concerns specific to the segment. CSU is more than forty years old, and many of its campuses have matured. There are thirteen campuses with engineering programs—probably too many. Excess capacity is also located in the wrong places, given population and workforce growth. It is not clear how or when CSU will deal with these issues, other than through the aggregated plans of the individual campuses.

PROGRAM INITIATIVES

Program initiatives can be divided into undergraduate, graduate, and cross-segmental categories. At the undergraduate level, more attention is paid to the issues of general education design, lower division transfer patterns (to facilitate transfers from community colleges), graduation rates, and learning assessment than to the development of new programs or degrees. Under the guidance of the regional accrediting commission, the Western Association of

Schools and Colleges, considerable energy is being devoted to assessment and to using assessment data to improve programs.

At the graduate level, major efforts focus on teacher education, particularly to develop blended programs that integrate undergraduate and graduate work, thus speeding progress toward a certificate and better integrating content with pedagogy. CSU is generally handicapped in expanding its graduate programs, both by its mission and because of state funding arrangements that do not fund graduate instruction any more richly than undergraduate instruction. This could change with the acceptance of the governor's 2006–7 budget proposal to base computations for a full-time graduate student on twelve credit units rather than fifteen, the formula used for undergraduates. Joint education doctorates, in cooperation with UC, have been an important graduate program initiative. How these will fare now that CSU has the authority to offer independent doctorates remains to be seen.

Perhaps the most important initiative during the past decade has been intersegmental reform, developed with the K–12 sector, to align eleventh-grade proficiency testing with entry-level CSU proficiency standards for English and math. Seen nationally as a model reform, the initiative is intended to provide eleventh graders with an early warning of deficiencies that can be overcome in their senior year, thus enabling CSU to reduce its remedial offerings. Currently about 60 percent of incoming freshmen have to take remedial courses in English or math.

ENROLLMENT PLANNING

Determining eligibility standards and admissions priorities is a joint effort of state-level actors, the CSU trustees, and the CSU campuses. Under the Master Plan, CSU is to draw its students from the top one-third of public high school graduates. Authority for operationalizing this one-third standard falls to the trustees. However, the legislature has adopted a set of priorities to guide CSU in its enrollment planning decisions. Existing law states that, to the extent practicable, UC and CSU should admit and enroll California residents at the undergraduate level in accord with the following priorities: (1) continuing students in good standing, (2) qualified community college transfer students, and (3) students entering at freshman or sophomore levels. State policy further requires that UC and CSU reserve 60 percent of systemwide undergraduate, upper division slots for community college transfers.

The trustees delegate the responsibility for developing admissions policies to the chancellor, who typically refers the task to the Admission Advisory

Council, which is chaired by a campus president and includes faculty, students, and administrators. The primary role of the council is to recommend admission policy changes to the chancellor that will result in the eligibility of the top one-third of high school graduates. CPEC periodically performs an eligibility study to determine how well admissions policies are conforming to the one-third standard. At present, in order to be eligible for freshman admission to CSU, high school graduates must (1) complete the same A through G high school course distribution requirements mandated by UC and (2) earn a specific combination of SAT I or ACT scores and their high school GPA. The 2004 CPEC eligibility study that found UC's requirements had allowed it to exceed its Master Plan standard of 12.5 percent of high school graduates eligible for admission to UC campuses also found that CSU was taking somewhat less than 33 percent of the high school graduates it was mandated to accept. This did not spark efforts to lower CSU admission requirements, however, because of concerns with the already-high rates of remediation for eligible students.

Most applicants who meet CSU's minimum eligibility requirements are admitted to their first-choice campus. However, there are certain high-demand majors, programs, and campuses that lack the capacity to accommodate all eligible applicants. CSU campuses use two primary enrollment management tools to match demand with available capacity. The first tool involves altering application deadlines and priority categories (e.g., not admitting any lower-division transfers in certain years) in such a way that no eligible students are actually denied admission to their campus or program of choice. The second is a formal designation of *impaction*, which allows a campus or program to institute higher academic standards. This does have the effect of denying admission to students who otherwise meet minimum CSU standards. Individual campuses have different policies and practices for using these enrollment management tools.

The major enrollment planning issues facing CSU campuses today are impaction and its associated consequences for eligible students (including eligible community college transfers), remediation (i.e., reducing the huge need for remedial coursework through high school alignment, outreach, and other means), improving graduation rates, and curriculum alignments with CCC to facilitate student transfers. CSU is the key linchpin in the design of a state higher education system that requires most students entering public institutions to begin in a community college. Five out of every six transfer students from a CCC institution go to CSU. As enrollment grows rapidly, there are serious questions about the capacity of CSU to accommodate all who want to attend. CCC's refusal to distinguish work intended for transfer from everything else that they do is a constant source of complaint within CSU.

INFORMATION

CSU administrators who have worked in other state systems are surprised by the quality of data in California. However, each public segment continues to supply its own information, and no data are provided by the private sector. The institutions and segments all guard their own data carefully, and policy leaders pay little attention to the information that is provided. Some now question whether the state has the capacity to generate data that would be essential to an accountability policy.

CSU's internal accountability system provides trustees with the information they feel is essential for managing their campuses, and the segment publishes good and accessible data on its website about enrollment, proficiency, and other topics of general interest. CSU's system is a type of dual accountability system that might work in a state like California, where segments have evolved into such highly differentiated and autonomous sets of institutions. No one, however, is optimistic that the key elements of a statewide system are likely to be implemented any time soon.

BUDGETING

The internal CSU budgeting process is similar to the one for UC. Campus presidents suggest priorities to the trustees but do not submit campus budget requests. A Trustees Budget is prepared and submitted first to the DOF, and then to the legislature. As part of the legislative review process, the Legislative Analyst's Office conducts its own thorough analysis and issues recommendations that typically address enrollment funding, fees, and financial aid issues. In the absence of defined statewide goals and priorities, the annual budget negotiations become the most important arena for higher education planning and policy. The outcomes depend upon the balance of power among the legislature, the governor, and the segments. Generally, CSU is most effective if it can find a common set of interests with UC.

Enrollment issues are negotiated under the constraints of the Master Plan and its tenets on segment mission, access, and student eligibility. As an example, facing an unprecedented fiscal crisis, in January 2004 Governor Schwarzenegger proposed a budget for the following fiscal year that, among other features, recommended violating the Master Plan for the first time in history by redirecting a total of 10,000 students who were UC- or CSU-eligible to CCC for their first two years before admission to a four-year public institution.

That May, the governor plus UC and CSU agreed on a new partnership that maintained the proposed budget reductions for 2004–5 but provided for subsequent annual enrollment growth funding, steady fee increases, and related financial aid provisions. In June, the CSU chancellor was taken to task by Democratic state legislators for accepting a compact that involved reductions in support, higher student fees, and the diversion of eligible students to community colleges. A June 8, 2004, article in the main Sacramento newspaper quoted the chair of the Senate Subcommittee on Higher Education as being critical of the leaders of both CSU and UC for "rolling over and ignoring lawmakers who had vowed to fight cuts." In return, the CSU chancellor reminded legislators that previous efforts by UC and CSU had not been successful in warding off reductions, and that he had been told by a lawmaker, "until you turn students away, you will never get support for higher education."

In August, the governor and legislators agreed to restore funds to both segments to accommodate all eligible students. However, the decision was too late to admit many students who had already enrolled elsewhere. A threat to deny access for eligible students to its public four-year segments is the most powerful tool a segment can deploy. The threat is enhanced when both senior public segments stand together. In the end, the budget process for 2004–5 followed patterns in place for more than a decade. Yet to the extent that a governor agrees to compacts with the segments that ignore the Master Plan, such compacts are themselves vulnerable. The Legislative Analyst's Office has recently recommended that the legislature ignore the new compacts, because it is not clear if and how they relate to the Master Plan requirements on access and eligibility, underlying enrollment growth, or legislative priorities.

The same process used for General Fund appropriations is applied to capital projects, but the latter are funded through general obligation bonds that require voter approval. Given the access issues highlighted during the 2004–5 budget process, it is not surprising that voters have generally approved such requests by wide margins. CSU has considerable freedom in building facilities that generate revenues that can be used to pay off the associated bonds. CSU's current priority is building dormitories on some of its smaller campuses. These campuses can accommodate increased student enrollment, but they tend to be more residential than the larger campuses and thus need more dormitory space in order to attract students.

California Community Colleges

The California Community Colleges segment serves more than 2.6 million students annually, through 110 community colleges located in 72 districts. The Master Plan, in its vision of maintaining open access to a baccalaureate degree while preserving the quality associated with elite universities, assigned the majority of California students to CCC campuses. Three-fourths of California's public college students are enrolled in community colleges, compared to the national average of 40 percent. The percentage rises to almost 80 percent for blacks and Latinos (Shulock and Moore 2004). The majority of students—again almost 80 percent—work while attending CCC. Because of the number of students who attend part time, headcount enrollment is much higher than full-time equivalencies.

CCC institutions have multiple missions that center on their historic functions of academic transfer to institutions offering a baccalaureate degree and of technical/vocational preparation. But over the years since the Master Plan was adopted, CCC services and clientele have become increasingly diverse. Most legislators believe CCC should focus on transfer, basic skills, and workforce training, but CCC leaders advocate a much longer list, including lifetime learning, adult education, and community and economic development.

CCC is not a segment in the sense of UC and CSU. With seventy-two locally elected boards governing many aspects of college activity, its central board and administration play a far different and smaller role than in the two senior segments. This is one reason why CCC governance remains one of the most problematic higher education issues plaguing California policymakers. Because the individual college districts are "local education agencies" under California law, any centralized authorization for CCC becomes a "state-mandated cost" and is subject to reimbursement by the state. The DOF typically opposes such central mandates in an effort to avoid the fiscal implications of reimbursing the local districts for compliance costs.

CCC Actors

The principal actors for CCC include the state Board of Governors, the segmental Chancellor's Office, locally elected district trustees, local presidents and chancellors, and faculty.

BOARD OF GOVERNORS

Appointed by the governor, CCC's seventeen-member Board of Governors has legislatively granted authority to develop and implement policy for the seventy-two CCC districts. However, there have long been tensions between the Board of Governors and the locally elected district boards about policy responsibilities. Local CCC leaders want authority, yet complain that a weak Board of Governors seriously diminishes CCC's political influence compared to that for the four-year public segments (Shulock 2002). In the words of a former chancellor, "the Board of Governors lacks the capacity to adopt regulations that would cause community colleges to act more like a system."

Close oversight by the DOF further constrains the regulating authority of the board. DOF reviews all board-proposed actions to change regulations in the Education Code and, as noted above, it can block a proposal if it determines that such a plan involves a mandated cost for local districts for which funds are not made available. The DOF also exercises position control over the Board of Governors' staff, which greatly impedes the board's ability to make personnel decisions. All top-level appointments are subject to confirmation by the DOF, which limits the board's discretion to appoint its own management team.

CHANCELLOR'S OFFICE

The Chancellor's Office carries out three broad types of activity under the guidance of the Board of Governors: policy development, segmental compliance and accountability, and fulfillment of statutory responsibilities. In 1989–90, the Chancellor's Office had 250 authorized staff members. By 2005, the number of positions had declined to about 140. A review of the office by an external team found that as a result of these staffing problems, there were severe problems in state and federal governmental relations, accountability, compliance monitoring, research in the state's interest, technical assistance, and legal advice. A 2003 finding by an investigative reporter highlighted weaknesses in legal and staffing capabilities. Subsequently, the DOF discovered that secondary-school students were concurrently enrolled in CCC credit classes in gym and dance, in clear violation of state statutes. As a result, the colleges lost $25 million in state funding and gained "another black eye" (California Community Colleges 2004).

The Chancellor's Office has a tradition of erecting elaborate bureaucratic procedures for fulfilling its compliance and accountability functions. These procedures have not been relaxed, even though staffing has fallen precipitously. As a result, many of the procedures and reports that are required from the districts are no longer subject to segmental-level review. This leads to frustration at the local level, where officials would prefer to reallocate the administrative costs of compliance to more productive purposes.

CONSULTATION COUNCIL

The CCC governance structure, created by community college reform legislation in 1988 (Assembly Bill 1725), requires the Board of Governors to establish and maintain a consultation process at the state level to ensure local district participation in policymaking for this segment, and local districts must employ participatory governance within their districts. The process established by the Board of Governors has evolved over the years into a Consultation Council involving eighteen representatives of institutional groups—such as trustees, executive officers, students, administrators, business officers, student services officers, and instructional officers—and organizations such as faculty and staff unions and associations. The Consultation Council is chaired by the chancellor, and meets once each month to review and evaluate policy proposals, as well as to review and provide advice on both policy issues currently in development and the work of standing committees in such segment-wide areas as the budget and legislative programs.

The Board of Governors has created a consultation handbook to guide this complex process and reserves the right to make a decision in the absence of consensus. However, if the chancellor and the board make decisions counter to the council's recommendations, they do so at great political peril. Stakeholders and observers are either strongly for, or strongly against, the formal consultation structure, but all would probably agree that it complicates and slows decision making greatly. Many go so far as to define it as a major part of the ongoing problem of CCC governance.

TRUSTEES AND CHIEF EXECUTIVE OFFICERS

Each of the seventy-two CCC districts has a locally elected Board of Trustees that is charged with operating its local college in response to community needs. Boards employ a district CEO who is responsible for recommending policy (in consultation with the faculty, staff, and students) and implementing approved policy. CCC trustees and CEOs are represented by separate statewide organizations. These, in turn, are the key constituents of the Community College League of California, a Sacramento-based organization that helps local districts define and pursue common interests. The league coordinates its lobbying efforts with those of the Board of Governors, as long as the two are in agreement.

Most local boards have five or seven members. Members of fifty-four of the boards received the maximum compensation permitted by law in 2003; only seven received no compensation. Because local board members negotiate collective bargaining agreements but are not responsible for levying the taxes to pay for them, employees frequently spend money and time to ensure that those favorable to their interests are elected. This arrangement sometimes leads to short and difficult presidential tenures. It also leads to frequent budget shortfalls when the cost-of-living increases allocated in the state budget process are not sufficient to fulfill negotiated salary obligations. Some CEOs have complained that board members, who no longer have any responsibility for raising local tax revenue, spend much of their time involved in campus micromanagement. With the advent of term limits in the 1980s, membership on CCC boards has become more of a stepping stone to the state legislature.

CCC FACULTY

Assembly Bill 1725 guarantees CCC faculty the right to participate effectively in district and college decision making in eleven defined areas of professional rights and responsibilities, doing so through an academic senate whose primary responsibility is to make recommendations to the governing board on curriculum and academic standards. The act further mandates that increased faculty involvement in institutional governance should not conflict with faculty rights in collective bargaining. The faculty senate is very active in segmental policy issues. It produces a variety of substantive reports on topics such as basic skills, general education, and the meaning of an associate's degree. These reports, which rely heavily on data supplied by both segmental and campus research units, are major factors in planning efforts.

Virtually all CCC employees that are authorized to participate in collective bargaining do so. Districts are limited in their ability to use personnel resources most productively, because the variety of union contracts that are negotiated with them include restrictions on such things as transferring or reassigning staff. In Sacramento, faculty members are represented by their respective unions and by the statewide CCC Academic Senate. Under the best of circumstances, these groups join together with the Board of Governors to support policies on which consultation has created a consensus. In the worst-case scenario, they and the individual districts speak with many voices, adding to the difficulties the Community College League and the Board of Governors must overcome to represent CCC effectively.

There is both a statutory guideline and an implementing regulation, dating from 1988 legislation, that severely limits a college's flexibility with respect to the use of its faculty. The guideline states that districts should have 75 percent of all student credit hours taught by full-time faculty. Even more binding is the implementing regulation that computes an *obligation* of full-time faculty positions that each district must maintain. If a district falls short of its obligation, it must pay monies back to the state's General Fund, at a specified rate equivalent to an average full-time faculty salary. In high priority areas, this can force some districts to hire full-time faculty while laying off adjunct faculty and classified staff. Districts are also required to spend at least 50 percent of their operating budgets on direct instruction. This presents constraints in serving student needs, since many of the direct student services important to student success do not count toward this 50 percent.

Rules for CCC

A weak Chancellor's Office, a legislatively mandated consultation process at both the state and local district levels, and locally elected trustees with responsibility for spending money but not for levying the taxes required to raise it—these are only some of the contextual factors that make community colleges highly problematic outposts for the loosely coordinated California public system of higher education. As one state official said, "it takes the community colleges forever to agree on anything," and a faculty member on a CCC campus in an earlier study described the district decision process as "ready, aim, aim."

The key CCC characteristics are (1) a high degree of state regulation that recalls remnants of its history as part of the public school system, (2) a central office that is held accountable for segmental outcomes yet has little influence over those outcomes, (3) a central office culture that promotes increased internal regulation as an apparent protection against legal challenges, and (4) consensus governance structures that struggle to reach consensus in a highly contentious environment. The difference in the regulation of CCC, compared with that for UC and CSU, is best seen in their alternate approaches to partnerships and accountability. While the partnerships for UC and CSU, in the last three administrations, have been general agreements to provide incremental funding increases in exchange for *reporting* performance information, the counterpart for CCC was the Partnership for Excellence—a formulaic performance-budgeting tool, complete with targets and audits. That has now been discarded in favor of new legislation, signed by the governor in 2004, mandating a detailed district-level accountability system that would permit close state monitoring of district performance across the districts.

PLANNING

Statewide planning for CCC is inhibited by such factors as the sheer size of the CCC segment, the belief by many that statewide planning is unnecessary or inappropriate for colleges that serve *local* communities, its multitude of missions that are valued differently by various stakeholders, the open access mission many interpret as prohibiting priorities from being set, and weak central leadership. The very low per-student subsidy provided to CCC's campuses also diverts planning discussions toward calls for more funding.

A recent internal review of CCC's central office, commissioned by a new chancellor, recommended that (1) the Chancellor's Office develop the capacity for strategic analysis, planning, and futures analysis, and (2) a mission and values statement be adopted and employed as a management tool. In response, the central office obtained funding from a major foundation to support a strategic planning process. The plan has been completed and its implementation phase has begun. While participants in the process appear ready to make significant changes, the governance problems already described make it unlikely that much will change soon. For example, the implementation teams include representatives from most of the major internal stakeholders, turning the process into more of a political battle than a strategic effort to improve outcomes for the whole segment.

Instances of high-quality planning can be found in some individual CCC districts. For example, the cochair of the agency review steering committee was a former CEO of the Foothill–De Anza Community College District, which was nationally known for its leadership in planning during his tenure. Unlike CSU and UC, however, CCC has yet to extend its *institutional* capacity for planning to the segmental level.

PROGRAM INITIATIVES

The list of program regulatory responsibilities for the Board of Governors is a long one. The board approves new degrees and certificates, credit courses that are not part of an approved program, and noncredit (adult education) courses. The board also maintains inventories of approved programs and noncredit courses, as well as conducting research and providing policy leadership in the areas of basic skills and ESL, global/immigrant education, and various other fields related to distance education. In addition, it deals with probation and dismissal, course standards, degree and certificate requirements, applications for the approval of new educational centers and new colleges, and the instructional aspects of grading issues. The board's segment-level role, however, does not foster central programmatic leadership. Under current operating procedures, the Board of Governors simply coordinates and approves initiatives that arise from the local districts by means of a prescribed consultation process.

The internal management review of the Chancellor's Office argues that this office's role should shift from a focus on approval to one targeting leadership, technical support, and arbitration (when colleges and regions need such intervention). The report also calls for a plan to transfer aspects of curriculum approval, including that for new career and technical programs, to the regional level. In keeping with the culture of consultation, the report proposed—and the Board of Governors sanctioned—the creation of an advisory committee to monitor the newly delegated, conditional authority for local boards to approve new stand-alone courses. Some of the envisioned changes will require modifications to the Educational Code through which the legislature has tightly bound CCC.

ENROLLMENT PLANNING

Rules governing enrollment planning are shaped by four factors: (1) community colleges are open-door institutions with multiple missions, serving any student age eighteen or over "who can benefit from" enrollment; (2) a large proportion of those who enroll are seeking no degree or certificate, and many already hold a baccalaureate degree; (3) students move around from institution to institution; and (4) the political/cultural environment in the state gives rise to a strong resistance to assigning students to goals or program tracks. These factors combine to make "enrollment planning" primarily the art of maximizing enrollments subject to budget constraints.

Unlike UC and CSU, CCC cannot alter eligibility criteria to match its capacity with enrollment demand. The principal enrollment planning tool at its disposal is the class schedule, which expands or contracts as resources permit. In recent years, high demand and shrinking budgets have led to major mismatches between course offerings and student demand. Course reductions have had the biggest impact on low-income and underrepresented minority students, who tend to have less knowledge of the system, less flexibility, and fewer resources to devote to negotiating the increasingly competitive environment for gaining access to needed classes (Hayward et al. 2004, p. 40).

State-level discussions of enrollment in the public higher education system focus heavily on its transfer function. The governor and the legislature have undertaken no fewer than eight initiatives to improve transfer during the past two decades, but despite the attention California has given to this area, the results remain mixed. The three segments continue to resist a statewide transfer policy, relying instead on campus-to-campus articulation agreements. Those CCC campuses with strong reputations for transfer have good articulation, and a small number of institutions account for 60 percent of the state's transfer students. Within CCC, support for transfer as an institutional priority differs greatly, depending on each school's commitment and capacity. Collaborations between community colleges and four-year colleges and universities are also highly variable. Information to assess and improve transfer is lacking (Hayward et al. 2004), a shortcoming that serves as a major barrier to the development of a comprehensive approach to enrollment planning.

INFORMATION

The Chancellor's Office has a highly sophisticated information management system that is severely hampered by the CCC sector's resistance to identifying students according to their programmatic goals. Vast amounts of data can be reported about the numbers of students who complete a transfer preparation curriculum, a vocational certificate, or basic skills courses. Information on *course* completion rates and term-to-term persistence is accurate and plentiful. However, there is no capacity to report rates of transfer or completion of associate's degrees, certificates, or basic skills, because the system does not categorize students according to their educational goals.

The system is dependent on seventy-two districts to self-report accurate and timely data. Data collection is done through an information management services unit that collects semester and annual data from the local districts; maintains the data element dictionary; reports data to federal and state agencies; and provides data warehousing and systems development, ad hoc data querying services, and decision support systems. Most districts have institutional research offices. Local researchers have organized into an effective statewide research and planning group that shares data issues and methods.

Despite various shortcomings, good progress in sharing such information across sectors is being made at the regional level, spearheaded by select community colleges. The review of the Chancellor's Office, commissioned by the last chancellor, includes a strong recommendation for improving oversight of the CCC sector "to ensure taxpayers' monies are being used legally and effectively" and for clarifying the Education Code to require the chancellor to investigate when there is reasonable cause to assume the existence of an irregularity (California Community Colleges 2004).

BUDGETING

About 95 percent of funding for the CCC segment is determined through a complicated apportionment formula, leaving the Board of Governors with very limited authority over the remaining elements in the budget. Annual budget negotiations thus revolve around the overall education funding levels provided to the K–12 and CCC sectors under the terms of this formula, which is governed by an equally complicated voter-enacted funding initiative. The apportionment formula pits CCC against K–12 for its share of the total funding authorized under Proposition 98. Some argue that CCC will never be adequately funded under this arrangement, while others fear that removing CCC from the protection of this proposition (which mandates minimum funding levels) would leave this segment in an even more vulnerable position.

The Board of Governors' wish to gain more authority over segmental resources was an important factor in the 1998 Partnership for Excellence (PFE), the statutory counterpart to the more informal partnerships negotiated by the governor for UC and CSU. The PFE provided categorical funding to CCC in exchange for improving performance in the areas of student transfers, degrees and certificates awarded, successful course completion, workforce development, and basic skills. Specific goals and measures for these five categories were adopted in fall 1998, with targets to be achieved by 2005–6. Initially set at $100 million, funding increased to $300 million for several years, until the program was terminated due to overall state funding constraints.

PFE legislation specified that for the first three years, funds were to be allocated to districts based on enrollments. The Board of Governors was to develop a contingent funding mechanism that could be implemented to link allocations to district performance if, after three years, the board determined that CCC was not making sufficient progress toward its goals. The board chose not to activate the contingent funding mechanism, arguing that the CCC segment had been making satisfactory progress. Observers report that neither the board nor legislators wanted to take the political risk of implementing a contingent funding plan, preferring a predictable and stable full-time-equivalent (FTE) share to a performance-based competition in which individual districts could lose funding (Shulock and Moore 2002). This illustrates the extent to which formulas, rather than priorities, drive budgeting in this segment. In sum, CCC's experience with the PFE did not produce any real change in either accountability or performance.

Increasingly, policy attention is given to the very low rates of subsidy for CCC students, as well as to the finance mechanisms that reward access rather than success and are insufficiently responsive to regional differences in growth rates. Needed policy reforms include adequate funding, equity across colleges with similar program and student characteristics, simplicity, transparent incentives and disincentives, rewards for collaboration across programs and segments, and rewards for success (Hayward et. al. 2004, p. 40). In testimony to the legislature in March 2004, the chancellor emphasized that the state ranked forty-fifth in the nation in terms of state funding per community college student, the CCC segment received only $1.00 per student for every $1.83 for CSU and $3.62 for UC, and CCC had over 15,000 unfunded full-time-equivalent students in 2003–4. Proposition 92, a three-and-a-half-year effort by the Community College League to set aside a specific share of state appropriations for CCC while having this segment concurrently cut its tuition rates, was soundly defeated by voters in 2008.

CCC facilities are funded through general obligation bond issues, passed either on a statewide basis or by local districts. Local bond issues have become a favored form of capital financing since a voter's tax initiative reduced the majority required for approval from two-thirds to 55 percent (state initiatives require only a simple majority, but getting in the queue can involve significant delays). A planning unit in the Chancellor's Office oversees new construction, renovations, and related tasks by means of detailed policies and procedures that mirror the extensive regulations found in other areas of CCC operation. In January 2003, new legislation took effect permitting certain local districts more flexibility in designing and building capital projects.

Support for CCC facilities is evident from the pass rate of proposals. In 2002, community colleges received $745.9 million to fund more than 150 projects. In the same election, fourteen out of fifteen local districts passed bond issues providing another $3.2 billion. Despite the fiscal problems in California, seventeen months later voters statewide approved yet another $900 million, and ten out of twelve districts passed an additional $2.3 billion in funding for new facilities.

Clearly, Californians are proud of the quality of the University of California and see its campuses as engines of economic development. The California State University serves as the primary integrating force for state higher education. Its ubiquitous presence, comprehensiveness, size, and commitment to serving community college transfers help bridge the chasm between an elite, highly focused, and very selective UC and the underfunded, open-access, and multipurpose California Community Colleges. CSU deserves much of the credit for the benefits California enjoys—an educated workforce and well-prepared teachers. It is also the closest instrument to an integrating agency for all of education that the state currently possesses. CSU works with UC to offer applied doctorates; with the K–12 sector to define academic preparation and devise strategies for improvement; and with CCC to improve articulation and transfer, a core feature of the Master Plan.

CCC deserves considerable credit for its contributions to a trained workforce, especially for employed and place-bound working adults. It also meet the language, literacy, and job-skills requirements of a large immigrant population. There are at least two factors, apart from state funding, that prevent these benefits from being even greater. The first is uneven quality across the CCC segment. The second is the lack of a state agency with the authority to link programs to desired outcomes. As one interviewee noted: "There is a culture in community colleges that inhibits the effective pursuit of any priority. Nothing happens unless everybody gets a little piece of the action."

Governance arrangements in California rely primarily on institutional processes to represent the public interest. Segmental goals consistently trump state priorities, and accountability arrangements are sufficiently loose so that whatever happens can be interpreted as evidence of satisfactory performance. Quality, measured by inputs (including enrollment), is the core value. Access is celebrated in spite of serious problems with completion, particularly in CCC.

California institutions consistently receive outstanding reviews from academics, who resonate with an arrangement that gives primacy to professionals. While policy leaders in California may sometimes wonder about the relationship between what they spend and what they are told they get, the prevailing consensus is that the segments do a very good job of carrying out the missions assigned to them in the Master Plan. While policy leaders acknowledge the characteristics and problems of the system described in our study, they do not think that most Californians believe the overall system is broken. Absent such an agreement, these leaders are not sanguine about the probabilities for significant change in the foreseeable future.

CHAPTER FIVE

South Dakota

*South Dakota is near the median in terms of state effort and achieves a level
of performance that overall seems better than either that of California or New
Mexico. How can one account for such performance, given the state's economic
resources and geographic characteristics? South Dakota has clearly been in
the forefront nationally in bringing political leaders together with professional
educators to establish goals and priorities for higher education that reflect
multiple stakeholders. State budgets and their associated allocations closely
track these priorities in the decision-making processes. All of this is organized
by a unified governing board that operates, with at least one eye on efficiency,
in the shadow of the state capitol. While its state system, as in other states,
evolved from a collection of existing institutions, South Dakota, unlike most
other states, has successfully moved toward greater centralization and made
decisions unheard of elsewhere—such as closing an institution. Nonetheless, its
lack of a network of comprehensive community colleges may hurt South Dakota
on some of the indicators used in our study.*

South Dakota has long been associated with agricultural and rural communities. The state is small, with just over 775,000 residents (U.S. Census Bureau
2005). Several prominent legislators and community leaders have strong ties
to the agricultural industry. Over the last decade, however, economic trends in
South Dakota seem to be following the general patterns of the U.S. economy.
According to the 2000 Decennial Census, employment in South Dakota's agriculture and manufacturing industries shrank between 1990 and 2000, while
overall employment in the state experienced a moderate increase (QuickFacts).
Government classifications by occupation and industry have changed over
time, making precise year-to-year comparisons difficult, but it appears that
retail trade and professionally related occupations have contributed to the
state's modest growth.

The shift in South Dakota's economy has been taking place for some time, steadily drawing attention to the importance of postsecondary education. Yet it is only within the last ten years that higher education policy has taken on heightened importance, as evidenced by consistent policymaker engagement on issues ranging from performance to the implementation of a new merit-based aid program.

The challenges for postsecondary education are tied not only to economic shifts, but also to demographic realities. South Dakota's population growth from 2000 to 2003 was just 1.3 percent, compared to a 3.3 percent growth rate for the entire United States. In addition, by some estimates, there will actually be a decline in the eighteen- to twenty-four-year-old age group population by 2015 (Martinez 2004). The educational attainment status of the state's adult population also is a signal that postsecondary education must adapt to meet future challenges. The percentage of people twenty-five and older with a high school degree (84.6%) is larger than the national average (80.4%), yet those over twenty-five holding a bachelor's degree (21.5%) is lower than the national average (24.4%). In addition, the American Indian population in the state, at 8.5 percent, is South Dakota's largest minority, and several of the institutional and state leaders interviewed for our study spoke of the need to provide more effective opportunities for this population. All of these indicators signal coming challenges for higher education.

As with any state, higher education policy is the result of available resources, competing priorities, and political interplay among various individuals and groups. Within South Dakota's six-institution university system, however, structured dialogues between the system's and the state's leaders have created a purposeful framework on which to base higher education policy. These dialogues, commonly referred to in the state as roundtables, have occurred since the mid-1990s and have included discussions about how to prepare South Dakota's citizens for work that extends beyond the traditional occupations that are part of its history. The governor and state legislators are also concerned about the utilization of state resources and, as such, have participated in the dialogues and directly helped to define higher education policy priorities, starting in earnest in 1995.

South Dakota's postsecondary landscape is not limited to the university system. Four technical institutes are state supported and enjoy favorable reputations among many legislators. The private sector has several liberal arts schools, and there are tribal colleges that focus on the American Indian population. South Dakota is a small state, so institutional leaders from the private, tribal, and technical institutions are able to maintain personal contact with policymakers, although this contact is less formalized and systematic than is true for the university system.

Perhaps because of its small size, those who work in higher education generally express satisfaction with their interactions with state policymakers. This is particularly true for those belonging to the university system and the technical institutes. Policymakers commonly speak of economic development in the same breath as they talk about technical institutes. And many of those interviewed for our study were able to identify policy priorities for the universities, which include participation, retention, the efficient use of resources, and improved quality.

There is evidence, written and otherwise, of these policy priorities in South Dakota—particularly for the public universities. In 1997, state leaders formalized a set of goals for higher education, and the process by which these priorities emerged continues today, with refinements and improvements that allow decision makers to learn from the past while keeping an eye on the future. For example, the five original policy priorities that were tied to incentive funding in 1997 were reduced to three target ones in 2003. The state has also created new initiatives to coincide with evolving concerns, such as the 2004 implementation of a merit-based aid program intended to reform public schools and improve incentives for high school graduates to attend college in the state. It is largely through the interests and actions of state actors that higher education policy issues remain visible throughout South Dakota.

STATE ACTORS
The Governor

Governor Mike Rounds took office in January 2003. Governor Rounds was previously in the legislature and succeeded Governor Bill Janklow. Janklow served four terms as governor of South Dakota and is credited by many as laying the foundation for a strong Board of Regents through his appointments. During his tenure, Governor Janklow actively participated in higher-education-related discussions and was described as supportive. One legislator described Janklow as often critical of higher education in public but praising it in private.

Governor Rounds's initial approach contrasted somewhat with his predecessor's. Janklow had very specific solutions in mind and was somewhat confrontational; Governor Rounds, according to several sources, made it a point to listen to different ideas and gather input. A staff member in the governor's office said Governor Rounds is ready to make decisions and go in a certain direction, but first he likes to garner information from various sources. Interested observers think that any significant changes in higher education policy will require the governor's approval to be successful, regardless of who is in the governor's seat.

Staff members for the Board of Regents, as well as the governor's own staff, believe that the governor's office will continue to be actively engaged in higher education policy. The current governor attended roundtable discussions as a state legislator and has maintained conversations with higher education officials. Governor Rounds's interest in higher education is evidenced by the fact that he introduced legislation for student aid in 2003, his first year in office. Although the legislation did not pass, it is significant that the governor gave this issue his attention.

The Legislature

South Dakota has a part-time legislature, which meets between thirty-five to forty days per year. The legislature, as a body, has involved itself in issues of higher education policy, and this involvement has led to actions that have directly influenced institutional behavior. For example, in 1995 the legislature passed a resolution calling on higher education to be more efficient. There were no initial budget cuts, but the Board of Regents pushed institutions toward a unified approach in managing their academic resources. Institutions were asked to achieve savings through a number of strategies: cut low-enrollment programs, consolidate administratively, and change business practices.

Individual legislators have long been involved in higher education policy, especially with issues related to efficiency and the prudent use of state resources. South Dakota previously had seven universities, and one former legislator, who had a long career in both the House and the Senate, described how he worked with other legislators to help close one of these schools. Several respondents pointed out that it was not just single legislators who have influenced higher education, but rather the legislature as a whole. This body has, over the years, been particularly involved in pushing for efficiency and broaching the subject of accountability.

Legislators also communicate with top administrators from the four vocational institutes in the state, but this communication is not systematic or formal—a legislator might visit a technical institute, or interact with institute presidents during the legislative session. When asked, legislators were unable to identify specific examples of policy-driven change at the technical institutes, although most note their favorable impression of them.

Bureau of Finance and Management and Legislative Research Council

The Bureau of Finance and Management (BFM) is part of the executive branch. The commissioner and his staff work directly with the governor to identify executive priorities, including those for higher education. The BFM does not construct its own estimate of the higher education budget. Each institution has its own internal budgeting process that culminates in a request transmitted to the South Dakota University System Board of Regents. Next, the board compiles a cumulative budget for the six universities and two special schools it governs, and submits this budget for the state's university system to the BFM. The BFM then screens the Board of Regent's final budget request and examines it within the context of the governor's priorities. The Board of Regents works closely with BFM to provide information and defend its request. The BFM eventually constructs the governor's total state budget, which includes amounts for all of higher education.

The Legislative Research Council (LRC) is the legislative equivalent of the BFM, although its role in the budget process differs. The LRC tends to focus on issues raised by the governor's budget recommendation, which, in some respects, may be perceived as reacting to the governor's budget. LRC's staff also works on analysis and issues of interest to either individual legislators or the legislature as a whole.

South Dakota Board of Regents

The South Dakota University System Board of Regents is a constitutional board responsible for all aspects of university education. The university system dominates the postsecondary landscape in the state in terms of funding, enrollment, and public attention. The Board of Regents governs six public four-year institutions and two specialized schools (the South Dakota School for the Deaf and the South Dakota School for the Visually Handicapped). The six universities are spread throughout the state and operate as a true system, with the administration at each institution reporting directly to the board's executive director.

The nine members on the board are appointed by the governor and confirmed by the Senate. Regents serve six-year terms. The board is responsible for systemwide and state-level planning initiatives, and it also sets tuition at the six universities. Governor Rounds appointed six of the nine current board members during his first year in office. In contrast, it took Governor Janklow four years to appoint a majority during his tenure. Most administrators and legislators indicated that Janklow's appointments were very effective. A few board members reported some conflict with Janklow as they began to express divergent opinions, and some in higher education believe that Janklow's past criticisms of higher education reflected his disagreements with individuals within the system. One official said Janklow expected conformity, yet, inevitably, any regent might eventually take a different position from that of the governor who appointed him. The relationship between Governor Rounds and the regents has been positive, not only because of his opportunity to appoint a majority of board members in such a short time, but also because two of the continuing board members also support his goals.

Executive Director of the Board of Regents

One of the most critical duties of the Board of Regents is to appoint an executive director. The current executive director has presided over the implementation of roundtables, the shift away from enrollment-driven formulas, and the establishment of incentive funding. He is viewed almost unanimously as an effective state-level leader who has built bridges with policymakers, K–12 leaders, and institutional presidents. Many respondents in South Dakota believe that the university system has made great strides since 1995 and attribute much of that success to the executive director's leadership and the capable staff he has built.

The executive director and his staff provide an effective interface between public universities and state officials. The regents and executive director are active and influential state-level actors who have been involved in leading South Dakota's higher education policy discussions and translating subsequent policy into institutional action.

South Dakota Department of Education and Technical Institutes

The South Dakota Department of Education governs K–12 education and the state's four vocational institutes. The South Dakota Board of Education has nine members and focuses primarily on K–12 policy, ensuring that the many school districts that report to it meet state and federal requirements. Additional responsibilities that fall within the board's domain include accountability, teacher quality, and the fulfillment of No Child Left Behind requirements. The Board of Education, as a state actor, is primarily a voice for K–12 education.

Although the Board of Education governs the state's four technical institutes, their operations continue to be under the administrative control of the K–12 school district boards that first initiated them as area vocational schools in 1965. The duties of the state board encompass setting tuition rates, overseeing programs, monitoring budgets, and examining requests for maintenance and repairs. However, the relationships between the technical institutes and any other state actors are conducted outside of the Board of Education.

Although South Dakota has no community colleges, many in the state feel that some of the institutes provide several of the functions of a community college. Unlike community colleges, however, the technical institutes do not have a liberal arts track, only a career and technology track. A former legislator recalled what he said might have been a mistake when he tried to turn the technical institutes into colleges by trying to force students into an area of emphasis that could be transferred to universities. His current belief is that this would make it harder for those who want a marketable skill but not necessarily a college degree.

There is some difference of opinion about what the role of the technical institutes should be in the state, but from a policymaker's perspective, they are viewed quite favorably. Policymakers believe the technical institutes meet economic development needs and respond well to legislative concerns. According to one of their presidents, the institutes have an integral tie to industry, especially when one considers that "95 percent of our students are placed in a job after they graduate, and 87 percent of them are in South Dakota."

The presidents from the technical institutes are in regular contact with each other, meeting once a month. It is not clear how these meetings influence individual campus activities, but the meetings seem to be a vehicle for communication, where leaders can discuss common issues and concerns. According to one administrator, the meetings also help the technical institutes work toward a common legislative package.

Private Higher Education

Although the six public universities dominate formal higher education policy at the state level, it is interesting to note that almost 20 percent of the state's enrollments are in its five private universities and four tribal colleges. Legislators rarely mentioned private institutions in South Dakota, but they clearly are a part of the overall state postsecondary puzzle and appear to fill a niche role.

The five private universities are primarily liberal arts institutions, some of which have received national recognition. Augustana College, with a headcount enrollment of over 1,800 students, is regularly recognized in the *U.S. News and World Report*'s special issue on colleges and universities. The University of Sioux Falls, with a current enrollment of about 1,500 students, serves a niche market as a private Christian university, while its "academic programs simultaneously meet community needs," according to its president. Seventy percent of the institution's students are in-state. Campus leaders from the private liberal arts institutions do meet and talk to each other, but their contact with state legislators occurs mainly during the legislative session.

Tribal colleges also serve a niche market. One tribal college president described these institutions as providing "education to Indian people who have not fared well in the traditional educational system." A member of the state's Board of Regents, when asked about the importance of the tribal colleges, reflected on the public university experience, noting that "we have not been as successful with the Native American population as we should." Of the four tribal colleges, two are accredited and offer four-year degrees and graduate education. Informal articulation agreements exist with the public universities, but they are institution-to-institution. The tribal college president also described having little contact with state policymakers. One tribal administrator said that there was a public appropriation for tribal colleges in the late 1970s, but it was challenged by some lawmakers and subsequently never funded. In his opinion, the state policies that affect tribal colleges most directly are only those for areas in which students must complete a state exam—nursing and teaching.

The planning and budgeting activities of the liberal arts universities and tribal colleges are very specific to each institution. The presidents from the liberal arts colleges meet periodically, but the type of formal meetings found among technical institute presidents is less evident in the private sector. The presidents of the tribal colleges do not appear to have any forum where they meet to discuss state-level issues, although each of the institutions belongs to a national organization called the American Indian Higher Education Consortium.

The role of both liberal arts and tribal colleges in South Dakota seems destined to grow. A state merit scholarship program, first funded in the 2004 legislative session, allows scholarships to be used at public or private institutions. With the implementation of this program, many believe private institutions will play a more prominent role in state policy conversations. Recently, the Board of Regents hosted a meeting with presidents of the private institutions to discuss common issues.

STATE RULES

The rules that determine the roles of higher education actors, the ways in which they interact, and the impact of the policies they administer have evolved over time, based on constitutional provisions, statutes, court decisions, political culture, the state's economy, governing coalition priorities, and statutes that specify the design of the higher education system, including institutional governance arrangements. The next section of this chapter describes South Dakota's rules within eight different categories: planning, program review and approval, information, academic preparation, student assistance, fiscal policies, and economic development.

Planning

Among state actors, the clearest planning activity takes place between the Board of Regents and state policymakers. The board has proactively initiated state-level conversations through roundtables. The roundtables began in 1995 and continue to provide a forum where higher education stakeholders discuss issues of state concern. The board provides direction for the roundtable discussions, but it has commonly used a third party to moderate the meetings in order to create an atmosphere of goodwill and objectivity. Higher education respondents described legislative involvement in current roundtables as excellent.

Policymakers across the state uniformly agree that public universities in

South Dakota have had state-level policy goals since 1997. The roundtable process has enhanced communication among policymakers, higher education administrators, and business and community leaders. The legislature and the governor actively communicate with the Board of Regents and consistently convey concerns and issues from a state perspective. For example, state-level input often emphasizes efficiency, which is one reason the board directed the individual campuses to collaborate on course and program offerings. Although one former state senator estimated that only 25 percent of the legislators were really involved in higher education at any given time, he felt that South Dakota policymakers in general give higher education appropriate consideration during legislative sessions.

The early roundtables culminated with the creation of the following nine state policy goals in 1997:

1. Access for all qualified South Dakotans
2. Enrollment in economic growth programs
3. Improvement in academic performance
4. Attraction and retention of qualified professionals
5. Development of faculty professionals
6. Collaboration among the universities
7. Enhancement of the current technological infrastructure
8. Maintenance of current facilities and equipment
9. Generation of external funds

The Board of Regents, in its annual fact book (available online at www.sdbor .edu), provides a quantitative assessment of each of these goals. Although nine state policy goals guided South Dakota higher education from 1997 to 2002, policymakers who were interviewed for our study were more likely to emphasize goals that addressed participation, efficiency, and collaboration. After 2002, the policy goals were revisited, and the state now has three major priorities: external funding (grants and contracts), retention, and individual university measures that help improve quality (South Dakota Board of Regents, 2004, 2005c). The roundtables and the various avenues of purposeful communications have fostered the evolution of these priorities.

Currently, there is one major roundtable annually, usually at the end of the year. Invitees include the governor and some of his staff, legislators, regents, and institutional presidents. The end-of-year roundtable is always well attended, and legislators and the governor are commonly present. These roundtables are, manifestly, the locations where meaningful policy is discussed and broad plans are developed to carry out the agreements that emerge. The Board of Regents takes the results of every roundtable and translates them into actions that can be implemented across the universities.

The annual roundtable is not the only opportunity that legislators have to be involved in general discussions about higher education. In the summer, mini-roundtables are held regionally throughout the state; about 40 percent of the legislators who are invited actually attend. Because of their positive reception by policymakers, the initial set four mini-roundtables has expanded to six.

As an additional mechanism to engage legislators and the public in policy discussions, the Board of Regents recently began sponsoring town meetings, arranged by board's staff, that involve local community leaders and the public. The meetings are held in a community building and run by the local state legislator, who reaps the added benefit of presiding over a forum that provides an opportunity to communicate with constituents. From the perspective of the board's executive director, town meetings have been successful; they are an important vehicle to get people to talk about higher education.

There are many people in the state who believe that legislative hearings and draft bills during the session are reflective of the ideas, concerns, and conversations that happen at the roundtables. Over the last nine to ten years, all statewide policy on higher education that has resulted from legislative action can, in a real sense, be traced back to the roundtable discussions. For example, major topics at past roundtables have included issues of funding and program efficiency, both of which produced either legislation or board policy.

Policy and planning discussions between the K–12 sector and higher education are also beginning to surface. Communication has improved during the past two years, despite a history of resistance to collaboration by K–12 regional and state leaders that led one legislator to describe the K–12 sector as a stumbling block. The Board of Regents meets annually with the state Board of Education, and the executive director for the Board of Regents meets with K–12 leaders once a month. The Board of Regents' staff is now located in a building owned by the South Dakota Association of School Boards, a location they share with the South Dakota Association of School Administrators. This physical proximity has enhanced ties, particularly in terms of engaging the K–12 community in dialogues. Some regents have also led state-level task forces involving K–12 and higher education, further strengthening communication between the two entities.

There is little evidence of state-level planning for the technical institutes and private colleges and universities. There is no single office, representing either the private sector or the technical institutes, that serves as a convener or provides input to legislators for planning purposes. South Dakota is a small state, however, so administrators from the various postsecondary sectors often know legislators and interact with them on an ad hoc basis. It is also typical that presidents from these sectors visit with policymakers during the budget season or testify at legislative hearings.

The discussion of articulation and transfer of credits from technical institutes to the universities represents an interesting development during the last two to three years. For many years, administrators from technical institutes regularly voiced concerns to policymakers that the university system did not accept credits from their students and complained that those credits that were accepted did not count toward any degree programs within the university, in effect nullifying the coursework students had taken at the institutes. University officials had various worries about the quality of the credits and whether courses were taught by appropriate faculty, but the legislature had little sympathy for these arguments. After meaningful dialogues between the Board of Regents and the technical institutes, the universities entered into an agreement to certify the transfer requirements in general education offered by the technical institutes. Talks continue, with a focus on improving the articulation and transfer of specific technical program credits.

Program Review and Approval

State policymakers do not deal with individual programs, but because of their concerns about efficiency, policymakers are indirectly involved in university-level program review and approval. The fingerprint of efficiency has left its mark on programs in general, and even on institutions. The state used to have seven public universities, but one of those was closed in the 1980s, effectively shutting down an entire array of program offerings that many felt were duplicative.

The Board of Regents, not the institutions, works with policymakers at the state level to answer questions about efficiency and collaboration, at least as they pertain to programs. University administrators are sometimes involved in state-level conversations when an issue directly touches on their institutions. The 7/10 rule is an example of how legislative concern for efficiency affects program offerings and stimulates collaboration. The 7/10 rule stipulates that the Board of Regents will not fund graduate courses containing less than seven students and undergraduate courses with fewer than ten students. These actions encouraged collaboration among the state's six universities, which have worked to combine enrollments when there is a perceived need to continue a program or a course offering. Interinstitutional programs have developed in certain areas when it is clear that one university cannot maintain a program on its own, but where the demand from multiple institutions signals that the program should continue. Universities have also shared facilities to offer courses that draw on the strengths of the different institutions.

Information

The BMF and the LRC both rely on the Board of Regents to provide information that helps the governor and legislature make both yearly funding and broad policy decisions. The credibility legislators attach to this regent-generated information has increased over time. One staff member on the board said that the continuing dialogue and the relationships higher education leaders have built with legislators translates into trust and belief in the printed information the board offers.

The Board of Regents puts out an annual fact book that provides a general description of state-level funding and enrollment, as well as the general conditions under which higher education operates. There is also an assessment of state policy goals that reaches to the institutional level. Most of the assessments are based on numerical data, although there are areas that rely on qualitative descriptions. In addition, the board has recently put out accountability reports for the system (South Dakota Board of Regents 2005a) and management reports specific to different universities may also be derived as needed. According to the executive director, all of the reports the board produces are meant to circulate information, get people talking about higher education, and help policymakers as well as institutional leaders use that information to enhance decision making and realize state policy goals. The lack of state-level summary information from the technical institutes and private universities reflects the absence of any statewide entity that serves to coordinate these sectors.

Academic Preparation

Despite the concern of individual legislators, it is only during the past few years that South Dakota has begun systematic efforts to increase college preparation for secondary students. While the governor's office provided discretionary dollars to improve technology in K–12 schools during Janklow's tenure, the connection between the grants and common measures of preparation was indirect, at best. Now there are annual meetings between the Board of Regents and the state Board of Education, and monthly meetings between the Board of Regents' executive director and K–12 leaders. One outcome of these meetings, in addition to communication and goodwill, was an agreement that secondary students needed three years of math instead of two.

One of the state's largest efforts to improve preparation culminated in early 2003, largely because of ongoing talks between K–12 and higher education officials and state policymakers. The Board of Regents' staff completed a project that sent out mailers to all junior high and high school students, outlining the types of courses students needed to take to get ready for college. The most arduous part of the project, according to several interviewees, was obtaining the database with the names and addresses of these students. K–12 officials, for various reasons, were reluctant to provide this information. Launching the project involved a two-year conversation, which included interaction at the roundtables. The project gained political momentum as the governor and individual legislators became more concerned about preparation and participation. Eventually all the pieces came together, and the Board of Regents' staff obtained money from the legislature to publish and distribute the mailer.

Student Assistance

Compared to other states, students in South Dakota have always financed more of their education with loans. The state has never had a significant investment in student financial aid, although in the early 1990s, then governor Mickelson championed a small scholarship program which was 21 percent need based and 79 percent merit based. The program was phased out in 1999.

The state's policymakers are more concerned today with the lack of state-funded financial aid than ever before. South Dakota is losing quality students to other states, and most believe that the lack of state student aid contributes to that result. There are also several indications that a growing number of individual state leaders are concerned about student aid. Two scholarship programs were introduced in the 2003 legislative session, one sponsored by the governor and the other by the Board of Regents. The latter program won legislative approval, but it was not funded. However, the infrastructure was set in place, and funding for the program was authorized in 2004. Merit-based aid provided by South Dakota Opportunity Scholarships can be used at any public or private institution (South Dakota Board of Regents 2003). Interestingly, tribal colleges have elected not to participate in the scholarships, possibly because the required ACT score would make most of their students ineligible.

Several individuals involved in higher education issues—from staff members for the Board of Regents to institutional administrators to legislators—have mixed feelings about the new merit-based program, preferring more emphasis on need-based student aid. To qualify for a South Dakota Opportunity Scholarship, students must score 24 or higher on the ACT, perform at a B level, and attend an in-state college. A key criterion for receiving the award requires students to take the Regents Scholar curriculum, in which high school coursework reflects regent-specified requirements designed to prepare students for college. These requirements are described in the mailers that were sent out to all junior high and high school students. The rules for student assistance and academic preparation, then, work in tandem with the merit aid component. In this sense, the goal of the merit aid program is to reform public schools and improve academic preparation—a goal that many policymakers feel is being achieved.

Institutional efforts to provide student aid are garnering state attention, since they represent attempts to attract students from across the state. In one private scholarship program praised by a regent, South Dakota State University awarded $1,000 apiece to eligible students, based on their ACT scores. The awards continue if the students maintain good grades. Several interviewees in our study identified this program as being successful in helping students and effective in generating good publicity for the institution.

Despite differences in opinion about the details of merit- versus need-based assistance, just about everyone feels that student aid now must somehow figure into the higher education funding equation in South Dakota. In the words of one policymaker, "student aid is now on the radar screen." Legislators are particularly interested in keeping quality students in the state as a means of attracting business and industry, and they increasingly believe that student financial assistance can help.

Fiscal Policies

South Dakota's funding approach for higher education has long focused on providing operating support directly to institutions. Policymakers and higher education administrators alike believe that over the years the state has made strong efforts to support public institutions. Grapevine (Palmer 2005) data indicate that from 2000 to 2005, South Dakota's five-year change in state appropriations for higher education rose 24.5 percent, much higher than the national average of 10.7 percent, lending credibility to these perceptions.

Most respondents also think that tuition in the state is affordable, probably linking this belief to their favorable opinions about state efforts to directly fund higher education institutions. The Board of Regents sets tuition at the six public universities, and the rate is the same for each of them. There are some at the institutional level who disagree with this approach and believe it inevitable that different universities will someday require different tuition rates. The institutions do have different missions, and one interviewee contrasted South Dakota State University (SDSU) with Black Hills State University (BHSU)—SDSU will continue to emphasize research and competitive sports programs, while BHSU is largely regional and focuses on associate's, baccalaureate, and limited master's degree programs.

Although operating support and tuition are topics of interest in South Dakota, funding discussions are dominated by and unmistakably linked to notions of planning and accountability. It is here that roundtable priorities and the state's current funding approach are tied together. In the 1970s, the state implemented an enrollment-driven formula, as was the trend in many states around the country at the time. As South Dakota began formulating state policy goals in the mid-1990s, the Board of Regents worked with the legislature to change the way funds were allocated to the institutions. The board—in consultation with the legislature, through the roundtable process—approved and implemented a funding approach that is really a product of two components. The first, called *base-plus*, funds general expenses and operations. It is no longer predicated on enrollment and is adjusted for inflationary increases over time. This base-plus appropriation comprises the majority of institutional funding from the state and provides stability and predictability for the universities. Base-plus appropriations are intended to support all state policy goals by encouraging long-term planning, since the funding fluctuations associated with enrollments have been eliminated.

A second, performance-based component, called the State Policy Incentive Funding Program, was in effect from 1997 to 2002. Five state policy priorities, arrived at in consultation with the legislature, determined institutional eligibility. The Board of Regents worked to establish institutional goals for access, economic growth, academic improvement, collaboration, and increases in nonstate funds. Each priority was worth 1 percent of the funds from the total funding pool allocated to higher education. If a university met or exceeded a goal, they received 1 percent from the pool of funds; if they did not meet a goal, they did not receive funding in that area. These incentive goals corresponded with the direct measures detailed in table 5.1 (South Dakota Board of Regents 2002).

In the early phase of this performance-funding approach, there were different opinions as to whether the incentive portion of the new fiscal policy would be effective. Now that the program has run its course, the general consensus from state-level respondents is favorable. Even those who are not fully convinced that incentive funding was as effective as it might have been still believe that the state is better off than it was in 1997. One legislator even said the 5 percent maximum in additional funding from meeting the state's five performance goals probably was not enough, and that higher education could have been pushed further. The Board of Regents' staff indicated mostly positive responses from policymakers; symbolically, it appears that incentive funding has done much to elevate higher education's image. One analyst said that the yearly production of information builds credibility over time and shows an effort to assess performance. Institutional responses are less enthusiastic, with some expressing doubt about the relevance of quantitative measures for objectives calling for collaboration or quality.

South Dakota's willingness to revise and modify state policy goals is just as interesting as the state's process for deriving these goals. In 2002–3, state policymakers and the Board of Regents worked to incorporate the lessons they learned from the first five years of setting higher education policy by modifying and refining their priorities. As a result of the various policy discussions that continue to happen in the state, the number of priorities has now decreased to three, and the focus of each is somewhat altered. The emphasis on external funding was retained, and it now represents 40 percent of the total evaluation for each institution. Student retention has lately been identified as a priority, and it now accounts for 40 percent of the incentive funds. The remaining 20 percent is based on a quality measure defined by each institution, which allows for differences and provides a degree of freedom for each university. The accommodation for institutional differences is important

TABLE 5.1
State Incentive Funding Goals and Associated Measures

Goal	Measures
South Dakota resident enrollment	% change in fall enrollment
Students enrolled in economic growth programs	% change in fall enrollment in targeted programs
Academic improvement	Comparison of student improvement on a national proficiency exam relative to a national norm
Collaboration	Number of institutions sharing faculty/ facilities
External funds	Yearly external funds

in South Dakota, because the board has worked hard, in consultation with policymakers, to eliminate unnecessary duplication and create mission differentiation. The individual measures signal an appreciation of the possibility that universities can achieve quality in different ways. They also reflect the important insight that it is not possible to standardize every measure for all institutions.

The new priorities—external funding, retention, and quality—are known as the Resource Compact. There is general agreement, even among university administrators, that the amount of money tied to the priorities in the compact is not very important. Yet priorities and incentive funding continue to assure the legislature that the system is responsive to state policymakers' concerns.

The ways in which South Dakota appropriates funds for higher education sends signals about policy priorities. During his tenure, Governor Janklow created awards that gave faculty time and resources for redesigning courses so that technology was integrated into their disciplines. Starting in 1998, faculty members from a host of disciplines and across the six university campuses received these awards and were able to use them for compensation, training, equipment, and software. Governor Rounds has continued supplying discretionary money for faculty awards, even though these new awards have a different purpose than the Janklow ones. According to both one of the governor's administrators and the executive director for the Board of Regents, the new grants encourage professional development by awarding money to faculty who work together across campuses. The purpose of such collaborations is to develop campus-based courses that draw on the expertise of faculty from different institutions. State officials also hope that faculty collaboration across campuses will reduce duplication and encourage efficiency within the system.

Before 2001, capital project requests for the South Dakota university system reached the legislature one project at a time, even though the proposals were still made through the Board of Regents. Project submissions were based on whichever institution's turn it was to send a request to the legislature. In 2001, the board developed its first ten-year capital plan. First, the universities identify their capital needs and present them to the board. The board then prioritizes these needs from a systems perspective. Some capital projects are fully funded; for others, the board may, upon review, ask institutional administrators if it is possible to either scale back their plans or raise private monies to help realize a project. The state's approach to capital project development is more coordinated now, and the legislature is able to look at a larger picture of multiple projects without getting into the detail of each project as it pertains to individual campuses.

Economic Development

Policymakers have signaled that economic growth and development in South Dakota are linked with the state's technical institutes and its universities. Legislators spoke favorably of the technical institutes and their ability to produce students who make immediate contributions to the state's economy. The institutes also engender favor with most policymakers because they have stressed that their graduates tend to stay in South Dakota. There are many indications that the state's four technical institutes are supported politically, and they continue to be viewed as critical to South Dakota's evolution away from agriculture and into new and emerging industries.

The effort to connect the state's public universities to its economic development was embedded in an incentive that rewarded these institutions for building enrollments in designated economic growth programs. While it seemed conceptually sound at the time to provide incentive funding for specified programs, it was never clear that the designated economic growth programs were based on any systematic analysis that incorporated industry input. Interview transcripts from our study suggest that the Board of Regents engaged in a dialogue with each institution to arrive at targeted programs, but that the rationale for the decisions was never obvious.

PUBLIC HIGHER EDUCATION SYSTEM

South Dakota's six public institutions, governed by the state's Board of Regents, accounts for two-thirds of the state's postsecondary enrollment, with a total headcount of approximately 30,000 students over the last several years. The six institutions are geographically dispersed, with many in rural areas. These universities have, over the years, differentiated their missions and focused their campus-level activities to realize those missions. For example, the South Dakota School of Mines and Technology emphasizes engineering and science; South Dakota State University is the state's largest institution with a land grant mission and has a full offering of bachelor's, master's, and doctoral programs; and the University of South Dakota is the state's designated liberal arts university. Despite mission differentiation among the institutions, it seems that both state leaders and university administrators agree that the evolution of higher education will continue. One administrator voiced a common sentiment among policymakers when she openly questioned the need for five business schools and five teacher programs. Overall, both institutional administrators and the Board of Regents' staff share a common sense of direction, while remaining open to the inevitable changes that may result from emerging needs or new developments.

There are many examples of how the universities and the Board of Regents collaborate to achieve a common purpose. In the mid-1990s, the board worked with the institutions to proactively generate savings across the system during a time when elected policymakers were raising efficiency concerns and warning agencies that this would be a legislative priority. Higher education successfully met its self-imposed savings goal, clearly demonstrating to the governor and the legislature that it was serious about state priorities. The governor then bought into the board's recommendation that the universities keep the savings and reinvest them to create Centers of Excellence in areas defined as priorities. The six institutions chose different areas of excellence for their centers, largely aligned with each institution's mission. The University of South Dakota, for example, focused on information technology, while the School of Mines expanded its efforts in science and engineering. The process demonstrated how savings could be used to increase new areas of quality and expertise, reflecting state priorities, at each university.

System Actors

Trustees

The Board of Regents serves as the interface between state policymakers and South Dakota's six public institutions. Once the Board of Regents translates such information into policy goals or action items, one university president commented, state-level or even national information is converted to action for these institutions. In essence the board plays a state role, but it is also involved at the institutional level.

The board maintains close communications with administrators and faculty from each of the six universities, primarily through the executive director and his staff. In 1994, concurrent with employing the present executive director, the board laid the groundwork for increased central oversight by granting the executive director enlarged responsibility in relation to institutional CEOs. The executive director works with university presidents on budgeting, capital planning, and programmatic issues.

Administrators

Each of the six public universities is lead by its own president. These positions have been characterized by great stability. Although presidents are hired and fired by the Board of Regents, the approach to hiring a new president very much involves the entire university community. The executive director, with a number of regents, will travel to the institution in question. Community and university representatives participate in an open forum to talk about the process of a new search, which involves gathering input from all stakeholders. That process, once established, is followed as closely as possible as the regents deliberately and collaboratively seek to fill the post.

While it is apparent that the South Dakota Board of Regents practices centralized decision making across the system, most institutional administrators do not see this as a problem. Some felt that reporting requirements were occasionally tedious, and there were different opinions about the wisdom of such practices as charging equivalent tuitions across campuses. For the most part, however, university administrators feel that they have latitude in leading their campuses, and agree with both the system's overall goals and the need for efficiency.

Faculty

Individual faculty, and even institutions, may communicate with each other, but often such communication is task oriented and tied to some purpose that the Board of Regents and university presidents have established. One prominent example of how faculty communicate and collaborate across institutions is *discipline councils,* which are essentially groups of faculty organized by academic discipline. The councils meet to address concerns about efficiency, ' quality, and learning. There is one council per academic discipline or professional field across the campuses, and each university has two representatives on each council. The discipline councils reviewed every undergraduate course, and 3,100 institutional courses have been merged into 1,600 common courses.

Faculty are also unionized, an arrangement that could provide an additional vehicle for enhancing faculty participation in decision making. In reality, however, the South Dakota collective bargaining arrangements are very weak and probably better described as "meet and confer." The executive director for the Board of Regents, as the employer's representative, negotiates directly with the faculty union. If an agreement cannot be negotiated, the executive director decides on the actual contract terms. There is no appeal to an outside agency, and no mediation or authorized fact-finding. Union meetings on campus are sparsely attended, and only about 10 to 15 percent of the eligible faculty members belong.

Lastly, South Dakota institutions provide different options for their academic workforce. Faculty members can be promoted with or without tenure, so the system accommodates full professors who are not tenured. Professors who achieve their rank without tenure are expected to focus on teaching and on service areas that reflect both their expertise and institutional needs.

Institutional Rules

Planning

Each institution has flexibility in planning, but the mission differentiation among the six public universities, coupled with the centralized authority of the Board of Regents, creates the parameters within which these plans develop. One administrator acknowledged that institutions must look to their missions and work within those parameters, but he also gave several examples of initiatives at his university that help promote quality and enrollment. His conclusion: the ends are fairly clear, but the means allow for creativity.

Program Initiatives

Universities do not initiate new programs in isolation, without meaningful discussions with the Board of Regents or other institutions. There are several reasons for this, including a sensitivity to mission differentiation among the six universities, legislative concern over efficiency, and an effort to create programs and collaborations that will maximize enrollment. Administrators can create programs that fit within their institution's mission, but any program proposal is considered by the Academic Affairs Council, a committee of the Board of Regents, headed by a member of the executive director's staff. Proposals passed by this council go to the full board for final approval.

The Electronic University Consortium (EUC) is one example of a collaborative effort to expand educational opportunities by the creative delivery of new or existing offerings. Inaugurated in 2000 by the Board of Regents, the mission of the EUC is to leverage state technology investments and draw on the individual strengths of the different universities by coordinating the distance education course offerings of all six public institutions. Internet course offerings through the EUC started off strong and have continued to rise.

The Sioux Falls Center is a partnership through which the University of South Dakota, South Dakota State University, and Dakota State University deliver onsite courses and programs on the campus of the Sioux Falls Technical Institute. Sioux Falls is the largest city in the state, and enrollments in the partnership program have steadily increased. This collaboration between a technical institute and public universities is regarded by almost everyone as an unqualified success.

Personnel and Evaluation

Between 1997 and 2002, one of the state's policy goals was to attract and retain qualified personnel within the six public universities. Part of this goal involved addressing the low pay for professionals and faculty. The South Dakota system lags behind both national and regional averages. The regents have publicly tried to address this issue, leaving many with the impression that they are attempting to do everything possible in this area. In 1998, the board initiated a salary competitiveness program to increase salaries over a three-year period. The three-year plan did not require additional state appropriations and was funded through a combination of employee reductions, savings from previous years, and increases in tuition and fees. In order not to loose ground, the board has used increases in student fees to continue funding salary increases.

From an institutional perspective, two conditions make evaluations for individual pay increases difficult: (1) the existence of tenured and nontenured tracks and (2) unionization. According to one administrator, these conditions make it more challenging to define standards, particularly for faculty raises.

Enrollment Planning

Given that South Dakota's demographic trends do not anticipate growth in the eighteen- to twenty-four-year-old population, it would be misleading to suggest that institutions "manage enrollment" in the traditional sense. Most universities do their best to recruit students and thus increase their enrollments, and even the Board of Regents' executive director and his staff are involved in creative efforts to accomplish this objective. One such strategy is for system- and institutional-level administrators to recruit potential students from Southern California. California's space constraints and enrollment problems have been well publicized, and many higher education officials in South Dakota have worked to convince some of these students to attend a South Dakota institution.

There is talk within and across the state's universities about issues related to enrollment management. Given that the public universities have different missions, some have wondered whether institutions granting doctoral degrees should increase admissions requirements, cap enrollments, charge differential tuition, or implement some combination thereof. Such actions could conceivably further distill institutional missions and help more regionally based universities that are having trouble maintaining their enrollment levels.

Information

Generating information at the individual university level has quantified results, which in turn may lead to the important objective of increased funding. From 1997 to 2002, institutional information that aligned with the five policy goals in the State Funding Incentive Program was highlighted annually in the Board of Regents' fact book. The universities gather and produce much of the information in the fact book, which the board's staff then consolidates and checks before releasing the annual report. As previously noted, institutions are not in agreement as to whether the data collected to measure performance validly reflect such important behaviors as collaboration, a major value in the South Dakota system. However, the board's staff and university administrators generally concur that incentives and performance measures do create a mechanism for accountability and build political credibility.

Fiscal Policies

South Dakota's six public universities have internal budget processes that accommodate departmental and college requests. Each institution holds an internal budget hearing and develops priorities based on that hearing. The priorities and requests are then submitted to the Board of Regents in the same broad general budget categories that the board subsequently presents to the state's executive and legislative branches. The board develops a systemwide budget to avoid, to whatever extent possible, budget requests that focus on individual campuses. The board obtains a pool of funds that it then distributes to the campuses.

At the institutional level, administrative involvement in the progress of the various stages of capital planning is not always necessary, as this procedure is less systematic and formalized than the budgeting process for operational requirements. The universities do, however, identify and rank their structural needs. In 2001, all university lists were presented to the Board of Regents, and the board produced its final priority list for South Dakota's ten-year capital plan for its public institutions.

South Dakota has state public higher education priorities, with reporting, information, and funding all tied to them. The entire process has evolved through communication and collaboration. Public priorities, past and present, are developed through the various dialogues that happen each year. From 1997 to 2002, communications between policymakers and public university leaders, along with information and the results of the Incentive Funding Program, all contributed to the thinking that shaped the 2003 Resource Compact and the three priorities contained within it. South Dakota's leaders specifically took the lessons from the first five-year period and adjusted the state's higher education goals to reflect the current climate. This process, and the perception of accountability engendered by it, will continue to evolve.

Private institutions and technical institutes are slowly making inroads into the broader state conversations about higher education. For example, private institutions have been vocal about their belief that students attending them should be eligible for state aid; South Dakota's newly created merit scholarships may be used at any institution, public or private, within the state. The technical institutes have long voiced concerns about the university system's denial of transfer credits to institute students; today there is an agreement regarding the transfer and articulation of general education credits to the public universities.

Perhaps the biggest lesson in South Dakota is that a collaborative relationship between state policymakers and higher education leaders, or among higher education leaders from different sectors, takes time. South Dakota has had the luxury of consistent leadership—in higher education and in the executive and legislative branches—committed to fostering that relationship. Most in the state have also recognized that priorities and accountability systems must be revised and adjusted as times change.

CHAPTER SIX

New York

✤

New York is a low-effort, high-performing state. A strong coordinating agency
has responsibility and authority for all educational institutions and related
cultural agencies. The problems of excessive centralization in a populous state
with a large and unusual geographic area are largely avoided by grouping
higher education institutions into two heterogeneous, regionally focused
segments, each of which is overseen by its own unified governing board. Thanks
to the nation's most generous program of need-based student aid, choice has
been preserved, with students distributed in fairly equal numbers among
community colleges, public four-year colleges and universities, and a very
large and vigorous private sector. Private colleges and universities are well
integrated into the state plan for providing services. The two public segments
distribute appropriated funds in ways that respond to their individually
determined priorities while remaining within the scope of a comprehensive plan
created and administered by the coordinating agency. Legislative regulation
of tuition charges, and linking changes in charges to offsetting adjustments in
financial aid, help to keep New York's public institutions affordable to low-
income students, but these measures also weaken the market forces available
for steering these institutions. There is growing evidence that the state may be
underfunding public research universities.

✤

Politics and the budget process are the principal drivers of higher education
policy in New York. In the words of one lobbyist, "all programmatic issues get
sucked into the budget." The political and budget processes are opaque and
highly centralized. There is high discipline in both the Assembly, controlled
by Democrats, and the Senate, controlled since 1974 by Republicans. While
their respective caucuses may incorporate significant dissension, once a decision is taken, enormous authority is delegated to the leaders. New York also
has a very strong executive who, in cooperation with the two legislative lead-

ers, often makes the most difficult policy and budget decisions. Ordinarily, the governor's executive budget dominates policy discussions. Attempts by other actors to influence the decision process make little headway.

While the state constitution endows the governor with considerable power, including the executive budget and a line-item veto, it also provides for significant checks and balances. The governor's power to reorganize the executive branch is more limited than in most other states, and the regents of the state's umbrella interface agency for all education, the University of the State of New York, are elected by a legislature that is dominated numerically by Democrats from New York City.

Because people perceive this state's political process as byzantine, higher education leaders during former governor Pataki's administration were often selected from individuals who had been active in state government or in agencies that interface with state government. During much of our study, the chancellor of the State University of New York (SUNY), previously the director of the New York State Division of the Budget, was a long-term colleague of the governor. Both the executive director of the student assistance agency and the president of the Commission on Independent Colleges and Universities had extensive legislative experience. Beyond political experience, relationships are central. When people know and trust one another, "a lot of neat stuff happens," said a Senate staff member, "and if people don't get along, it shuts the policy process down."

It is little wonder that outsiders have difficulty understanding how higher education works in New York. The entire complex system is bound together at the policy level by social relationships that provide early warning of impending issues as well as opportunities to test alternatives and build coalitions. The system seems uniquely designed around the issues confronting a state with vast diversity and frequent contentiousness between established groups and those seeking to move from the periphery to the center.

New York City has its own public higher education system, the City University of New York (CUNY). CUNY's focus on New York City means that it aims to serve 40 percent of the state's population, including many who belong to minority groups or are recent immigrants. The state's city-dominated Assembly views CUNY as its special protectorate. In no small measure, the needs of urban minorities and immigrants, and the representatives they elect, explain the role of politics in higher education in the state.

While many we interviewed had difficulty identifying state priorities for higher education, our interviews suggested a working consensus among key policy leaders during the past several years about the importance of economic development, infrastructure investment, accountability, affordability, choice, and improvements in quality. Not all actors share all priorities. The state struggled for many years to respond to a court mandate requiring significantly more funding for the public schools in the City of New York. Now, the agreement that resolved that struggle is threatened by declining state revenues in yet another economic downturn. The governor, nonetheless, is in a pivotal position to use both executive and appointive powers to articulate and drive a higher education agenda. Governor Pataki used these powers effectively during his tenure and, before his abrupt resignation, Governor Spitzer did so as well, despite some early missteps (*Poughkeepsie Journal* 2007).

State Actors

State-level actors who significantly impact higher education include elected officials, executive and administrative agencies, and stakeholder interest groups. The major state-level actors we consider here are the governor, the Division of the Budget, the Department of Economic Development, the legislature, the Higher Education Service Corporation, the State Education Department, unions, and the Commission on Independent Colleges and Universities. We discuss governing boards for the state's two public higher education segments, along with their executive staffs, under institutional governance.

The Governor

The governor is a key policymaker for public higher education. He appoints all trustees for SUNY-operated institutions, as well as their largely advisory local college councils. He sets budget and policy priorities, directs collective bargaining negotiations with faculty and employee unions, and uses direct relationships with system officers and trustees to emphasize values and directions. The governor's influence extends to CUNY, as well, where he appoints ten of the seventeen trustees. As with his SUNY appointments, then governor Pataki chose individuals he knew personally or who had established a track record for supporting the goals and values he believed important.

Conservative initiatives by activist boards are often resented and sometimes resisted by faculty groups. The stance of the SUNY board on requiring a university-wide general education requirement brought formal condemnation from faculty. The CUNY board's removal of remedial education from senior institutions in the system also raised protests. In neither instance were trustees deterred. In both cases, both System Administrations, the trustees, and the governor maintained the unity essential to face down their critics.

Pataki consistently supported economic development, high-technology and infrastructure investments, high standards, and accountability. His strategies were not, however, aimed at directly influencing campus policy. Nor did the governor show much interest in master planning, a process that in New York is overseen by the assembly-elected Board of Regents. Pataki also did not appear to place much faith in the budget process as the principal way to get systems to change. Instead, he relied most heavily on the initiatives and leadership of trustees and system leaders who shared his values. Not surprisingly, the governor spent time and money where he had control and discretion. The Higher Education Service Corporation (HESC), for example, was designated as the agency to submit the state's federal GEAR UP proposal. The director reports to the governor, who also appoints the HESC board.

Broader decisions regarding higher education policy are made within the governor's office by a well-prepared professional staff who work in collaboration with analysts from the Division of the Budget, also part of the executive office. The process is confidential. Policy advice is carefully calibrated to respect the governor's priorities. We were told, for example, that Pataki never considered raising tuition during his first seven years in office. In a time of fiscal crisis, however, the tuition increase scenario was on the agenda and ultimately adopted.

Many, of course, disagreed with the Pataki agenda, but it is hard to fault it on the basis of its impact on discernible system change. As a case in point, an executive compensation plan mandated by the governor's office is now in statewide application, including throughout CUNY and SUNY. Each system must submit its plan to the governor's office for "blessing." Plans have been tied to such system objectives as enrollment management and to the attainment of specific objectives that are defined in individual institutional plans (which must be consistent with system priorities). While respondents expressed widely varying estimates of the early effectiveness of this design, it was refreshing to be able to trace the priorities articulated by an elected state leader directly into the internal planning and operations of a campus.

The governor also provided money, the prestige of his office, personal involvement, and coordinated statewide infrastructure to support an impressive set of economic development initiatives for which others, including the state senate, also justifiably claim credit. The crown jewel of the effort was the attraction of International Sematech to the Albany area, described by one writer as "equal in importance to the opening of the Erie Canal in 1825." This accomplishment was aided by a Pataki-sponsored, $250 million state investment in five high technology Centers of Excellence (with two more on the drawing boards), including one at SUNY Albany in nanoelectronics and several at independent institutions. The governor also helped to lay the groundwork for the partnership with Sematech through personal conversations with its president. The governor's staff coordinated workforce development programs and convened representatives from the centers of excellence.

Former governor Pataki used all of the levers at his disposal to shape higher education. Early in his tenure, he used significant budget cuts to reshape system finance and programmatic priorities. He combined this tactic with the appointment of carefully screened trustees to change standards and priorities. Toward the end of his last term, the governor unsuccessfully proposed withholding one-third of the state's need-based grants pending student graduation. Such actions clearly outline the role a governor interested in higher education can play in New York.

Division of the Budget

State law requires that the governor seek and coordinate appropriation requests from state agencies and present a balanced budget to the legislature, along with related revenue and appropriation bills. Agencies, including the two public university systems, follow their own internal budgeting procedures and submit their requests to the Division of the Budget (DOB) in early fall, after the DOB issues a "call letter" outlining the governor's priorities for the coming year and identifying expected fiscal constraints.

After a series of constitutionally prescribed formal budget hearings at which selected agency heads present their requests in written and oral formats, DOB staff and analysts, in close consultation with the governor, prepare a financial plan and recommendations on revenues and expenditures. After receiving the executive budget, the legislature holds joint public hearings, establishes its own estimates and priorities, and eventually acts on the appropriation bills. Differences are typically worked out at last-minute meetings involving the Senate Majority Leader, the Speaker of the Assembly and the governor. The process is not quite as undemocratic as it sounds, since the two legislative leaders are widely credited, in these discussions, with faithfully representing the priorities to which those they represent have previously agreed. In 2003–4 budget discussions, however, no agreement was forthcoming, and ultimately both houses of the legislature voted to override the governor's veto of appropriation bills that, among other actions, restored many of the cuts to higher education originally proposed in the executive budget.

The delayed adoption of the annual state budget contributes to its heavy influence on higher education policy. While many initiatives require no or only small appropriations, most are held hostage to the passage of the state budget. By the time the state budget is adopted, it is typically too late to pass any other bills involving appropriations. While the budget process in New York incorporates a five-year capital plan, there is no similar foresight devoted to operating support. In fairness, fiscal strategies can be discerned from a review of state funding priorities over the past several years, and these have clearly influenced institutional behaviors.

Department of Economic Development

To promote economic development, New York has created an infrastructure for stimulating business, state, and academic research partnerships under the oversight of its Department of Economic Development. A separate public authority, the Empire State Development Corporation (ESDC) partners with the department to develop enticing packages for businesses and helps universities to work collaboratively with the other organizations needed to attract a major employer. The ESDC provides technical assistance, helps with bonding, and manages the economic development fund. It also oversees a jobs creation program (Jobs Now), tax-free zones, and the development of tax-attraction sites. The New York State Office of Technology and Applied Research (NY-STAR) provides competitive capital grants to develop an infrastructure that enhances the capabilities of academic research centers to compete for federal basic research dollars, as well as assisting them in transforming research into commercially valuable initiatives that produce high-tech jobs. Gen*NY*sis is an initiative that funds incubators and accelerators for young and expanding technology firms that partner with higher education institutions. While there is understandable competition among elected officials in claiming credit for successes, there is also considerable cooperation and collaboration in moving the economic development agenda forward.

The Legislature

When difficult choices must be made among tax cuts, health care, and education, champions for higher education are needed. Despite the importance of New York's governor and his executive staff, it has been the legislature that has served in this role in the recent past. Legislators in the state believe they can influence higher education performance, and they take their policy role seriously.

Choosing among policy alternatives is not an easy task. "Legislative districts vary from an average income of $17,000 to over $125,000. The percentage of nonwhite residents within districts varies from 1 percent to over 99 percent. Some districts are completely rural and others are densely urban. These differences create conflicts among legislators about which policies should be pursued, what taxes should be imposed, and how benefits should be distributed" (Stonecash 2001, p. 143).

For the Republican-dominated Senate, priority for higher education has traditionally ranked just below health care and K–12 issues. This has been particularly important in the recent past, as the Senate has provided leadership for NYSTAR and Gen*NY*sis. The Senate has also historically defended the statewide Tuition Assistance Program (TAP) because of its importance to independent institutions and to economic development. SUNY, which operates institutions in most upstate districts, is also high on the Senate's agenda.

While the Assembly is widely and accurately regarded as the foremost advocate for CUNY, Senate minority members also reside in the New York City metropolitan area. Their interest in CUNY and in keeping tuition low influences the actions of the Senate's majority, especially when such controversial items as an override vote on the budget are under consideration. In addition to CUNY, the Democratic-led Assembly cares most about opportunity programs, multiyear community college funding (because of its impact on local funding), TAP, tuition, and funding for more full-time faculty. Accessibility and affordability also remain important, as reflected in Assembly support for tutoring and services for students with disabilities.

The differences in political affiliations of the majorities in the Assembly and Senate would seem to be an invitation to conflict. The reality is more one of constructive interaction around a shared agenda. While differing on details and priorities, the two chambers are in agreement about the importance of higher education and the legislative role of protecting educational systems and sectors from gubernatorial cuts. The legislature has carefully guarded its responsibility for oversight and for providing broad direction and accountability for higher education. The capacity to work together is also enhanced by strong (some would say absolute) leadership in both chambers.

The general consensus is that no one voice speaks for higher education. Given this reality, it falls to the legislature to convene the differing stakeholders and mediate among them in the interest of identifying acceptable policy. For example, the legislature established a joint chancellor-and-trustee committee to develop a plan for revising tuition policy. At the same time, the legislature is widely credited with rarely attempting to influence internal system priorities or meddle with curriculum or academic freedom issues. As in other states, New York's institutions have their own needs and communicate these directly to their legislators. In normal budget years, legislators can arrange special-initiative grants outside of the budget process. One staff member told us, "there is no difference between that and helping a little league team build a baseball field."

The centrality of the legislature in the higher education policy process guarantees frequent visits from representatives of stakeholders. Legislative staffers perceive such groups as being highly sophisticated about lobbying. While legislators understand both the weaknesses and the strengths of the way higher education is structured in New York, there are no strong convictions that anything should change.

Higher Education Services Corporation

The Higher Education Services Corporation (HESC) is a state executive agency created in 1974 to administer the Tuition Assistance Program established in that year by the legislature. State Education Department (SED) student assistance programs and staff were transferred to the new agency in 1975. HESC is primarily responsible for administering student financial aid programs. The agency also coordinates the federal loan guarantee program and administers New York's college savings program. HESC is the nation's fifth largest guarantor of federal student loans. The agency administers fifteen scholarship award programs for the state and the federal government, helps to oversee a college choice tuition savings program, and recently has become more involved in early awareness programs.

A fourteen-member Board of Trustees, appointed by the governor, oversees HESC. The SED commissioner is a member of the board, as is the president of the Commission on Independent Colleges and Universities, the chancellors for CUNY and SUNY, and a representative from the proprietary sector. The governor appoints nonstatutory members of the board, as well as the agency's president. HESC representatives emphasize the agency's role as policy *implementing*, not policy recommending.

Much of HESC's interaction with potential borrowers and aid recipients occurs through online services. Students and their parents can apply for both state and federal grants in a single online web session, without ever having to complete a paper form. Applications for a College Choice Tuition Account or a student loan are also fully electronic. Through the website, high school students, college and graduate students, parents, schools, and lenders have access to the information they need.

University of the State of New York/State Education Department

The State Education Department (SED) is the administrative agency for the Board of Regents (BOR) of the University of the State of New York (USNY). SED also serves as custodian of the State Archives, and as the primary state government interface agency for more than 7,000 public and private elementary schools, nearly 7,000 libraries, 750 museums, and 25 public broadcasting facilities. SED licenses more than a half million professionals in a variety of fields and certifies 200,000 public school teachers, counselors, and administrators, among other responsibilities. The Board of Regents is comprised of sixteen members, who are elected by a joint session of the legislature to staggered five-year terms. The board elects a chancellor from its membership and appoints a chief administrative officer, who has the joint title of Commissioner for the Department and President of the University.

The method of electing regents contributes to credibility issues with the Republican-controlled Senate and Republican governors. While in theory the Senate and Assembly elect board members by concurrent resolution, in practice a joint session is held to conduct the election if the two chambers cannot agree on candidates. In the joint session, the Assembly's wishes inevitably prevail, because of their overwhelming numbers. According to a Senate staff member: "Every current regent is a choice of the Assembly. Senate Republicans don't even show up for the vote."

SED is organized into five offices: elementary, middle, secondary, and continuing education (EMSC); higher education (OHE); cultural education (OCE); the professions (OP); and vocational and educational services for individuals with disabilities (VESID). The department has almost 2,800 positions, all but 15 percent of which are supported by dedicated fees, charge-backs, and federal grants. In addition to the main office in Albany, SED has branch offices throughout the state. About 150 staff members work in higher education. SED administers a budget of more than $20 billion annually, including aid to localities and capital projects.

Under the state constitution, all colleges and universities—public, independent, and proprietary—are members of USNY by virtue of their authority to award degrees. It is this membership that enables New York to integrate independent, proprietary, and public higher education with elementary and secondary education, libraries, museums, public broadcasting, and the learned professions to serve the needs of the state and its people. As one example of this integrating capacity, the Board of Regents convened a Summit on New York Education in late 2005, following a series of regional meetings. The summit involved 700 representatives from its membership sectors—together with students and participants from business, industry, labor, and other branches of state government—to discuss and make commitments to finding ways of closing the achievement gap between white students and students of color at all levels, from pre-kindergarten through graduate school. The New York Online Virtual Electronic Library Network and teacher preparation are other recent examples of how SED uses its broad convening authority to bring together groups across different jurisdictions—groups who, in other states, often do not talk to each other.

SED is certainly not the only source of information about higher education, but it is the most credible source for data that transcends individual systems. SED picks its battles carefully, and otherwise collaborates and networks with individuals having technical expertise in areas of importance to the activities it coordinates. Whenever possible, SED avoids actions that would galvanize opposition from the public systems or the powerful independents and their supporters. This strategy doesn't always work, as evidenced by the CUNY remedial education debate referenced at the beginning of the chapter. When the regents are drawn into public debate, they are heavily lobbied, which suggests their importance. Their decisions can be controversial.

Most of the Board of Regents' time in recent years has been spent on K–12 issues, a focus that was used as a rationale for a proposal by former governor Pataki to reorganize SED, concentrating its responsibilities on the K–12 sector, and authorize gubernatorial appointment of a majority of the regents. Not surprisingly, the Assembly blocked this proposal. Subsequently, the board's commissioner reactivated an advisory council on higher education, composed of college and university presidents from all sectors, asking the group to identify and prioritize critical issues and to provide advice. The chancellors of both public university systems usually attend these meetings. The advisory council also helps to develop the statewide plan and to formulate advocacy positions all sectors can support. The commissioner uses task forces, appointed after consultation with sector heads, to revise standards and procedures and to consider issues such as off-campus instruction, transfer articulation, and distance education. Task force reports become the basis for revising policy.

In addition, the commissioner has a sector-head meeting, which serves in part as an informal executive committee for the advisory council. Information about this group's actions is closely held. Because the commissioner is not dependent on the governor in the same way as the leaders whose boards the governor appoints, he can and has spoken against a number of the governor's proposals on higher education. He has also addressed the legislature at fiscal hearings, emphasizing points acceptable to all sectors and staying away from anything controversial. In his move to become a more important player within the higher education community, the commissioner has been helped by a popular deputy commissioner for the Office of Higher Education, who in her first year in office met with seventy-four presidents, as well as with business councils and unions, to gather priorities and concerns which were then reflected in the office's agenda.

Despite having more freedom than executive agencies, SED is not entirely divorced from responding to the priorities of the governor and the Senate majority. The DOB's director controls the disbursement of funds by issuing certificates of allocation, a process that gives the DOB considerable influence over all state agencies. Hence positions in the SED budget can be eliminated. While the governor can decide that an SED function will no longer be performed, he cannot transfer that function to another agency without amending the Constitution, an action that is particularly difficult in New York. The checks and balances built into the powers of these actors encourage both the governor and the Board of Regents to keep differences within reasonable boundaries, as does the responsibility they share for a common enterprise that neither desires to harm.

Unions

With the exception of executive staff, virtually all employees in the public sector are organized for collective bargaining. The governor's office is the employer of record for SUNY, negotiating its collective bargaining agreements. New York City's Mayor's Office negotiates for CUNY. The unions are major players in state politics. Unless they sign off on an issue, it usually means nothing will happen. "Even if you don't take their money," we were told by a legislative staff member, "their ability to influence local elections prevents most legislative actions they strongly oppose." The Professional Staff Congress (PSC) represents 20,000 full-time and adjunct professionals within CUNY. Professionals in SUNY are represented by the 25,000-member United University Professions (UUP). Both unions are affiliated with the American Federation of Teachers (AFT), and both work closely with the 450,000-member New York State United Teachers (NYSUT), as well as with the AFL-CIO. Information and publications on priorities such as improving conditions for adjunct faculty are shared with AFT affiliates in other large industrialized states, such as California, Washington, Pennsylvania, and Illinois.

The unions are an important source of information for legislators. Even though they may not agree with specific initiatives, the unions enjoy generally good relationships with the governor and the legislature, and union officials have ready access to top staff members in state government. The legislature looks to the unions and asks them for their agenda, and the public system chancellors may occasionally ask the unions for assistance on issues where their legislative agendas coincide. The extent of administrative-union cooperation during our study was somewhat limited by the generally antagonistic relationships between faculty and Pataki-appointed trustees in both SUNY and CUNY, sparked by such issues as remedial education, general education, and assessment.

Union leaders describe faculty senates as a "weak influence on policy issues." Historically there have been turf battles between the UUP and the University Faculty Senate (UFS). A union official, after describing the UFS as "without legal authority" and "funded by SUNY," referred to the organization as the "tail of the chancellor." Despite the view of the UFS as "politically ineffectual," union leaders maintain cordial and collegial relationships with its leaders.

The state's largest unions join forces on issues of importance. The legislative strategy in recent years has been to keep the agenda short, no more than five or six items, and to present it through NYSUT. Both the PSC and the UUP have professional staffs that solicit ideas from members and coordinate lobbying efforts. The UUP also has its own political action committee. SUNY's professional union alone contributes approximately $150,000 annually to legislative campaigns. The unions may also lobby the Board of Regents on such issues as ending remedial education among CUNY's four-year institutions.

Commission on Independent Colleges and Universities

Private, nonprofit, higher education institutions are an integral part of New York's higher education system. Collectively, more than a hundred institutions enroll 426,000 students, including 290,000 from New York City. Private institutions award 55 percent of the state's baccalaureate degrees, 70 percent of its master's degrees, and 77 percent of doctoral and first professional degrees. Significantly, 51 percent of the bachelor's degrees awarded to African-Americans and Latino students are earned in independent institutions. Forty percent of the state residents attending private institutions come from families who earn less than $60,000 per year.

Private institutions dominated the New York higher education scene until well into the latter half of the twentieth century. They are still very important, but political leaders have redefined the public-private relationship to one of relative parity. While educational leaders continue to feud from time to time over the allocation of resources, both public and private sectors agree on the importance of TAP, the nation's largest need-based student aid venture. However, some long-term public college presidents still complain about what they perceive as a disproportionate share of student aid flowing to the private institutions.

The Commission on Independent Colleges and Universities (CICU) is chartered by the New York State Board of Regents to develop consensus among an extremely diverse group of institutions and to influence higher education policy. CICU is led by an experienced veteran of New York politics, who previously served as the fiscal analyst for the state's Senate Finance Committee, as secretary to this committee, and as the budget director for former mayor Giuliani. His job was described by a former legislator as rolling a wheelbarrow down the street with 103 frogs in it while keeping them from jumping out. CICU coordinates its advocacy activity with a statewide council of governing boards that represents more than 3,000 trustees.

New York supports private higher education primarily through TAP. At the time of our study, the maximum award to students was $5,000, and direct institutional (Bundy) aid provides colleges and universities with a sum for each degree awarded to a state resident. Two smaller programs—the Higher Education Opportunity Program (HEOP) and the College Science and Technology Entry Program (CSTEP)—provide assistance to academically and economically disadvantaged students. For some time, CICU has advocated capital funding from the state for private, nonprofit institutions on a basis similar to the arrangements for SUNY and CUNY. This initiative was included in the budgets of both Governor Pataki and the legislature in 2004, but the measure was ultimately vetoed by the governor because of a lack of agreement on how the funds should be distributed. The program was finally approved in 2005. Independent institutions already participate in state economic development initiatives. And in 2002, SED received $3.4 million from the federal government for alternative teacher certification programs for New York City teachers to pursue graduate study at independent institutions.

While relationships between the public university systems and the independent sector are less contentious now than they have been historically, these relationships probably cannot be described as collaborative. A former private university president told us collaboration between public and private institutions simply isn't on the radar screen in New York, because of both the way the legislature operates and the fault lines produced by policy decisions negotiated at the very top. Despite this pessimistic assessment, there are literally thousands of degree programs offered jointly between public and independent colleges, and many are dual-degree ones in which students making satisfactory academic progress move into the second institution without a second admission review. The Board of Regents has also authorized four independent colleges to operate branch campuses or extension centers on the campuses of public community colleges.

Proprietary Colleges

New York distinguishes between proprietary *schools*, which do not award degrees and are supervised by SED, and proprietary *colleges*, which are authorized to award degrees and are regulated by SED. The state's twenty-eight proprietary colleges operate thirty-eight campuses that serve about 35,000 students. Most (90%) award associate's degrees, but a small and growing number award baccalaureate or master's degrees. More proprietary colleges are also seeking Middle States accreditation, partly because SUNY refuses to recognize transfer credits from institutions without regional accreditation. After a review by SED staff, the Board of Regents approves requests for new programs and authorizes degree-granting status for the proprietary colleges.

Proprietary colleges have their own statewide association. This organization is represented on the HESC board and on the SED chancellor's advisory group. Its executive director, like her counterparts in several other statewide higher education agencies, has extensive experience working with the legislature. Recently, the association has begun referring to its member institutions as the fourth sector of higher education in New York. Proprietary college students are eligible for maximum TAP awards, but the institutions do not receive Bundy Aid.

STATE RULES

The next section describes eight categories of rules in New York: planning, program review and approval, information, academic preparation, student assistance, fiscal policies, and economic development.

Planning

Statewide planning and program regulation are high on the list of SED responsibilities affecting higher education. The regents also can close an independent institution or replace its trustees. While the arrangements for public and private institutions are similar, the two large public systems operate through central offices that provide a certain degree of insulation for member campuses. SED can be formidable in its relationship with any institution. An application filed by the University of Phoenix in 1998 to offer master's degrees was still under review as this book was written. SED denied them authorization to offer baccalaureate programs, stating that their liberal arts and science coursework did not meet state standards.

Each of the 236 individual colleges within the state must file a plan with the regents, every four years for public institutions and every eight for private ones. CICU also submits a plan for the independent sector as a whole (Commission on Independent Colleges and Universities 2004). Master plans must address goals and priorities within the Board of Regents' plan and must spell out standards, such as those for admission. All programs (including any new ones to be proposed) must be in the plan. The regents accept plans for independent institutions and approve them for public institutions. Regardless of whether plans are accepted or approved, every institution must seek an amendment to its plan in order to gain approval for a program that changes its mission, alters standards, or is offered in a new location. Perhaps two dozen times each year, the regents consider such proposed amendments.

A change in admission standards triggered the Board of Regents' review of CUNY plans for ending remedial education in its senior colleges, an initiative pushed by trustees appointed by the incumbents at that time, Governor Pataki and Mayor Giuliani. Opponents of the initiative, supported by many members of the Assembly, heavily lobbied the regents to reject the proposed change. Permission to implement the new admission standards on a trial basis was given by a bare minimum of nine votes when first considered in 2000. In 2002, the regents voted unanimously for unqualified continuation. An example of a less-controversial mission change for public sector institutions was the Board of Regents' authorization for five institutions that were previously two-year SUNY colleges of technology to award baccalaureate degrees.

The regents' priorities for 2004–12 include the following: quality; articulation; affordability; closure of performance gaps related to economic status, ethnicity, race, or gender; services for students with disabilities; preparation for college; and provision of an adequate supply of qualified professionals, including teachers and school leaders. Each year the regents host a public policy conference focused on some defined priority. In their own planning processes, institutions use self-study and assessment to address the Board of Regents' priorities (University of the State of New York 2005).

Program Review and Approval

SED policies emphasize the use of program approval authority, primarily to preserve quality and ensure compliance with TAP-related regulations. SED's staff can look in depth at such questions as whether faculty members who teach in a program have qualifications appropriate to the standards for the degree they plan to offer. The regents have the authority to close existing programs, although they rarely exercise it. SED staff members use outside consultants for difficult calls or when no one in the department has the expertise to make a judgment.

Before an institution may advertise or enroll students, the commissioner of the Board of Regents must register every one of its programs that either leads to a degree or carries degree credit as meeting quality standards. *Quality standards* address resources, faculty, curricula and awards, admissions, administration, and other requirements; further standards are applicable to programs leading to teacher certification or professional licensure. SED has registered more than 26,000 programs and receives 1,500 to 2,000 proposals a year to register new programs or replace existing ones.

The prevention of unnecessary duplication is implicit within the program approval process. Proposed programs must be consistent with the statewide plan, and a new offering by an institution, at a different level of study or in a different disciplinary area from existing programs, must undergo an additional planning review. For the fewer than fifty such programs reaching SED in a typical year, the planning review examines (1) evidence regarding the need for the proposed program, (2) its potential effect on the proposing institution, and (3) its potential effect on other institutions. While a single institution can request and receive a hearing on a proposal, objections to a program are usually resolved through a process of negotiation, during which there is considerable pressure to work out differences outside of the formal hearing process.

SED argues that it does not micromanage programs, and those we interviewed from the public systems generally agreed. SUNY developed a program review process that emphasized mission, market, and quality. Speed became one of its objectives, with proposals forwarded to SED thirty to sixty days after receipt from a campus. SUNY's System Administration worked with SED to secure agreement on a common format and a timeline, with the timeline buttressed by an accountability report. SED generally accepts SUNY recommendations. The relationship between CUNY and SED is similarly straightforward. SED's goal is to respond to program proposals within a month. They generally keep to this schedule, a significant improvement over years past.

Information

New York's state government lacks a nonpartisan office, charged with providing information and analysis for legislators, found in some other large states. Both minority and majority committees in the legislature have their own partisan staffs. The governor relies on the DOB, where ten to fifteen staff members focus on higher education. Their sources of information include state agencies, the two public systems, CICU, business groups, unions, public information advocates, national databases, and the *Chronicle of Higher Education*. The search for information inevitably produces conflicting figures that are reconciled in the form of educated guesses, taking into account the credibility and motives of the various sources.

Among sources, SED is regarded with special affection by Assembly staffers and by Senate minority committees, because "they either provide requested information or tell you where you can get it." By contrast, recipients believe the public systems "negotiate" the data they provide. The Senate majority, while also using SED data, has some of the same reservations about it as the governor, because of the way members of the Board of Regents are selected.

CUNY generally receives high marks from legislative analysts as "unbelievably proactive and a willing source of information." SUNY, a larger and more complex system with greater campus autonomy, takes longer to respond to data requests and is perceived as less likely to supply information in a useful form. Legislators believe that both systems provide information with a spin, and they take that into account on fiscally related issues. Getting necessary data is a process that may take several weeks, involving multiple sources and much probing and questioning.

SED's Office of Research and Information Systems (ORIS) manages a comprehensive data system that collects and distributes information on the status of higher education. ORIS collects data from public and private degree-granting institutions (except federal units) and from 250 non-degree-granting proprietary schools on enrollment, degrees conferred, admissions, finances, financial aid, student charges, and graduation rates. The process was not automated at the time of our study, creating the need for a major data-entry effort. ORIS also develops performance indicators, administers institutional aid programs, and responds to requests for information from the governor's office, legislators, statewide offices for independent colleges and universities, and the proprietary sector, as well as the general public.

High on the ORIS wish list is a unit record information system. Representatives from SUNY and CUNY (who already have unit record systems) have historically resisted a student record system for SED for a variety of reasons, including concerns about cost, redundancy, and the possibility of endless discussions about whose data is correct. Recently, however, both systems have signed on to an effort to create a statewide unit record system.

Elected state policy leaders also rely on HESC for information obtained from the TAP database and from ISAR, a database generated from the financial aid forms for student assistance that each student must submit. HESC verifies the FAFSA information for all residents through the New York State Income Tax Department. In the absence of a state unit record system, HESC also requested data from SUNY and CUNY. SUNY's data was then used as a proxy for nonexistent data from the independent sector.

Academic Preparation

SED's Office of K–16 Initiatives and Access Programs (KIAP) provides technical assistance on innovative strategies, organizes and coordinates cross-sector partnerships, and administers about $120 million annually in grants, contracts, and scholarships. Three operational units carry out the work of the office: Precollegiate Preparation Programs, Collegiate and Professional Development Programs, and Grants Administration and Scholarship Processing. KIAP is currently the only organizational unit that spans the entire range of education represented in SED.

KIAP's strategy is to get programs with related objectives to work together to achieve synergy. The Liberty Partnerships provide a good example. Each program must have—as a minimum—a college, a school district, and a community-based organization working together. Once the partnership receives a grant, it must involve parents (New York State Education Department 2007).

The list of access and opportunity programs administered by KIAP is lengthy and includes initiatives especially designed for independent institutions (Higher Education Opportunity Program/HEOP), as well as those that span all sectors, such as the College Science and Technology Entry Program (CSTEP). The unit also administers Perkins Vocational and Technical Education Act grants and a range of small, special-purpose scholarships established over time by the legislature. Some of these award programs, such as the Regents Health Care Scholarships in Medicine and Dentistry, were created on the basis of less-than-adequate information about needs and demands, so they find few takers (these awards require recipients to practice for a period after graduation in areas designated by the regents as under-served).

KIAP's responsibilities provide clues to anomalies in the design of New York's system of higher education, as well as to the behaviors that have evolved for coping with them. SUNY and CUNY administer their own opportunity programs, while SED administers the program for independent institutions. SED also uses its convening authority to bring together leadership from all three. While KIAP would seem a logical choice for coordinating the state's five-year, $21 million, federal Gaining Early Awareness and Readiness for Undergraduate Programs (GEAR UP) proposal, the governor assigned that responsibility to the Higher Education Services Corporation. As a result, HESC is responsible for administering a program that is preparing more than 200,000 low-income and at-risk high school sophomores for college admission. SED, in its turn, administers many small scholarship programs that would more logically seem to be the responsibility of HESC. Fortunately, HESC and SED work together closely, sharing the same information base, and meeting regularly.

Student Assistance

New York invests heavily in need-based student assistance as its primary strategy for preserving accessibility. Its tuition assistance program, which provided $675 million to more than 350,000 students in 2001–2, is the largest in the nation. Full-time students attending New York institutions with family net incomes of up to $80,000 can apply to TAP. Awards are calculated on a sliding scale, with students from families with the lowest incomes being eligible for a maximum of full tuition in the public sector or of $5,000 in the independent sector. Awards are not duplicative of other financial assistance, so students with high needs may use a TAP grant to pay for tuition and a concurrent Pell award to pay for other costs. Senior administrators in public institutions sometimes describe TAP as a program that primarily channels public funds to independent institutions, a major purpose of TAP's predecessor, the Scholar Incentive Program created in the late 1960s. However, in 2001–2, more undergraduate dollars (59%) flowed to SUNY and CUNY students than to all the independent institutions combined.

New York offers much smaller need-based assistance programs for part-time undergraduates (about $12 million) and for full-time graduate students (about $3 million). The lion's share of part-time aid ($2,000 maximum) goes to SUNY and CUNY students (78%), while independent college students receive the largest share of the graduate awards (55%). Students attending proprietary schools are eligible for both full-time and part-time awards.

The state also administers a variety of small merit- and need-based programs, which together accounted for less than 5 percent of total state assistance in 2001–2. Overall, 20 percent of the state's higher education budget is devoted to student assistance, compared with the 8 percent national average. Because New York's commitment to need-based assistance is so high, conventional wisdom has it that the governor regularly proposes cuts, in the sure knowledge that the legislature will restore them.

HESC administers TAP, coordinates the federal loan guarantee program, and administers New York's college savings program—which, by August 2002, had more than 250,000 accounts with $1.1 billion in assets. The College Choice Tuition Savings Program, enacted in 1997, encourages families to save for their children's college education by providing tax benefits on contributions and on interest earned for college savings accounts. State policy leaders treat need-based assistance for full-time undergraduate students as an entitlement (New York State Higher Education Services Corporation 2006).

Fiscal Policies

Policy leaders have committed to a TAP award for the neediest students that, at a minimum, is equal to or higher than the cost of tuition at a public uni-

versity. All state revenues, including tuition and research revenues earned by
the two public higher education systems, must be appropriated by the legislature before they can be spent. To live with this arrangement, both university
systems have established research foundations. These legal entities allow the
systems to spend funds raised through sponsored research without having
the legislature appropriate them first. Employees of the foundations are not
eligible for university pension benefits, nor do they belong to the university
unions. This arrangement has become a source of contention.

When Pataki was first elected governor, his perception was that SUNY was
too big, too inefficient, too costly, and poorly managed. Thus his first strike
was at SUNY's budget, under the assumption that what you don't have you
can't waste. He proposed sharp reductions in state operating support, to be
partially or fully offset by tuition increases. SUNY and CUNY are authorized
to charge differential tuitions for graduate programs, provided that the same
tuition is charged at all institutions offering the same program within the system.

Reductions in state operating support and greater reliance on tuition have
been accompanied by increased flexibility in budgeting for the two systems.
The legislature appropriates funds to the SUNY system, which allocates them
to the state-operated campuses on the basis of an internally designed budget
allocation process. Legislative and DOB analysts believe this arrangement incorporates elements of performance funding appropriate to the New York
context. State-appropriated funds for the community colleges SUNY coordinates are distributed using a historical formula that includes base and per
capita allocations.

Arrangements are somewhat different and considerably more complex for
CUNY, because the system receives city as well as state funding. In addition,
CUNY's fiscal year coincides with New York City's budget cycle, rather than
the state's, so the city prefinances the operating expenses for CUNY's senior
colleges and pays its local share for CUNY's community colleges.

While everyone understands that the diverse characteristics of students
attending the systems justify different priorities, programs, and support services, the appropriations process inevitably results in consistently proportional
shares for the two systems. Despite such politically inspired, evenhanded
treatment, the issues for CUNY have never been the same as for SUNY.

A new, five-year, $2.5 billion plan for capital investments for SUNY and
$1.2 billion for CUNY was approved in the 2004–5 budget. The state finances
all capital projects for all CUNY senior colleges except Medgar Evers, and

shares the capital costs for Medgar Evers and CUNY's community colleges with the City of New York. CUNY issues its own bonds under state-authorized appropriations for academic facilities and infrastructure improvement. A statewide Dormitory Authority issues bonds to cover the state's share of revenue-producing facilities.

Under arrangements similar to those for CUNY, the state also funds facilities and infrastructure for the state-operated SUNY senior and community college campuses and provides appropriation authority for self-funded capital improvements for revenue-generating facilities, such as residence halls. A separate SUNY legal entity, the Construction Fund, is responsible for receiving the investments and proceeds from bonds and for building all facilities. Spending grants or donations from nonstate sources for capital improvements require appropriation authority from the legislature.

Because New York law does not require the electorate's approval to issue bonds, it has not been as difficult here as in some other states to provide the facilities required for public higher education. In fact, for a period of time, the SUNY funding formula for operations rewarded the construction of space whether it was required or not. During the 1990s, the structure for SUNY's capital and debt service was revised to make it more predictable and more accountable. Bonding authority was collapsed so that bonds were issued by agencies like the Dormitory Authority. Now tuition dollars go to offset appropriations for operating costs rather than being pledged to support ongoing capital projects. In addition, the state currently provides capital support for facilities construction in independent, nonprofit colleges and universities.

Economic Development

The state funds five university-based or -supported centers of excellence: at SUNY Albany in nanoelectronics; at Buffalo in bioinformatics; at SUNY Stony Brook in wireless internet and information technology; at Rochester in photonics and optoelectronics; and at Syracuse in environmental systems. There is also a joint venture in structural biology at CUNY's City College that involves five other New York City institutions. The structural biology initiative illustrates the importance of state leadership that goes beyond providing dollars.

New York has also created Empire Zones to attract business and create jobs through special incentives, and Liberty Zones to rebuild businesses in lower Manhattan, as well as establishing a $100 million Empire Opportunity

Fund. The Griffiss Institute for Information Assurance is an example of how different political actors come together under the state infrastructure to support significant high-tech initiatives without losing the opportunity to claim credit for their participation. The Institute was created with $1.5 million in capital support from the governor, $1 million from the Assembly, and a like amount from the Senate, along with $500,000 in startup aid. Another example is the recent CUNY Business Incubator Network, funded with a $7.5 million startup grant from the Assembly. An Economic Development Corporation established with a startup grant from the Sloan Foundation will lead the CUNY network program, which will focus activities through community colleges, with LaGuardia as the demonstration institution.

Economic development initiatives in New York State are interesting and complex because of the multiple strategies they employ. State leadership somehow coordinates and oversees the involvement of an incredible variety of business, academic, and governmental actors. There is a process for awarding grants for capital outlay and operating expenses that permits the governor, the Senate, and the Assembly to each claim credit for specific contributions and look out for special constituencies without spreading state resources so thinly that projects fail to achieve critical mass. All in all, the structure and processes are impressive, if not mind-boggling. Higher-education-focused economic development initiatives date back at least to the 1980s, when the legislature and then governor Cuomo, acting on a recommendation from the Board of Regents, established and funded ten Centers for Advanced Technology operated by a consortia of public and/or independent research universities. Tangible results have produced considerable political support.

HIGHER EDUCATION SYSTEMS

The New York system of higher education encompasses 254 degree-granting institutions: 61 campuses of the State University of New York, 21 campuses of the City University of New York, 141 independent colleges and universities, and 31 proprietary schools. The system is very decentralized. There are different centers of power, some responsible primarily to the governor and others to the legislature. Divided power is not necessarily seen as a bad idea, since it provides checks and balances to the authority exercised by individual actors in the decision-making processes. The 2003–4 executive budget proposed more than $7.7 billion to serve the more than one million students enrolled in these public and private higher education institutions.

There are no significant linkages between the two public systems of higher education. The two chancellors are friends, talk to each other on a regular basis, and try to be helpful; but no one in New York speaks with a single voice for public higher education, let alone all of the higher education community. Each sector or system, through its lobbying representatives, interacts directly with the governor's office and with at least the majority in each chamber of the legislature. The interface is formal in relation to the budget process and informal on other policy matters. Nevertheless, there are issues, concerns, and programs on which most public and nonpublic colleges agree. In testimony to the legislative fiscal committees' joint hearings on the executive budget, the commissioner of education addresses individual sector needs (faculty lines for SUNY or CUNY) as well as cross-sector issues (student aid) on which there is reasonable agreement.

New York's system of higher education assumed its current form in 1961, when SUNY was made independent of SED except as part of the larger University of the State of New York. Current relationships within the system continue to be colored by the fact that the regents resisted this change. CUNY's four-year institutions became fully state funded only in 1982, following New York City's fiscal crisis. The higher education system in New York now enrolls more students from outside the state than the state exports, and it boasts of at least three public universities on course to become among the most respected in the nation. These efforts, combined with those of a well-established and highly regarded independent sector, create enormous potential for the future. While the unusual system design clearly generates tensions, it also seems capable of managing them.

State University of New York

The State University of New York's geographically dispersed campuses (located, with only highly specialized exceptions, outside New York City) bring educational opportunity within commuting distance of virtually all New Yorkers not served by CUNY. SUNY is the nation's largest comprehensive system of public higher education. Campuses are divided into four categories—doctoral institutions, the technology sector, comprehensive colleges, and community colleges—based on educational mission, the kinds of academic opportunities available, and degrees offered. There is no single flagship campus. SUNY trustees serve as a coordinating board for the system's thirty community colleges, each of which has a local governing board. Trustee policy guarantees admission to a four-year institution to students who earn a two-year degree from a SUNY campus. However, this guarantee does not specify campus or program.

With some 6,650 degree and certificate programs overall, SUNY offers access to almost every field of academic or professional study somewhere within the system. These programs enroll more than 410,000 students (approximately 37 percent of the state's higher education student population) either in traditional classrooms and laboratories or working at their own pace through the SUNY Learning Network or through Empire State College. About 18 percent of the students are minorities, in comparison with 12 percent of the full-time faculty.

New York governors, both past and present, have had a major impact on the SUNY system. Dewey is known for the establishment of SUNY; Rockefeller for SUNY's expansion and for providing institutional support for independent campuses; Cuomo for declines in that support and for neglecting his role in the planning process; and Pataki for budget cutbacks and severe reductions in state funding in 1995–96 and 2003–4.

Trustees

The first SUNY trustees appointed by Pataki, especially the chair, were determined to realize the Rockefeller vision. The trustees also added their own objective of placing SUNY in the front ranks of American higher education to Rockefeller's general vision for the system. The "Pataki trustees," as they came to be called, developed a strategic plan, *Rethinking SUNY*, that set forth their values and goals for the university (State University of New York 1995). Within two years, they became a national model for "activist trustees" determined to put their stamp on the institutions they controlled. Two of their more controversial and conservative actions included adopting a university-wide general education requirement and establishing a campus accountability system that compares the performances of individual institutions. For the most part, however, majority trustee actions during the Pataki era led the system in directions most actors wanted it to go. One or two trustees consistently and verbally supported intrusive policies, which were effectively rejected by the board majority and the chancellor. The amount of media attention devoted to sharp exchanges around the proposals introduced by this faction made the board seem more divided than was actually the case.

Administrators

The chancellor and sitting governor during much of our study were long-time colleagues, and their relationship provided stability as well as predictability for SUNY. The way the chancellor defined his role gave latitude to a new provost charged with implementing the academic initiatives stemming from *Rethinking SUNY*, including Mission Review, the SUNY Learning Network, and SUNY Connect (an integrated electronic library initiative). The chancellor was strongly supportive of the emphasis on planning and accountability which preceded his appointment. He also maintained considerable influence over the budget process. And he seized upon presidential evaluation for institutions governed by the SUNY board as a key strategy for enhancing enrollment management and fiscal processes aimed at making SUNY as highly regarded for its quality as for its size.

The implementation strategies for *Rethinking SUNY* called for a framework for accountability and strategic direction within which individual colleges and universities would be free to make decisions about how to best achieve their goals. Part of the strategy entailed having a liaison within the Office of the Provost who worked with each campus. Teams of campus specialists, by sector, were used to guide the process of Mission Review. The senior leadership team that designed and carried out these strategies turned over toward the end of the Pataki era. A replacement chancellor, chosen from within the SUNY system, has now departed as well. The imprint that the Paterson administration will impose is yet to be determined, but the opportunity to influence leadership choices will clearly be present.

During our study, a separatist movement among community college presidents who felt ignored within the SUNY system led to the decision to reestablish a vice chancellor for community colleges. External consultants advised presidents that they would be better off staying within a system where they were represented by a vice-chancellor authorized to work with a permanent ad hoc committee of the SUNY Board of Trustees than they would be trying to bring issues of importance to community colleges to the entire board. These changes were implemented and have generally proven effective. In situations where community colleges have experienced financial difficulty because of excessive regulation or inadequate appropriations by their county legislatures, SUNY, in cooperation with the Middle States Association, sent in a visiting team to help resolve the problems.

Faculty

Despite their "advisory-only" status, faculty members influence SUNY decisions in several ways. First, faculty governing bodies create resolutions that become the formal mechanisms for influencing the decision-making process. In rare instances where the policy process is deadlocked, resolutions can take the form of "votes of no confidence." Second, faculty governance leaders utilize informal strategies—such as behind-the-scenes negotiations with System Administration, trustees, and legislators—to get policy mandates revised or reconsidered (Smalling 2006, pp. 128, 132). Faculty governance leaders do not occupy a position on SUNY's Board of Trustees, in contrast to the CUNY system. However, they have served on several board and System Administration committees and task forces. Recent legislation makes the president of the Faculty Senate a nonvoting member on the board.

Faculty members also influence policy decisions through their faculty union, United University Professions. UUP and its more powerful parent union, NYSUT, collaborate to develop an influential policy agenda using grassroots lobbying, face time with legislators sympathetic to their agenda, political endorsements, strategic employment of information and the media, and collective and coordinated action (Smalling 2006, pp. 97–98). The union generally resists granting more management authority to the chancellor, on the grounds that greater flexibility in such areas as purchasing equipment without bidding might subsequently lead to greater authority on personnel issues such as hiring and firing. Arguments by the SUNY administration for variable tuition and for privatizing the hospitals within the system were successfully opposed by UUP and key legislators. UUP has tried to get the chancellor to change the budget distribution policy and has advocated a "rational" tuition policy.

Under Pataki, UUP perceived SUNY trustees as being meddlesome, partly because of their 1998 effort to impose a required curriculum on campuses and, several years later, to mandate a systemwide assessment of that curriculum. As the relations among the actors grew more contentious, dissention over these controversial policies encompassed a larger debate over the nature of shared governance in the SUNY system, as well as a broader dispute over SUNY's original mission of access and service versus calls for excellence, efficiency, and market responsiveness (Smalling 2006, p. 72). By mid-1999, trustee actions had produced a major effort by the faculty to compel the removal of the board, or at the very least to force a change in SUNY.

The ratio of full-time faculty to adjunct faculty has been a predominant issue. Under the then newly elected Governor Spitzer, former Chancellor Ryan and the legislature agreed on funding for a new initiative designed to bolster full-time faculty numbers in areas involving research and high-needs occupations. Individual campuses have also used *cluster* hiring practices, where faculty are recruited in groups built around common research or academic themes, to facilitate campus-based instructional initiatives. As an accepted part of the budget process, a representative from a faculty senate committee attends all budget presentations and may ask questions.

Rules for SUNY

PLANNING

Rethinking SUNY called for a 30 percent smaller system office that would be more responsible for policy and for monitoring educational results, less controlling of campus operations, and more focused on serving the Board of Trustees. Concurrently, campuses would be empowered to more directly manage their academic and financial affairs. The plan called for the elimination of disincentives to the prudent use of campus and system resources and for increased teaching productivity. The plan also advocated increased cooperation among units, a stronger focus on quality and customer satisfaction, and differential tuition measures aimed at reducing the amount of time students took to earn degrees.

Mission Review, the process developed by the Office of the Provost to implement the plan, was designed to (1) clarify goals and market niches for each campus, with a focus on distinctiveness; (2) enhance the quality of academic programs through effective programming and the resolution of programmatic overlaps; and (3) increase opportunities for and support of intercampus collaboration (State University of New York 2004b). This process culminates in the development of strategic plans, which serve as the basis for memoranda of understanding designed both to measure progress and to hold presidents accountable for their institution's progress toward the goals in their strategic plans.

SUNY's priorities have shifted over the past six years to include recognition of the system as a critical economic driver, increased fundraising activity from the campuses, and greater public recognition. Its systemwide academic direction aims at raising SUNY's academic quality and overall profile, with the intention that New York should have a state university competitive with the country's best (State University of New York 2004a).

PROGRAM INITIATIVES

Rethinking SUNY recommended a review of degree programs at all levels to eliminate unnecessary duplication of programs with low enrollment and high costs while maintaining access through the use of distance learning technologies. Within this context, program review and approval and the enrollment management process have become two of the principal levers for harnessing strategic direction and achieving the goals established through Mission Review.

Assessment of academic majors includes self-study and the use of outside reviewers drawn from current peers, as well as a report. Campus academic officers send the SUNY provost a copy of the review and a brief response to it. In their response, academic officers are asked to address two questions: What did you learn? and What are you going to do about it? Contingent upon these answers, there is an informal agreement about how weaknesses are to be addressed. Assessment of academic majors is tied into the program review process and is becoming a part of that review, just as enrollment management is a component in the allocation of fiscal resources. A campus with programs that are not in compliance with this process is not able to secure approvals for new programs.

The program review process verifies that programs are consistent with the institution's mission and that appropriate standards have been addressed in proposing new programs. After a review by SUNY, new programs are forwarded to the State Education Department, which generally accepts the SUNY recommendation. Each campus has the responsibility for deciding which programs it will advance and which, if any, it will close.

PERSONNEL AND EVALUATION

The presidential evaluation process is an important source of accountability. The chancellor evaluates the presidents of SUNY's four-year institutions annually, particularly in terms of progress toward meeting the goals set forth in the memorandum of understanding created at the end of their university's Mission Review. An effort is underway to eliminate redundant administrative services through voluntary strategic alliances that would link some of SUNY's relatively small campuses. SUNY is working to establish a formal assessment process for community college presidents, who also report to their own county college boards. In addition, there is talk of rewards and incentives for this sector. SUNY's effort to increase accountability for community colleges is a delicate exercise in balancing the use of power against possible political consequences. The chancellor is the key person in making such decisions.

ENROLLMENT PLANNING

As previously noted, enrollment planning is one of the primary components of strategic direction. Through this process, campuses are charged with the task of mapping out their short- and long-term enrollment plans in terms of the numbers and academic profiles of admitted students. SUNY has developed a two-way selectivity matrix, with five categories derived from grade point averages and SAT scores. During Mission Review, each campus identifies its targeted selectivity level and the timeline for achieving its goals. The Office of the Provost and the chancellor negotiate those targets with the SUNY campuses and monitor each campus's progress toward reaching them.

The Office of the Provost leads the decision-making process about enrollments through a committee called the Enrollment Planning Group (EPG), which has representatives from the areas of budget and finance, enrollment management, institutional research, opportunity programs, and program review and assessment. The EPG forecasts attainable levels of state-funded enrollment that are consistent with SUNY's overall System Administration and individual campus goals and yet remain within the level of available state support. The group engages campuses in dialogue and reviews and recommends approval of campus plans to the provost.

Enrollment planning is aimed at keeping campuses from an unrestrained pursuit of the incentives for enrollment growth built into the formula used for funding, as well as monitoring progress toward achieving such planning goals as the targeted selectivity profile. It can also be used as a tool to help institutions with low enrollment problems. Campuses submit their enrollment plans to the EPG, and approved enrollment targets drive the funding for state-operated campuses. The EPG's deliberations take into account the amount of state operating money SUNY receives, as well as campus performance.

SUNY's minority enrollment has increased, even with higher admission standards and dramatically improved selectivity, yet some of our interviewees suggested that it might be time for a special look at diversity. There are no university-wide policies outlining objectives, and campus-specific efforts achieve varying degrees of success. Interviewees told us that more systematic attention will be paid to diversity in the second cycle of Mission Review (MRII), and the university system's commitment to maintaining access and diversity was reaffirmed in SUNY's 2004–8 Master Plan. SUNY has also opened a Metropolitan Recruitment Center that focuses on the recruitment of high school students from the New York City metropolitan area.

The attention SUNY campuses give to attracting community college transfer students also varies, even though the SUNY Master Plan calls for "the 'seamless' transfer of community college graduates as bona fide third-year students at state-operated campuses." Articulation is a matter of institution-to-institution arrangements. Some state-operated campuses receive very high grades from adjacent community colleges, while others have a reputation for being basically unresponsive.

INFORMATION

SUNY's Institutional Research Office (IR) maintains a comprehensive information system. Census data is available for each campus, including those community colleges for which SUNY manages the distribution of state appropriations. The unit record system includes data from the National Clearinghouse, which can be used in a variety of ways to track applicants and graduates. The office also conducts surveys of students, alumni, and faculty on a cyclical basis.

Any information needed for decision-making / policy formation purposes can quickly be made available. For example, IR can readily provide student-to-staff ratios by campus, as well as information about campus rankings on the student opinion survey. SUNY's System Administration is cautious about releasing information outside the system before consulting with campus leaders. IR works with campuses to provide required information to the federal government and to the State Education Department.

BUDGETING AND FISCAL POLICIES

The fiscal allocation process has changed and evolved over time. Over forty years ago, funds were appropriated to each campus on the basis of detailed categories. In the 1970s, the system moved to a faculty/student ratio based on four instruction levels and ten discipline groups. With increased fiscal autonomy in 1985, SUNY incorporated the basic structure of the full-time-equivalent-based matrix model—along with funding in relation to headcount enrollments, sponsored program activity, the square footage of campus facilities, and the actual cost of utilities—into a benchmark approach.

By 1995, the complex benchmark approach was out of sync with the total amount of funding available from the state. After committee study, the Board of Trustees adopted a new financial allocation plan in 1998, centered on campus retention of tuition, rewarding enrollment growth, rewarding increases in student quality, rewarding growth in externally sponsored research, increasing public service, and increasing mission distinctiveness. While the distribution of operating funds is based primarily on enrollment, the budget allocation process (BAP) is consistent with SUNY's shift toward greater campus autonomy while also taking performance (retention) into account. Each campus now has discretion in the use of both state- and campus-generated funds. SUNY's full-time-equivalent enrollment declined from 190,000 to 183,000 during the period prior to the adoption of the new funding arrangements, but it has now returned to the 190,000 mark (headcount enrollment is over 410,000).

Now that there is no additional state funding to support enrollment growth, BAP incentives are impaired. Senior SUNY administrators believe that the formula needs to be modified to place greater emphasis on campus performance related to student selectivity, retention, and graduation rates. The BAP formula has caused campuses to pursue board-related priorities as long as doing so brings them the greatest rewards. Each campus has its own internal distribution process, and local control of tuition dollars has clearly made departments and campuses more entrepreneurial.

Most appropriations to SUNY community colleges are based on a per capita formula. SUNY officials believe they have the authority to alter the formula to add a performance element, but they have been hesitant to force the issue because of concern about possible political consequences. SUNY's System Administration is already battling a number of county legislatures over the maintenance of local effort and final authority on the selection of community college presidents.

City University of New York

The City University of New York is the largest urban university system in the nation, with nineteen campuses, approximately 219,000 fall headcount students, an operating budget that exceeds $1.5 billion, a billion dollars in capital funding, and 450 buildings located throughout New York City's five boroughs. Currently, CUNY is engaged in creating a flagship environment. The university system includes five competitive (and more selective) institutions, four comprehensive institutions, six community colleges, and two other campuses that do not fit easily into any of these groupings. CUNY also has a graduate center, a law school, and a school of biomedical education. The system is unique for its size, the geographical proximity of its campuses, and the availability of inexpensive and reliable public transportation. Historically, CUNY has been shaped by a series of debates involving open admissions, academic standards, and tuition charges.

CUNY must balance its accountability to the state against its responsibilities to the mayor and council of the City of New York. City government representatives influence hiring practices and the negotiation of collective bargaining agreements. The City Council receives formal reports from CUNY, but it also hears more informally from faculty and students. City Council staff members, including a policy analyst, check the reports against their own sources of information.

Trustees

The governor appoints ten of the sixteen voting members of the Board of Trustees; the mayor appoints five. State law requires that gubernatorial and mayoral appointments must minimally include one resident of each of the five boroughs. The board is responsible for appointing CUNY's chancellor as well as its college presidents. Trustees serve seven-year terms, renewable for one additional term. By law, meetings of the Board of Trustees are open, and they may attract a relatively large public audience, depending on the issue.

Trustees appointed by the incumbents at that time, Governor Pataki and Mayor Giuliani, pursued an agenda focused on high standards, improved performance, and accountability. This program was developed in response to the issues raised in *An Institution Adrift*, a report commissioned by the mayor that criticized CUNY for its low graduation rates and poor management structure (Mayor's Advisory Task Force on the City University of New York 1999). In January 1999, in the midst of intense protest, the Board of Trustees voted to end remedial education in the senior colleges, an action that was intended to restore CUNY to earlier standards of quality and prestige. From the perspective of a central office administrator, "unless CUNY started to raise the bridge instead of lowering the river, students would never learn how to swim." Although the battle to end remediation was highly contentious, it provided evidence of massive support for CUNY and contributed to increased respect and legitimacy for CUNY's leadership from the Board of Regents and other higher education actors.

Administrators

Matthew Goldstein, the current chancellor, is both the first graduate of the CUNY system to serve in this capacity and a former CUNY college president.

While president of Baruch, he gave a speech identifying accountability, an integrated university, a flagship environment, improved quality, and better management as necessary actions for CUNY to maintain its vitality as well as to improve its reputation and quality. After leaving CUNY to serve briefly as president of a private university, he was recruited by the board in 1999 to address the issues set forth in *An Institution Adrift*. Benno Schmidt, who chaired the committee that produced this report, subsequently became the chair of CUNY's board. The conclusions of the report bore a striking resemblance to the chancellor's earlier recommendations.

Once in office, the chancellor immediately began to make changes in CUNY's freshman admissions policies and management structure. To improve the management structure, the chancellor reduced the number of vice chancellors who reported directly to him from seven to four and implemented a program that rewards college presidents for the performance of their institutions. He also strengthened the presidents' capacity to hold faculty-elected department chairs accountable for addressing institutional priorities.

CUNY had long tested all entering freshmen. Now baccalaureate candidates had to pass these tests to be admitted, unless they were already exempt on the basis of SAT scores or the New York State Regents Examinations. Arguing that it has been historically underfunded by the state, CUNY has sought external funding and reallocated its existing resources to upgrade facilities and improve its technological capabilities. CUNY maintains close contact with the governor's budget office and does everything possible to influence the executive budget. In addition, administrators try to coordinate the efforts of the city and other interested parties in advocating for CUNY.

Faculty

The Board of Trustees' bylaws give faculty a role in the academic and administrative direction of CUNY. The Professional Staff Congress (PSC) negotiates with CUNY, the city, and the state on behalf of the more than 20,000 full-time and adjunct faculty and professional staff. The collective bargaining agreement, which is very comprehensive, includes workloads and class sizes. In addition to differences of opinion on such issues as ending remedial education, PSC priorities may or may not support those of the board. Recently, they emphasized academic achievement, graduate research, economic development, increased funding for educational opportunity programs, and expanded numbers of full-time faculty over a three-year period.

PSC works closely with the university system's central administration in advocating for CUNY during the state budget process. The union has more freedom to lobby legislators and the governor, since state directives that limit the actions of university representatives do not apply to the union. In a successful court case against New York City's mayor, PSC joined with CUNY's central administration to oppose an initiative to lower the "maintenance of effort" law that ensures city funding for CUNY. On the campus level, PSC works to prevent retrenchment and strongly advocates for low tuition.

Rules for CUNY

CUNY's board and central administration seek nothing short of transformation through new leadership, new policies, and new management processes, despite some skepticism and a certain level of resistance from the individual campuses. Central administrators are working to create an integrated and stratified system by re-engineering administrative processes. The strategy is to combine resources into a single system to be shared by all nineteen campuses. CUNY also expects to have student information, finance, and human resource processes available online. While this strategy publicly aims at strengthening the image of an integrated university, central administrators are not blind to the money-saving potential of consolidated systems. As one example, CUNY expects to save money on paper by creating an online purchasing system. CUNY also envisages that the restructuring processes will shrink its administration, leaving more money for academics. The following sections explore the implications of these re-engineering strategies for the rules under which the CUNY system operates.

PLANNING

CUNY's Master Plan is the driving document behind academic and financial planning. The 2000–4 plan committed CUNY to higher standards for admissions and graduation for all students. The plan emphasized creating a flagship environment, improving the full-time / part-time faculty ratio, increasing admissions standards, collaborating with government agencies and corporations to achieve economic and technological goals, and increasing accountability (City University of New York 2000). Academic and budgetary planning have been organized around these objectives and linked to accountability and performance. The 2004–8 plan documents achievements in all of these areas and lays out a continuing agenda that emphasizes the interdependence of CUNY and the City of New York and aims at creating an integrated university to provide a truly seamless education for all New Yorkers (City University of New York 2004).

From the perspective of CUNY's central administrators, the planning process is very straightforward. The chancellor and his staff set goals and targets for each of the nineteen campuses and identify the indicators that will be used to audit progress. Presidents, in consultation with their senior staffs, set campus goals that include local as well as system priorities. Each campus reports its progress annually to the Chancellor's Office.

Academic planning entails an emphasis on saving dollars on the administrative side to create an improved academic infrastructure. There is also a focus on improving professional programs, increasing standards, and improving collaboration and articulation/transfer. Although CUNY was under a hiring freeze during our study, faculty lines were exempt from the freeze. Between 1999 and 2000, cluster hiring in such targeted areas as photonics, foreign languages, teacher education, new media, and computer science was adopted as a key strategy for strengthening the educational quality of the university system. In 1992–93, CUNY hired 100 new faculty members, and more than 400 the following year.

CUNY has also tried to structure its financial planning around Master Plan priorities, but some campus leaders reported difficulty in identifying a relationship between system and campus priorities and their annual budgets. One financial officer described her campus budget as primarily flatline, based on the previous year's allocation. This campus eliminated budget meetings because there were no dollars to fund new projects or initiatives.

PROGRAM INITIATIVES

The central goal of transforming a federation of colleges into an integrated university in an environment of scarce resources means that most new program initiatives are a product of central planning. The recently established Honors College provides one example. The Honors College, expected to grow ultimately to 1,600 students, provides academically talented students with opportunities to experience the expertise that exists across CUNY campuses. The program is currently offered on seven senior campuses. CUNY's central office planned the program, with selected faculty input. The central administration provides fundamental leadership and a set of ground rules to ensure uniformity across participating institutions. A similar approach was used to develop the more recent Accelerated Study in Associate Programs (ASAP), a city-supported initiative at CUNY's community colleges, to improve associate's degree completion rates by addressing many of the financial, academic, and administrative barriers students face.

To offset the impact of more selective admissions policies on underprepared students, and in hopes of facilitating a "seamless transition," CUNY has expanded instruction in New York City high schools through its twenty-year-old College Now program. Other collaborations include educational opportunity programs, a center for teaching and learning, and continuing education. A new CUNY Proficiency Exam (CPE), designed to improve writing and critical reading, requires students to meet specified standards to remain matriculated. To help prepare students, CUNY has introduced an extensive writing-across-the-curriculum program. As is true for the Honors College and ASAP, the writing program is offered on a variety of campuses, but it is centrally directed by the Office of Academic Affairs.

PERSONNEL ADMINISTRATION

Beginning in spring 2000, CUNY adopted a performance management process with five aims: (1) transform a federation of colleges into an integrated university; (2) ensure that the Master Plan guides the plans/priorities of all colleges, while each retains its own identity, mission, and governance; (3) inject accountability into the system; (4) recognize and acknowledge progress at all levels; and (5) ensure clarity about CUNY and college priorities and expectations for the year. The performance management process begins where the Master Plan leaves off and identifies specific CUNY goals and targets for each year. Plans for each campus translate CUNY's goals into specific indicators and targets for that college. Presidents submit year-end reports containing relevant performance data. The chancellor meets with each president to discuss past performance and set new goals and targets.

The performance management program holds campus presidents accountable for "bottom-line performance" and rewards them and their senior staff through an executive compensation plan when funds are available. This arrangement has significant symbolic value, as it demonstrates to the external community CUNY's system-level emphasis on accountability, assessment, and performance-based awards. CUNY's central administrators believe the system provides the data necessary to assess management performance and are using it to reward achievements by presidents and their management teams (City University of New York 2004).

The chancellor expects college presidents to hold department chairs to account. In turn chairs, who are members of the faculty union, are responsible for the overall administration of their departments and for establishing and achieving departmental goals. Since department faculty members elect chairs, their role in the accountability chain was murky until the chancellor sent a memo to presidents in October 2000, directing them to conduct annual evaluations. Faculty argued that such a review violated the trustees' bylaws, and filed a grievance. The outcome confirmed presidential authority to (1) accept or reject the faculty's recommendation for chairperson; (2) remove chairpersons in the best interests of the college; and (3) annually evaluate chairpersons. Central administrators believe that current accountability measures are an effective strategy for achieving systemwide priorities.

ENROLLMENT PLANNING

While remedial instruction is still offered at comprehensive colleges with associate's degree programs, the end of remedial education in the senior colleges mandated attention to admissions criteria. The chancellor made freshman assessment his first priority, arguing that existing CUNY tests lacked validity and reliability and should be replaced by examinations with national norms. The Academic Affairs Office evaluates admissions criteria each year to determine which students possess the characteristics for academic success at each institution and constructs an admission index for each college. Using this index, the Academic Affairs Office collaborates with senior colleges to help them design admission criteria for baccalaureate programs.

While many of the opponents to ending remedial education have argued that access was harmed, CUNY central administrators point out that the change was essential in improving graduation rates and attracting better-prepared students. CUNY administrators also submitted voluminous documentation to the State Education Department showing that access had not suffered, and that there has been no significant diversion of baccalaureate-degree applicants to community colleges. CUNY's current strategy has been to maintain access for a student body that reflects the population of New York City, both through collaboration with high schools (particularly in its College Now program) and through its greatly expanded summer immersion program.

This strategy places considerable pressure on articulation and transfer procedures, which have never functioned as effectively as was possible within a system where both community and senior colleges are governed by the same board. CUNY's central administrators say they are "putting teeth into articulation and transfer." Campus leaders agree that CUNY encourages collaboration and articulation, but they point out other constraints, including problems with information, that are barriers to better collaboration. CUNY has devoted substantial resources to a program which allows prospective transfer students to assess the credits they can receive from each prospective four-year campus for work completed at their home college. According to a spokesperson, transfer rates within CUNY are "quite high."

CUNY also attempts to maintain access through its educational opportunity programs for students considered "academically and economically disadvantaged." Search for Education, Elevation, and Knowledge (SEEK) is the primary program for senior colleges, and College Discovery is its counterpart for the community colleges. Since fall 2000, SEEK enrollments have grown by about 5 percent. The new admissions policies allow SEEK programs to admit students who do not pass CUNY's exams. Students then have a year to meet the requirements. Funding for both SEEK and College Discovery were under annual assault in the state's executive budget during the Pataki years, but they remained priorities for New York City's legislative representatives.

INFORMATION

Prior to the arrival of the new chancellor, the management information system in use at CUNY was widely regarded as inadequate. A December 1998 report by Pricewaterhouse Coopers recommended that CUNY itself develop the data system needed to support planning and budgeting and to provide management with information essential to effective decision making. The report added that a new system would require collective action by the state, the city, and CUNY to identify the substantial resources needed for it. In 1999, *An Institution Adrift* repeated this assessment, adding that CUNY lacked basic information to make sound judgments about the quality and effectiveness of its programs.

According to CUNY planning documents for 2000, the system had several stand-alone administrative systems: student information management, financial information and financial accounting, personnel, student financial aid, and admissions. These systems were described as "successful" in that they did what they were designed to do. At the same time, the document acknowledged the need to upgrade, link, and increase their functionality (City University of New York 2000). Three efforts have been undertaken to address these needs: (1) the development of a new relational database that incorporates college data into a student data warehouse; (2) web-enabling the current student information management system; and (3) partnering with private companies to develop a secure, scalable, prototypic purchasing application. CUNY is also acquiring Enterprise Resource Planning software, which will eventually produce integrated human resources, financial, and student information systems that will be much more useful in managing daily operations.

A CUNY portal was established in January 2003 with the aid of a special grant from the mayor's Office for Technology. The portal is a web-based system that was designed to provide 24-hour access to educational and administrative services for all members of the CUNY community. It includes an electronic procurement system that eliminates the use of paper requisitions. CUNY has shown more willingness to report factual information, and the system has begun collecting surveys of student satisfaction. Planning outcomes for each campus are also available on the web. There is a sense that the system is moving toward greater transparency, even if it is not there yet.

Clearly, CUNY provides substantial amounts of information about students as they enter the system, as well as about outcomes of the proficiency exam that students take to move from a two-year to a four-year institution or from the sophomore to the junior level in a senior institution. All campus institutional research directors have access to CUNY's data warehouse— which integrates data for every student on demographics, courses, grades, and degrees—although some directors choose not to use it. The system tracks graduation and retention rates at the college where a student starts, as well as at the college to which a student transfers within the system, with the help of the centralized application processing center. The system routinely looks at how long a student takes to complete remedial education and how much remediation CUNY offers.

More information is now available to the general public, but much remains closely held. The State Education Department made extensive data requests during the remedial education debate, virtually all of which were met by a limited staff through an information system that was not modern. One of the limits on providing more information is the sheer magnitude of the external demands.

BUDGETING AND FISCAL POLICIES

The task of the CUNY Budget and Finance Office is to estimate actual numbers for a budget that will not be perceived by an external audience as unrealistic, even when a larger budget request can be justified. In practice, the budget is a working and negotiating document. The themes emphasized in the 2007–8 budget request for CUNY are those highlighted in the Master Plan. The request represents the second year of a multiyear funding strategy called the CUNY Compact. The Compact asks the state and the city to use tax levies to cover 100 percent of mandated costs and at least 20 percent of the investment plan. CUNY, in turn, commits to funding the balance of the investment plan through philanthropy, productivity, efficiencies, targeted enrollment growth, and the revenue from modest and predictable annual tuition increases. The investment plan includes such Master Plan priorities as creating a flagship environment, fostering a research environment, supporting student success and academic achievement, upgrading the information management system, upgrading facilities, and workforce and economic development (City University of New York 2006).

Collective bargaining agreements impact the budget process, but they are not part of it. Contracts are negotiated outside the budget cycle with representatives from CUNY, the city, and the state, each of whom must approve any agreement. Approval of a contract by the city or the state does not carry a commitment for funding; either the city or the state may approve a contract and then refuse to adjust the baseline appropriation. In such cases, CUNY has to make up the difference, and it is prohibited from raising tuition to do so.

The capital budget request for 2006–7 asked for approximately $599 million for the senior colleges and $282 million for the community colleges. This budget is part of a five-year capital plan, which includes funds for major new construction, the rehabilitation of existing buildings, and capital equipment, especially to upgrade educational technology and the systemwide network infrastructure for telecommunication projects. Major bonded projects accounted for all but $11 million of the combined total. CUNY faced special needs in the aftermath of September 11, 2001. A building on the campus of Borough of Manhattan Community College collapsed, causing the loss of more than 250 classrooms and displacing nearly 25,000 people. The continuing impact of September 11th can be felt throughout the system. In addition, many campuses have dilapidated buildings that CUNY is fighting to have repaired or replaced.

Higher education in New York seems well designed to respond to state priorities. Public institutions are grouped under two governing boards, which serve geographically distinct regions. Both segments have a full range of institutional types, which helps to promote collaboration and transfer within the systems but not between them. A statewide coordinating board—with jurisdiction over K–12 districts, museums, and libraries, as well as both public and private higher education institutions—develops the goals and priorities to which institutions respond through a formal planning process. The coordinating board has the authority to prevent unnecessary program duplication and mission creep (the enhancement of institutional missions) and uses its convening authority to bring actors together across a variety of levels and missions. A system of checks and balances prevents any single state actor, including the governor, from dominating the higher education system in the absence of a working consensus about direction among the other key actors.

Because policy leaders believe that accountability is properly located at the governing-board level, there has been no state effort to implement performance funding. Each of the two public sectors has its own arrangements for holding presidents and their executive staffs accountable for institutional performance in relation to state and system goals.

New York uses multiple and coordinated strategies to improve student preparation for college. A separate statewide agency administers the nation's largest program of need-based student aid, a program that is treated as an individual entitlement. State student aid is coordinated with federal programs. The maximum student award is designed to cover full tuition for needy students at a public university, and Pell grants do not reduce student eligibility for state aid. Maximum state awards may be used at either public or private institutions. Private institutions receive state support for the state residents they serve.

Investment strategies, as well as active participation by the governor and legislature, have been effective in attracting industry and in competing for federal research dollars. Some public institution leaders believe that support to private institutions comes at the expense of adequate support to public institutions, and it is clear that the most distinguished research institutions in the State University of New York system receive far less than their counterparts in such states as California.

CHAPTER SEVEN

New Jersey

⌗

with contributions by Michael W. Klein

⌗

New Jersey is a low-effort, high-performing state. Prior to 1994, an exceptionally strong coordinating board gave the state's comprehensive four-year and community colleges the dubious distinction of being among the most heavily regulated institutions in the nation. A successor coordinating agency retains regulatory authority to plan and approve programs where mission change might be an issue, but it shares this responsibility with a Presidents' Council that includes representation from all nonprofit and for-profit institutions in the state. This arrangement, while widely questioned when implemented, has encouraged the use of market forces and steering strategies within a framework of benchmarking information and performance reporting to encourage institutions to choose their own strategies for achieving state goals and priorities. Institutions have been free to set tuition rates and use revenues to issue bonds for capital improvements. State appropriations are not linked to enrollment levels for the four-year institutions.

⌗

While New Jersey has a knowledge-based economy with signature high-tech telecommunications and pharmaceuticals industries, by 2005 the state's share of national employment in these areas was starting to fall "at a rapid rate" (Hughes and Seneca 2005, pp. 5, 8). The state budget has a growing structural deficit that has challenged governors and legislators over the past several years and jeopardized funding for higher education. New Jersey's significant debt compounds the structural deficit. In the past ten years, after issuing bonds to build schools, rebuild highways, and balance its budget, New Jersey had more than quadrupled its bonded indebtedness, from $8.1 billion to $33 billion, making it the third-biggest borrower among the states (Corzine 2006, p. 4; McNichol 2006).

Because the state constitution requires a balanced budget, Governor Corzine proposed a FY2007 budget that would cut funding for higher education by $169.1 million, or 7.9 percent. After the legislature restored $65.3 million in funding and $80 million in fringe benefit costs, higher education still suffered a $100 million cut in base appropriations, the largest such reduction in New Jersey's history. The reductions proposed for 2008 were even more severe.

New Jersey has the highest per capita property tax burden in the country (Tax Foundation 2006). No other state with a broad-based income or sales tax relies on property taxes to the same extent (Coleman, Hughes, and Kehler 2001, p. 19). The population is wealthy and well educated. The median household income of $61,359 in 2004 was first in the nation. One-third of the state's residents over the age of twenty-five have at least a bachelor's degree, the fifth highest of any state. Demographically, New Jersey's Latino population, which is now 15 percent, is growing faster than either the white (71%) or African American (13%) populations (U.S. Census Bureau 1990, 2005).

STATE ACTORS

Principal actors in New Jersey include the governor, the state treasurer, and the legislature. The state's coordinating board plays more of a planning than an advocacy role. A parallel Presidents' Council is designed to ensure an institutional voice in policy development and implementation for all sectors. The Higher Education Student Assistance Authority is an independent state agency that coordinates student aid programs, advances student aid policies, leverages state and federal resources, and provides direct services to students. All faculty members in public institutions are unionized. Fourteen private institutions enroll fewer than 20 percent of the state's students and are closely integrated into state plans for achieving higher education goals.

The Governor

The governor appoints all judges, does not share authority with a lieutenant governor, and has veto, conditional veto, and line-item veto authority. A representative of a higher education lobbying organization described the governor as a "czar," adding, "There are no other statewide elected officials. No one is equal to the governor."

Changes in the state's legal structure during the past decade and a half have strengthened the governor's influence over higher education in New Jersey. With no intervening regulatory system, the governor determines higher education policy, largely through the annual state budget. The governor sets pri-

orities by recommending an executive budget and presenting a budget message to a joint session of the legislature by the fourth Tuesday in February each
year. The governor also has the constitutional authority to certify revenues
for the budget, thus determining how much the state spends in addition to
directing how it is spent.

Success in implementing new initiatives has always depended upon leadership from the governor. Former governors Richard J. Hughes (1962–1970),
Tom Kean (1982–1990), and Christine Todd Whitman (1994–2001) accomplished the boldest initiatives. Hughes commissioned the Citizens Committee for Higher Education, chaired by Princeton University president Robert
Goheen. The committee's 1966 report outlined the steps needed to create
a system oriented toward the needs of all citizens in the last quarter of the
twentieth century and beyond.

> The state needs a much enlarged system of public two-year county colleges,
> a major expansion of Rutgers, the state university, a doubling of the en-
> rollment capacities of the six state colleges and their conversion to multi-
> purpose institutions, the establishment of new state colleges, a substantial
> increase in the graduate and professional offerings, and finally, provision for
> extensive research facilities to enrich the industrial and cultural life of the
> state. (Citizens Committee for Higher Education in New Jersey 1966, p. 6)

Implementing the recommendations of the Goheen committee, then governor Hughes established a Department of Higher Education under the oversight of a Board of Higher Education. The board selected a powerful chancellor, who served as a member of the governor's cabinet.

In 1985, during his tenure, Governor Kean signed legislation that granted
trustees significantly greater authority, including the right to appoint a CEO
without the approval of the chancellor. Personnel decisions related to mana-
gerial and professional staffs were separated from those for civil servants, and
institutions gained more financial and operational freedom. The Kean administration also decoupled state funding for four-year public institutions from
enrollments.

In 1994, then Governor Whitman removed even more regulation by elimi-
nating the Department of Higher Education and its board. In their place, she
created the New Jersey Commission on Higher Education (which provides
general coordination, planning, and policy development) and the Presidents'
Council (which collaborates with the commission on issues such as licensure
and policy development). Whitman also strengthened institutional govern-

ing boards; added responsibilities to sector organizations for community colleges, state colleges, and universities; and created an independent Office of Student Assistance, which has since become the Higher Education Student Assistance Authority. Perhaps most importantly, she emphasized a managed market model as the basis for state relationships with higher education.

In addition to directing policy and the budget, the governor, with the consent of the Senate, appoints the trustees of the twelve senior public institutions. The governor also designates two trustees for each of the county colleges. Governor Corzine, through an executive order in 2006, required the trustees of the twelve senior public institutions to file a conflict-of-interest form annually that identifies any personal interest they have in vendors doing business with the college or university that they serve.

Office of Management and Budget

The Office of Management and Budget (OMB), in the Department of the Treasury, plays a gatekeeping role in the budgets of the public institutions in New Jersey. Each of the twelve senior public institutions must prepare and present an annual budget to OMB in the fall preceding the governor's February budget address. Similarly, the New Jersey Council of County Colleges provides the state treasurer with an annual budget request for the county colleges. OMB makes findings and recommendations to the governor for the state's entire budget.

The Legislature

The legislature meets on Mondays and Thursdays, year round, in two-year sessions. New Jersey's legislators serve part time, and most members have other jobs. Unlike many states, New Jersey permits dual office holding, which results in several legislators also serving as mayors or county freeholders.

During our study, each house had a Democratic majority. Legislators traditionally assume a kind of defensive posture on higher education, which, according to one legislator, is "a second-tier priority grouped with environmental issues and health care." Another legislator noted that "the relationship between policy and higher education performance is not direct. Part of the process is to create expectations in the minds of the public. Higher education doesn't move quickly. It's not a sea change; more tinkering."

The legislature has several forums for higher education issues. Policy matters come before the Senate Education Committee and the Assembly Higher Education Committee, which was reestablished in 2006. Fiscal matters are heard in the Senate Budget and Appropriations Committee, the Assembly Budget Committee, and the Assembly Appropriations Committee.

The annual hearings in each house's budget committee on the governor's proposed budget for higher education generate the most significant—and high-profile—discussions between the legislature and the higher education community. As one legislator said, "Legislators focus on the budget. Policy guidance comes indirectly as a result of action on the budget." Topics raised during recent budget hearings included operational efficiencies, presidential and administrative salaries, enrollment, tuition costs for in-state and out-of-state students, graduation rates, and private fundraising.

Commission on Higher Education

The New Jersey Commission on Higher Education (CHE) is the state-level coordinating body, with the following as some of its more important responsibilities:

- statewide planning and research on higher education issues
- licensing institutions and granting university status
- rendering final administrative decisions, either on programs that go beyond or change the programmatic mission of an institution or on new academic programs referred to it by the Presidents' Council because they are unduly expensive or duplicative
- reviewing budget requests from institutions in terms of their missions and statewide goals
- proposing a coordinated budget policy statement to the governor and the legislature
- establishing the format and content of the annual reports to the public on the condition of each institution

The CHE consists of eleven members. Its six public members and a faculty member from an institution of higher education are appointed by the governor, with the advice and consent of the Senate. Two public members are appointed by the governor on the recommendation of the president of the Senate and the Speaker of the General Assembly, respectively. The chairpersons of the Presidents' Council and of the board of the Higher Education Student Assistance Authority are ex officio members. The governor also appoints two students, who serve one-year terms. The CHE's executive director is a nonvoting member.

The CHE has tried to provide a central voice and plan for higher education that balances institutional missions, visions, and ambitions with the state's interests and evolving needs. Many believe that its influence has been strengthened by the development of a long-range strategic plan. "This has been an important step," said one policy leader. "We are now measuring progress against objectives in the plan. The plan and subsequent buy-in by state government identified seven objectives that focused the work of the commission. They have done a good job with the plan."

Under the Higher Education Restructuring Act of 1994, the CHE must annually propose "a coordinated budget policy statement to the governor and the legislature," but the law does not specify how this will be done or who will provide the advocacy necessary for its translation into an appropriation. The CHE essentially has very little authority, yet it has the unenviable task of working with the Presidents' Council and the governor to produce a statement acceptable to both. Since both the council and the CHE generally have good access to the governor, they have some idea of what he would find acceptable.

The CHE has been handicapped by the loss and nonreplacement of strong staff members, with many positions remaining open for six to nine months after key individuals retired. To help compensate, the CHE has employed several highly competent and well-respected retired former officials. Its role has increasingly become one of advocating for the public interest, rather than for institutions. This direction has provoked criticism from institutional representatives, who believe that CHE's lean staffing has limited its effectiveness and led to a minimalist, no-risk approach. More extreme criticisms describe the CHE—in contrast to the President's Council—as a "huge disappointment," a "strange animal," and "too weak."

Some legislators agree that the CHE should have stronger authority. And Governor Corzine has recently tied the CHE more directly to his policy office by choosing as his senior advisor on higher education the same individual whom the CHE board subsequently appointed as its executive director. The CHE press release announcing the appointment said, "Given its responsibility to serve as the state's planning and coordinating agency for higher education, the CHE sees the establishment of a direct relationship with the governor's office and the state policy and planning table as a means of significantly enhancing New Jersey's higher education governance structure" (Beardsley 2006, p. 1).

Presidents' Council

The Presidents' Council is a member-funded advisory body consisting of the president of each New Jersey public institution of higher education and each independent institution that receives direct state aid. The council shares responsibilities with the CHE for the statewide coordination of higher education. While patterned conceptually after Michigan's Council of Presidents, which provides voluntary coordination to four-year public institutions, the New Jersey arrangements differ by bringing together under a single structure all sectors of higher education, including community colleges, independent colleges and universities, public four-year colleges and universities, and proprietary and theological institutions. The responsibilities of the Presidents' Council are varied:

- reviewing and making recommendations to the CHE on new programs that exceed an institution's programmatic mission, require substantial additional resources, or raise significant issues of duplication
- reviewing and making recommendations to the CHE concerning changes in the programmatic mission of an institution
- encouraging the formation of regional and cooperative programs among institutions and developing criteria for "full faith and credit" transfer agreements between county colleges and other institutions of higher education
- advising and assisting the CHE in adopting and updating a statewide plan for higher education
- providing recommendations concerning institutional licensure and university status when requested to do so by the CHE

It has taken time and much learning to develop an effective Presidents' Council. As a CHE board member said, "When we first got together after restructuring on issues that were controversial, the Presidents' Council would not take a position. And they might not support positions, once taken, behind the scenes. We have outgrown that. Meetings and the willingness to make decisions are much better."

The strength of the system is its capacity to get everyone together. The presidents have formed productive committees on transfer and articulation and on teacher education. And the council, through behind-the-scenes negotiations and with generally very good collaboration, has been able to coordinate the development and approval of new programs. "The New Jersey system should receive high marks for collaboration, but the adversarial characteristics are there as well," a CHE staff member commented. "It is a given that everyone is going to operate in their self-interest. Overarching initiatives and umbrella goals bring out the parochialism."

A proprietary college president told us, "There's been a tremendous change since restructuring. Because of the Presidents' Council and [its] executive committee, you really understand issues from other sectors. There's more collegiality; before restructuring I never knew anybody. As a result of restructuring, there's more synergy and more collaboration between institutions." The president of an independent university added, "College presidents know each other across sectors; this did not happen before. There is more emphasis on interpersonal relationships. Presidents personally know and like each other. The new voluntary alliance is more real than the structure it replaced."

A member of the executive committee of the Presidents' Council, who is president of an independent college, concurred with these assessments: "There is a sense of being part of a larger whole. Now you get to know the presidents of public institutions in a way I had not previously experienced. We work together on the budget. It is not just one sector screaming for itself." And a CHE staff member told us that New Jersey higher educational institutions have become more collaborative and cooperative since restructuring: "There are more joint degrees. There is also a lot more collaboration within and across sectors. Because of the Presidents' Council, presidents must, at least in some areas, take a statewide view."

As the structure has aged, some of its weaknesses have also become evident. Presidents of the more prestigious independent universities do not participate very much in council activities. New presidents from public institutions are perceived by some of their more experienced colleagues as lacking commitment. Attendance at council meetings is sometimes spotty. One county college president sensed an emerging parochialism. "New presidents need to establish credibility with their own boards," he said, "and start programs that are not necessarily collaborative."

Higher Education Student Assistance Authority

The Higher Education Student Assistance Authority (HESAA) is the most important of the remaining actors in the interface between institutions and state government. As an independent state authority, HESAA coordinates student aid programs, advances student aid policies, leverages state and federal resources, and provides direct services to students. HESAA is governed by an eighteen-member board, appointed by the governor, that includes voting representatives from all sectors of higher education as well as student and public members.

A representative of the CHE serves on the HESAA board.

HESAA administers four types of student assistance: savings programs, merit-based grants, student loans, and need-based grants. The largest program is the Tuition Assistance Grant (TAG) program, described in more detail under the student assistance section of this chapter. HESAA administers a number of smaller programs, the most important of which is the Outstanding Scholar Recruitment Program, designed to encourage high-achieving high school graduates in New Jersey to attend college within the state.

Of all the state agencies spun off from the 1994 restructuring, HESAA receives the highest marks. An administrator in one sector organization said, "The governor's office of policy and planning has a lot to say about what happens at HESAA. Financial aid has been a real shining light of restructuring. The HESAA board has been very effective in advocacy."

Unions

Campus chapters of the American Association of University Professors (AAUP) represent the faculty at New Jersey's three research institutions, with a separate unit at Rutgers for part-time lecturers. The faculty union at the state colleges and universities has separate units for full-time and adjunct faculty and is affiliated with the American Federation of Teachers. The powerful New Jersey Education Association (NJEA), which represents over 90,000 certified teachers, also includes the faculty at the majority of New Jersey's county colleges. The NJEA is respected for its political clout and its professionalism. It has one of the state's best-financed political action committees and works hard to get supportive candidates elected.

Collective bargaining is handled differently among New Jersey's higher education sectors. The research institutions and the county colleges each negotiate directly with their unions. At the state colleges and universities, however, the governor remains the employer of record, and negotiations are conducted by the governor's Office of Employee Relations.

Organized labor is a potent political force in New Jersey, and the labor representatives of higher education contribute to, and benefit from, that clout. In 2001, statewide labor leaders achieved a 9 percent increase in pensions for teachers and public employees. In 2003, higher education's faculty unions successfully lobbied for legislation that allows part-time and adjunct faculty and staff at public colleges and universities to purchase coverage under the State Health Benefits Plan. The AFT at the state level supports greater oversight from Trenton and union representation on boards of trustees. The AFT is also concerned that part-time faculty outnumber full-time faculty, and considers this imbalance a negative consequence of the marketing emphasis embedded in restructuring's push toward autonomy (Yovnello and Erickson 2006, pp. 1, 3).

Private Higher Education

Fourteen independent colleges and universities serve New Jersey, which is one of only seven states that provide direct aid to such institutions. A well-regarded Association of Independent Colleges and Universities provides coordination and advocacy, as well as a modest amount of information reporting. A policy leader stated that the current governance arrangements have treated independent institutions with fairness. "Given the state's funding constraints, the independent colleges have faced the same problems as everyone else. They have not been singled out," he said. Several years ago, the state did not pay independent colleges the money that was approved for them under the appropriations act, but subsequent efforts by the institutions and their advocates restored that money. Even though state operating support has not grown for independent institutions, financial aid has, and this has been a boon.

Their financial and political success notwithstanding, the independent sector has two serious concerns with the system implemented under restructuring: (1) it precludes regulatory controls on any one sector that would limit competition with another sector, and (2) it lacks a visible champion to represent higher education to state government. The old system protected the independent colleges and universities against expansionist aspirations of the public institutions, but now there is more direct competition. Public institutions have enlarged, and some are perceived to be widening their missions. Still, under restructuring, enough has gone well for the independent sector that most of its representatives are at least ambivalent about the desirability or feasibility of returning to the former arrangements.

Proprietary Institutions

New Jersey has four licensed proprietary colleges and universities. The legislature amended the authorizing statute of the Presidents' Council in 2003 to increase the number of proprietary institutions serving on the council, expanding it from the two largest to all those that were authorized to offer licensed degree programs before the amendment's effective date. The amendment also allowed one president from the proprietary schools to serve on the executive committee of the Presidents' Council. The University of Phoenix received its license to operate in New Jersey after the authorizing date, precluding its participation.

STATE RULES

A former executive staff member of CHE described New Jersey's current structure as coordinated autonomy. The goal is for institutions to work together harmoniously on a common effort. As a county college president argued, "Autonomy can't be chaos. It has to be coordinated." The components of coordinated autonomy add up to New Jersey's rules for planning, program review and approval, information, academic preparation, student assistance, fiscal policies, and economic development.

Planning

The CHE is responsible for statewide planning for higher education under the Higher Education Restructuring Act of 1994. It drafted its first long-range plan in 2003 and updated it in 2005 (New Jersey Commission on Higher Education 2005). The plan contains seven objectives:

1. Achieve and sustain higher levels of excellence in teaching and learning, research, and public service in all sectors
2. Support increases in capacity and specific programs to prepare a growing and increasingly diverse population for responsible citizenship in a democratic society and to attract more New Jersey students to the state's institutions and prepare them for high-demand occupations
3. Support financial aid programs that enable New Jersey students from all backgrounds to afford high quality higher education
4. Establish funding policies and methodologies for state operating and capital support for the public research universities, state colleges and universities, community colleges, and independent institutions
5. Encourage and enhance coordination and collaboration between and among all educational institutions in the state

6. Encourage and expedite partnerships between higher education and other sectors of society
7. Enhance the public research universities

In the 2005 update of its long-range plan, the CHE noted "considerable progress" (New Jersey Commission on Higher Education 2005, p. 49). Institutions had established internal goals and strategies to address key components of the plan, and they had identified peer groups to facilitate comparisons and improve strategies. Financial aid programs stood on more solid footing, and task forces were developing methodologies to support the twelve senior public institutions and a long-term policy for capital needs.

The specter of the state's structural deficit hangs over the prospects of the long-range plan. In 2005, the CHE wrote that the deficit's fiscal constraints "have hindered any serious discussion or consideration of significantly increasing the level of state support for higher education." Expanding New Jersey's higher education capacity—the second objective of the long-range plan—is the most significant cause of the state's budget struggle. In 2004, New Jersey's colleges and universities served 38 percent of recent high school graduates, up from 36 percent in 2002. Reaching the national average of 47 percent will be difficult. First, the state has the highest outmigration rate of baccalaureate-seeking students in the nation. Approximately 37 percent of New Jersey high school graduates who go to college attend college out of state (NCPPHE 2006, p. 7). Second, the number of high school graduates in New Jersey keeps growing. By 2017–18, about 103,092 students will graduate from the state's high schools, a 16 percent increase over 2001–2, the twelfth-highest percentage increase in the country (WICHE 2003).

A university president described the absence of state planning for additional capacity in light of this growth in high school graduates as a "dangerous game." He added, "The policy is to outsource higher education, and the current system maintains the status quo by decoupling changes in enrollment from changes in funding. There is no additional capacity except at community colleges."

Program Approval

Under New Jersey's market-based, coordinated-autonomy approach, new programs emerge through a two-step review process between the Presidents' Council and the CHE. The Presidents' Council reviews and makes recommendations to the CHE on new programs that exceed an institution's programmatic mission, require substantial added resources or raise significant issues of duplication. The CHE renders final administrative decisions on these issues; final approval rests with the President's Council for programs outside of these parameters.

There has been legislative concern that review by the Presidents' Council would amount to "mutual back scratching." At a public hearing in 2005, institutional representatives told members of the Senate Education Committee that the council's academic review committee conducts a serious screening process and does not approve programs that violate criteria. They also argued that the new program review process prevents unnecessary duplication and a waste of state resources. Mission differentiation and behind-the-scenes negotiations help to keep the formal rate of program rejection low, as questioned programs are pulled off the table before formal action is required.

The Presidents' Council and the CHE also work together to review applications for licensure. New Jersey has a reputation for having some of the most rigorous licensing standards in the nation. The CHE wants to maintain high standards while also making sure that the regulations take into account rapidly changing technology, communication modes, and demands for knowledge.

Information

New Jersey is an information-rich state. The rules generate information from the executive branch, the legislative branch, and the institutions themselves. A key component in developing good will—and achieving high performance using a market-oriented approach—is good information. New Jersey's shift from a regulatory to a predominantly market-driven system has placed heavy demands on communication. Consumers—students and their parents—need information to make better choices. State officials require details to administer and monitor a massive program of student assistance. Elected leaders ask for data assuring them that the system is producing reasonable outcomes in the absence of state regulation. Potential donors seek evidence of whether their contributions are making a difference in areas they value. Employers need facts to determine if the state's colleges and universities are producing workers with the skills needed in the marketplace.

The CHE has access to three databases: the Institutional Postsecondary Education Data System (IPEDS), a unit record system for enrollments and degrees (SURE), and the state financial aid system, to which SURE can be linked. If retention or graduation is defined in relation to student financial aid, data going back to 1981 is available. State databases cover all public and a few independent institutions. For these institutions, the CHE aggregates data and uses it to report to IPEDS.

The CHE is heavily involved in benchmarking, a process that is based on their accountability reports (the first was published in 1996, after restructuring) and institutional accountability reports, which are prepared in a format specified by the CHE and use CHE-generated data as well as that provided by the campuses. To track performance, the CHE employs national benchmarks in conjunction with state indicators, and it takes into account the magnitude and direction of change occurring both in New Jersey and in other states. The CHE's *7th Annual Systemwide Accountability Report* (New Jersey Commission on Higher Education 2004), for example, provided a long-term analysis of graduation rates, cost, benefits, and other outcomes, similar to the information provided in the National Center for Public Policy and Higher Education's *Measuring Up* report cards. Thus the grades awarded to New Jersey in these reports came as no surprise to policymakers or institutional leaders, as shown by the steps the state had already taken in such areas as need-based assistance for part-time students and community college articulation and transfer.

The Office of Legislative Services (OLS) uses the same databases at the CHE to generate reports that respond to requests for information from policymakers. Legislators consider the well-staffed and nonpartisan OLS to be an excellent source of information, especially on fiscal questions. Legislators also have a high regard for the CHE's reports, but they tend to view them as providing information supportive of the priorities and perspectives of the higher education community. The legislators' partisan staff supplement the work of the OLS and CHE by providing briefings and background papers, including political comments about who is likely to be supporting or opposing a bill. Such valuable information for elected lawmakers is outside of the scope of permissible activity for either the OLS or CHE. If legislators have a close interest in a bill, they talk to OLS and do their homework. Otherwise, they are likely to depend on the notes they get from their partisan staff.

The New Jersey information system also has its problems. Legislators sometimes report differences between the reports they receive from the CHE and comments from institutional leaders. In 2005, there were also perceptions that higher education lacked the central voice in state policy discussions enjoyed by other major areas of state government. It was partly to address this perceived deficiency that the current CHE executive director was also appointed as higher education advisor to the governor.

Academic Preparation

Much goodwill and many regional projects are aimed at improving students' preparation for college. The CHE estimates that over 500 collaborative projects involve the state's colleges, universities, and elementary and secondary schools. A representative of the Department of Education described its working relationship with the CHE as "very close, especially in teacher education." Also noted were the close ties between county colleges and K–12 schools; county superintendents serve on the colleges' boards of trustees to promote this linkage.

The Department of Education representative also praised the improved cooperation that characterizes the development of joint proposals between his department and higher education. Exhibit A in support of this assessment was the 1999 U.S. Department of Education's GEAR UP award of $10 million for the CHE, which used the grant for college preparation for 1,861 low-income students from ten middle and seven high schools in the cities of Camden, Jersey City, Newark, and Trenton. The proposal for this was built on existing state-funded College Bound programs. In 2005, New Jersey received a second GEAR UP grant, this one for $20.9 million allocated over six years, which expanded the project to ten more schools and added the city of Paterson. By spring 2005, 81.7 percent of graduates from the New Jersey GEAR UP program had enrolled in some form of postsecondary education, almost double the rate of low-income students across the state (Johnson 2005, p. 1).

The Presidents' Council and the CHE are working with the Office of the Governor, the Department of Education, and the business community on the American Diploma Project (ADP), a network of twenty-two states endeavoring to strengthen high school standards, curricula, assessments, and data and accountability systems so that more students graduate prepared for college and twenty-first-century jobs. The goal for New Jersey is to decrease college-level remediation for high school graduates by at least 20 percent by 2012. Within ADP, New Jersey is one of thirteen states participating in Alignment Institutes, which bring postsecondary and business leaders together with K–12 leaders to define the core English and math skills that graduates need for college and work and then to revise their high school standards as necessary (Achieve 2006).

Student Assistance

New Jersey's award programs fall into three distinct areas: need, disadvantage, and academics. New Jersey is consistently among the nation's leaders in providing need-based student assistance. New Jersey ranks second in the nation in the estimated need-based undergraduate dollars available per full-time undergraduate student, fourth nationally in the estimated undergraduate grant dollars per full-time-equivalent student, and twelfth in expenditures for need-based programs (New Jersey Commission on Higher Education 2005, p. 23). In 2003–4, New Jersey awarded 5 percent of all the need-based aid given out nationally and was among the few states that awarded more than $150 million in need-based student aid (National Association of State Student Grant and Aid Programs 2005, p. 21).

The most significant program in this area is the Tuition Aid Grant. Established in 1978, TAG provides eligible full-time undergraduates with up to 100 percent of the cost of tuition at public institutions in New Jersey and up to 50 percent of the average tuition at independent institutions in the state. Approximately 34 percent of full-time undergraduates attending college in New Jersey receive a TAG award. Of these, nearly 64 percent come from families with adjusted gross incomes of $22,200 or less. Over 350,000 students apply for TAG support annually, but only about 61,000 students receive these grants (New Jersey Higher Education Student Assistance Authority 2005).

Language within the FY 2004 budget, and in each budget thereafter, has authorized TAG awards for part-time students at county colleges. The proposed FY 2007 budget provides $4.9 million for these students, calculated to support 9,941 recipients with an average award of $497 (Corzine 2006, p. 30).

The New Jersey Educational Opportunity Fund (EOF) was created in 1968 to help students from economically and educationally disadvantaged backgrounds obtain a college education. EOF provides supplemental financial aid to help cover college costs—such as books, fees, and room and board—that are not covered by the state's TAG program. EOF sponsors an array of campus-based outreach and support services at twenty-eight public and thirteen independent institutions. The EOF program uses the services of HESAA to distribute grants totaling almost $22 million to over 13,000 eligible students (Mann and Forsberg 2006, p. 27).

While operating under the general supervision of the CHE, the EOF is governed by an eight-member board of directors appointed by the governor. The board sets policy, approves regulations for program operation and student eligibility, develops an annual budget request, and supports EOF programs at public and independent colleges and universities.

New Jersey has also expanded merit-based aid during the past decade, intending to stem the brain drain and keep academically talented students in the state. In 2004, New Jersey provided 12,000 merit-based scholarships through six separate programs. The most significant is the Outstanding Scholar Recruitment Program (OSRP), which provides annual scholarships ranging from $2,500 to $7,500 to students who achieve stipulated SAT and class-rank criteria. To retain the scholarship, students must maintain a B average. In 2004, nearly 4,900 students in this program received scholarships worth over $13.1 million.

That same year, New Jersey also launched a merit-based scholarship program for full-time county college students, called the New Jersey Student Tuition Assistance Reward Scholarship (NJ STARS). NJ STARS offers five semesters of county college tuition to students who graduate in the top 20 percent of their high school class and then maintain a 3.0 GPA in a county college, but these students must first apply for grant aid from all other available federal and state sources.

In a program which started in fall 2006, NJ STARS students who complete their associate's degree within five semesters are eligible for a NJ STARS II scholarship at a public four-year college or university in New Jersey. The state provides $4,000 per student per year toward tuition and approved fees, and the participating institution covers the balance. As with the original NJ STARS program, students must first apply for all other available federal and state aid grants.

Student aid funding now approaches about 15 percent of New Jersey's total appropriation for higher education. The proposed FY 2007 budget provided about $290 million for the state's student assistance programs, increasing funding for need-based student assistance programs by $6.3 million and reducing funding for other, non-need-based student aid programs by $5.7 million (Corzine 2006, p. 29).

Fiscal Policies

Until 1985, New Jersey allocated state funding for its public colleges and universities according to an explicit policy based on enrollment, student credit hours, building size, degree levels, and program fields. Under the 1985 State

College Autonomy Act, Kean—who was governor at that time—shifted New Jersey from formula funding to more incremental budgeting. Annual budget negotiations are based on the previous year's funding level, which is then increased or decreased by the governor and legislature depending on the state's fiscal condition and the advocacy efforts of the higher education community.

Former governor Whitman, who was committed to a market model of public higher education, allowed four-year institutions to set tuition without interfering in the process. Her successors, however, have taken action to combat tuition increases. In 2002, then governor McGreevey warned the twelve senior public institutions that they would face an audit by the CHE if they raised tuition by more than 10 percent. In FY 2004, the twelve senior public institutions faced a cap of 9 percent, imposed through the state budget. The budgets in fiscal years 2005 through 2007 each placed an 8 percent cap on tuition increases. The penalty for exceeding the cap in FY 2006 and FY 2007 was a reduction in state funds by 5 percent for each 1 percent in tuition increases that exceeded 8 percent.

Between FY 1990–91 and FY 2004–5, tuition and fees at public four-year colleges in New Jersey roughly tripled, from $2,654 to $7,879 a year (Mann and Forsberg 2006, p. 12). New Jersey's four-year public institutions have the second-highest average tuition and fee charges nationally, exceeded only by Pennsylvania (College Board 2005, p. 22). Even allowing for financial aid, the cost of attending one of New Jersey's public four-year institutions in 2004 amounted to 34 percent of an average family's income, up from 24 percent a decade earlier. Measured this way, only six states charge more.

The Independent College and University Assistance Act, passed in 1972 and amended in 1979, allocates state support to independent colleges and universities that "provide a level of education which is equivalent to the education provided by the state's public institutions of higher education." The funding is tied to the number of full-time-equivalent New Jersey undergraduates enrolled during the previous year at eligible independent institutions. The actual dollar amounts institutions receive are dependent on appropriations, and invariably they receive only some portion of the entitlement due to them under the act. In FY 2002, and again in FY 2007, language inserted in the state budget effectively made Princeton ineligible to receive aid. The funding that would have been allocated to Princeton was redistributed among the remaining independent colleges and universities.

The Higher Education Incentive Funding Act, established in 1999, provides state funds to match private endowment contributions or donations made to public and independent institutions of higher education. The amount of matching funds depends on the kind of gift and the type of institution. Governor Corzine planned to discontinue the program in FY 2007, because the state has seldom met its obligation to match endowment contributions, and a five-fold increase in appropriations would be required to fully match eligible contributions already received by the colleges and universities.

In contrast to the rules of the game for operating funds, which seem to have changed very little since restructuring, New Jersey clearly redesigned those for capital funding in order to encourage entrepreneurial activity and put both public and independent institutions on a more equal footing. Capital planning is now decentralized, with the primary responsibility for it vested in institutional governing boards. Restructuring eliminated the oversight role of the former Board of Higher Education, allowing institutions to address their campus facilities needs more quickly.

Institutions in New Jersey fund capital expenses in four ways—through direct state capital appropriations, general obligation bonds, bond programs administered by the Educational Facilities Authority (EFA), and campus-backed debt. From 1980 to 1999, direct state appropriations for capital maintenance and renewal amounted to about $147 million (New Jersey Commission on Higher Education and New Jersey Presidents' Council 1999, p. 9), but the state has not provided a separate capital budget for higher education since FY 1999. The last general obligation bond issue approved by the voters was in 1988. For the four-year institutions, the bulk of state capital support has been one-time-only, debt-financed programs dating at least to the mid-1980s, usually administered by the EFA.

Beginning in 1993, New Jersey developed a series of renewable debt-capacity programs for the four-year colleges and universities, which in some instances also included county colleges. These programs allow new bonds to be issued as old ones are retired. Public institutions have received between 89 and 94 percent of these funds, with the remainder going to the fourteen independent institutions (New Jersey Commission on Higher Education 2005, p. 32). All institutions have assumed a share of the cost of the debt on many of the state bond programs.

The EFA issues bonds and notes to finance campus construction, renovation projects, and capital purchases for the states' public and private colleges and universities. In 2005, EFA financing activity set a new record by issuing $960 million in debts (New Jersey Educational Facilities Authority 2005, p. 6).

The CHE's role in capital funding is limited to ensuring that proposals submitted under five of the debt-financed programs are consistent with legislative intent. The CHE also addresses the need for capital support in its long-range plan, its annual budget policy statements, and in testimony before the New Jersey Commission on Capital Budgeting and Planning, which recommends projects for inclusion in the annual budget to the governor and the legislature. In the past decade, these recommendations have been followed only rarely.

The senior public colleges and universities, in particular, have increasingly relied on their own debt for facility investment. They are now among the most leveraged public institutions in the nation, with the resulting debt service generally falling to students through tuition or fees.

Research and Development

The New Jersey Commission on Science and Technology (CST) was established in 1985. It develops and oversees policies and programs promoting science and technology research and entrepreneurship in New Jersey. The commission's mission statement (2006) calls for it to (1) promote ties between industry and universities to accelerate the commercialization of technology, (2) provide grants to entrepreneurial technology businesses in areas of strategic importance to the state, and (3) strengthen research collaborations among universities to create a new potential for increased federal funding and private investment.

In 2006, the CST provided $500,000 for a nanotechnology facility at Rutgers University; nearly $2.5 million for eighteen technology companies, including $1.3 million awarded under the Entrepreneurial Partnering Fund program to four companies partnering with New Jersey research universities; and $695,000 for nine postdoctoral Technology Fellowships, a program for companies hiring PhD graduates from New Jersey's research universities (Fineman 2006).

New Jersey is ranked twenty-first nationally in its aggregate share of federal research dollars for higher education. The CHE has set a ten-year goal for New Jersey to increase its share of available federal monies by a full percent (New Jersey Commission on Higher Education 2005). In September 2006, Governor Corzine established the $150 million Edison Innovation Fund, designed to build the capacity of New Jersey's research universities to complement economic development, support entrepreneurial efforts, increase access to startup capital, and support high-tech businesses.

The Economic Development Authority and the CST have created three Innovation Zones—in Camden, in Newark, and around New Brunswick—that include state universities, research institutions, and related businesses. Innovation Zones are designed to spur collaborative efforts and promptly transfer discoveries from the laboratory to market. Technology and life sciences businesses that move to these zones are eligible for financial incentives. Each zone features a commercialization facility, providing specifically designed office and lab space for companies' early-stage growth.

HIGHER EDUCATION SYSTEMS

Adaptation and incremental change informed by data analysis are the characteristics of higher education in New Jersey. The state's public higher education system includes three research institutions, nine state colleges and universities, and nineteen county colleges. We describe selected rules as they affect each of these sectors below.

Public Research Institutions

New Jersey has three public research institutions: Rutgers University, the New Jersey Institute of Technology, and the University of Medicine and Dentistry of New Jersey. Although they each have their own distinct history and operate under separate sets of statutes, there are rules that apply to all three.

Rutgers is New Jersey's largest and most comprehensive public university. It is one of America's oldest institutions of higher education, yet one of the newest nationally regarded research institutions. Founded in 1766 as Queen's College in New Brunswick, it was the eighth college established in the colonies. Rutgers was designated as New Jersey's land-grant institution under the Morrill Act of 1862; the Rutgers Scientific School, which has since become the agricultural school, was established in 1864. Rutgers was named the state university in 1945, but the state did not assume full control until 1956. In 1989, Rutgers became the fifty-eighth member of the Association of American Universities.

Rutgers grew into a three-campus system when it absorbed the University of Newark in 1946 and then the College of South Jersey in Camden in 1950. In fall 2005, Rutgers enrolled more than 37,000 undergraduates and almost 13,000 graduate students across its three campuses. More than 90 percent of Rutgers undergraduates are New Jersey residents.

The New Jersey Institute of Technology (NJIT) opened in 1884 as the New-ark Technical School. It grew to become the Newark College of Engineering in 1919, and expanded to a full-fledged technological university in 1975, when it was renamed the New Jersey Institute of Technology. NJIT enrolls approximately 5,500 undergraduates and about 2,800 graduate students.

Medical education in New Jersey developed along private and public tracks that converged in 1970. The Seton Hall College of Medicine and Dentistry opened in 1954 in Jersey City, and it was purchased by the state in 1965. Renamed the New Jersey College of Medicine and Dentistry (NJCMD), it moved to Newark in 1967. Meanwhile, Rutgers started Rutgers Medical School in 1966 as a two-year, basic science institution offering a master's degree in medical science. The Medical and Dental Education Act of 1970 merged NJCMD with Rutgers Medical School and created the College of Medicine and Dentistry of New Jersey. The institution was renamed the University of Medicine and Dentistry of New Jersey (UMDNJ) in 1981, and today it is the nation's largest public university for health sciences.

Governing Boards and Executive Leadership

The board of trustees of each public research institution has the authority to appoint the institution's president. As a result of negotiations during its transformation from a private to a public university, Rutgers has both a Board of Governors and a Board of Trustees. The Board of Trustees was the governing body of the institution from its founding until it became New Jersey's state university in 1956. Rutgers, the State University Act of 1956 created a Board of Governors to oversee the university. Under this act, the Board of Trustees was reduced to an advisory role, although it has certain fiduciary responsibilities over university assets that existed before 1956, including land and the school's name.

The Board of Governors is composed of eleven voting members, six appointed by the governor (with confirmation by the Senate) and five elected by and from the fifty-nine-member Board of Trustees. The president of the university is a nonvoting member. The University Senate elects two faculty members and one student as nonvoting representatives. Voting members of the Board of Governors serve six-year terms and may succeed themselves for one additional term.

NJIT's Board of Trustees may have up to fifteen voting members. Trustees must be citizens of New Jersey, and they are appointed by the governor with the advice and consent of the Senate. Trustees serve four-year terms and have no term limits. The governor and the mayor of Newark serve ex officio as nonvoting members. The board, by law, recommends potential new members to the governor.

Governance at UMDNJ changed significantly after a federal investigation for Medicaid fraud in 2005, a symbol to some policymakers that the market model was out of control. Under a deferred prosecution agreement, a federal monitor began overseeing the institution's operations in January 2006. Shortly thereafter, legislation expanded the board from eleven to nineteen members, and separated the governance of University Hospital from UMDNJ. Among the nineteen trustees, the governor now appoints two upon recommendation of the Senate president, two upon recommendation of the Speaker of the General Assembly, and fifteen with the advice and consent of the Senate. All but three of the trustees must be residents of New Jersey; they must represent the gender, racial, and ethnic diversity of the state; and there must be at least two trustees each from the northern, central, and southern regions of the state. Trustees serve five-year terms and may be reappointed. New Jersey's commissioner of health serves ex officio. UMDNJ is unique among the twelve senior public colleges and universities in New Jersey, since the governor designates one of the voting members as chair of the board.

In June 2006, the Middle States Commission on Higher Education placed UMDNJ on probation because of concerns regarding (1) the institution's finances, (2) the stability of the board and executive leaders, and (3) oversight and control over the institution and its activities. Between December 2005 and April 2006, three trustees resigned over conflicts of interest; the president was forced to resign in part because of no-bid contracts and hiring procedures that favored the politically connected; the senior vice president for academic affairs resigned over allegations of expense account violations; and the deans of all three medical schools left, including one who was forced to resign after the federal monitor reported a fraudulent accounting scheme that boosted his annual bonus. Governor Corzine, within his first week in office in January 2006, bypassed the Board of Trustees to negotiate the departure of the president and hand pick an interim president. The Board of Trustees later confirmed the governor's selection.

Faculty

Individual chapters of the AAUP represent the faculty at each of the research institutions, and each institution's Board of Trustees bargains with its respective chapter. Collective bargaining generally concludes after the state has completed its negotiations with the state employee unions, which set a pattern for salary and benefits.

In addition to the AAUP, the governance system at Rutgers includes a 196-member University Senate, which has representatives from the faculty, administrators, students, and alumni and is responsible for establishing minimum standards for admissions, scholarships, and honors. It also provides advice to the president on academic and administrative issues. On the New Brunswick and Newark campuses, Faculty Councils undertake that role for their campus leaders, and the arts and sciences faculty at the Camden campus has established a Faculty Senate.

At NJIT, an AAUP chapter represents most full- and part-time faculty and librarians. Under NJIT's governance structure, the faculty as a whole must approve major decisions affecting either themselves or the academic programs. The Faculty Council—a group elected from among the faculty—often considers and debates such issues.

At UMDNJ, the AAUP represents medical, dental, and nursing faculty, along with librarians. This institution abolished its Faculty Senate several years ago, because of the perception that the senate did not play a significant role in governance or in solving faculty concerns. "The faculty did not object to the demise of the Faculty Senate" (University of Medicine and Dentistry of New Jersey 2005, pp. 1-9 to 1-10).

Rules for Public Research Universities

PLANNING AND STRATEGIES

The 1994 Restructuring Act specified that the governing board of each public institution of higher education has the power to develop an institutional plan. Rutgers initiated its first university-wide master plan in 2001, in an effort to address enrollment growth, advancing technologies, and regional development across all three of its campuses. Two years later, it unveiled the Rutgers University Master Plan, which comprehensively assessed the university's facilities needs and physical growth. The plan is intended to guide institutional growth and development through 2012.

The New Jersey Institute of Technology Act of 1995 specifies that NJIT must develop an institutional plan and, consistent with that plan, determine the schools, departments, programs, and degree levels to be offered. In 2004, NJIT adopted a strategic plan valid through 2010. Its top priority is to develop a core of nationally recognized programs in mathematics, architecture, and wireless communications and networking.

UMDNJ had a strategic plan covering 1999–2004. Since 2000, each of its eight schools has prepared an individual strategic plan that is updated on an annual basis and submitted to the University Office of Academic Affairs. In its 2005 Middle States self-study report, UMDNJ acknowledged that it should write and publish a comprehensive, university-wide strategic planning document and disseminate it widely within and outside the institution.

PROGRAM INITIATIVES

The Restructuring Act confirmed the previously existing authority of the governing board for each public institution to determine the programs and degree levels to be offered by that institution, consistent with its individual strategic plan and mission. According to observers, since the 1994 act, Rutgers and NJIT have become more entrepreneurial, more concerned about the bottom line, and more willing to offer high-demand, low-cost programs with the potential for yielding a profit. Higher education officials have noticed that Rutgers, in particular, monitors other institutions more carefully than before and is seen as having a greater tendency to respond to the market and to potential competitors. By law, UMDNJ offers mostly graduate degrees, but since 1992 it has been required to partner with other institutions to offer new associate's or baccalaureate degree programs.

ENROLLMENT PLANNING

The 1994 Restructuring Act authorized boards of trustees of the public colleges and universities to establish standards and requirements for admission and for granting diplomas, certificates, and degrees. The legislature respects this authority. In programs like NJ STARS II, which encourage county college students to transfer to four-year public institutions, the underlying legislation states, "Nothing in this act shall be construed to require a four-year public institution of higher education to admit a student eligible for a scholarship under this act or to waive its admission standards and application procedures" (New Jersey Student Tuition Assistance Reward Scholarship II, § 18A:71B-86.7).

INFORMATION

The boards of trustees of the public colleges and universities in New Jersey, under the 1994 Restructuring Act, must prepare several documents for the public: (1) an annual financial statement; (2) a statement delineating the amount spent on government relations, public relations, and legal costs; (3) an annual independent financial audit, which, along with any management letters regarding that audit, are considered public documents; and (4) an annual report on "the condition of the institution" that must include the following:

a profile of the student body including graduation rates, SAT or other test scores, the percentage of New Jersey residents in the student body, the number of scholarship students and the number of Educational Opportunity Fund students in attendance; a profile of the faculty including the ratio of full- to part-time faculty members, and major research and public service activities; a profile of the trustees or governors as applicable; and a profile of the institution, including degree and certificate programs, status of accreditation, major capital projects and any other information which the commission and the institution deem appropriate. (Higher Education Restructuring Act, §18A:3B-35)

NJIT and UMDNJ have an additional responsibility. They must submit an annual report to the State Treasurer on the operation of all joint ventures, subsidiary corporations, partnerships, or other legal entities entered into or owned wholly or in part by their institution.

FISCAL POLICIES

"Influencing higher education," one legislator said, "becomes increasingly difficult as you move upward through the state colleges and universities and then the research institutions." Most of the state's influence comes from the power of the purse. The public research institutions, like other public colleges and universities, must submit a request for state support to the Department of the Treasury's Office of Management and Budget and to the CHE. The governor and legislature, of course, determine how much of the request is granted. State funding has a direct influence on tuition. In 2005–6, the average undergraduate in-state tuition was $7,336 at Rutgers and $8,472 at NJIT.

Once their appropriations are in place, the public research institutions have great flexibility in expending them. With no central control from Trenton, the institutions set their own priorities—with an eye toward statewide needs—and spend their funds accordingly, consistent with a market approach. They are subject only to potential state audits and to occasional legislative scrutiny.

State Colleges and Universities

New Jersey's nine state colleges and universities were established over a 120-year period. Three institutions—the College of New Jersey, Kean University, and William Paterson University—began as normal schools in 1855. Montclair State University (1908), Rowan University (1923), and New Jersey City University (1929) were founded in the first decades of the twentieth century.

In response to the baby boom in the late 1960s and early 1970s, New Jersey created two additional traditional institutions, Ramapo College and Richard Stockton College. Thomas Edison State College, a distance education institution geared toward adult learners, was also formed in response to the growing demand for higher education. The state colleges and universities are strategically located—especially given the state's compact geography and inexpensive and convenient public transportation—to provide baccalaureate and master's degrees to all residents.

In addition to institutional governing boards, the state colleges and universities have a professionally staffed, member-supported organization, the New Jersey Association of State Colleges and Universities, with statutory status as an advocate and advisor to the governor and legislature. Both the CHE and the Presidents' Council include sector organizations in their operations.

Trustees and Executive Leadership

The governing board for each institution determines its own size, between a minimum of seven and a maximum of fifteen. Members are appointed to six year terms by the governor and confirmed by the Senate. The senator representing a nominee's home county may block an appointment. Except for a maximum of three alumni, all must be citizens of the state. Two full-time students, elected by their fellow students, serve two-year terms as an alternate member during the first year and as a voting member during the second. Student trustees cannot participate in (1) employment issues involving any prospective or current officer or employee, (2) transactions of real property with public funds, the setting of banking rates, or the investment of public funds where disclosure could adversely affect the public interest; and (3) pending or anticipated litigation involving the board or attorney-client privilege. Trustees appoint and determine the compensation for their institution's president.

Faculty

Separate statewide bargaining units for full-time and part-time faculty are affiliated with the American Federation of Teachers and negotiate directly with the governor, as their public employer, through the Office of Employee Relations. The nine institutions recommend a single representative, who is then designated by the governor as a member of the negotiating team. Each campus AFT unit is allowed to appoint an observer to committees of its Board of Trustees and to college-wide committees. The union also has the right to speak at all public sessions of the board.

Rules for State Colleges and Universities

PLANNING

Like the public research institutions, the state colleges and universities are authorized to develop an institutional plan, and each institution does so. The nine institutions may also plan jointly through their sector organization. One such venture was College Bound 2008, a project to track enrollment trends and advocate for increasing college capacity in New Jersey. This initiative was shared with the legislature and governor, to the consternation of the CHE executive director at the time, who saw the project as infringing on an area of responsibility statutorily assigned to the CHE.

PROGRAM INITIATIVES

Since 1986, state colleges and universities have had the power to determine their curriculum and authorize new programs. They gained additional independence under the Restructuring Act, which eliminated oversight by a higher education chancellor. Institutions were encouraged to become distinctive. The College of New Jersey and Rowan University seized upon this opportunity in the mid-1990s, partly because their leaders had already committed them to such a course of action. A senior administrator at Rowan noted that before the university developed its engineering program and offered an EdD in Educational Leadership, neither of these options was available in South Jersey, which has 30 percent of the state's population.

Many believe that the state colleges and universities have attracted a new breed of leaders, more independent-minded and entrepreneurial yet still capable of working cooperatively with their colleagues. Sector leaders argue that their institutions want to be distinctive, reflect great diversity, and are committed to avoiding mission creep. Members of the legislature remain skeptical. One legislator suggested that "the state colleges and universities have lost their laser focus and are trying to be all things to all people." At a public hearing in 2005, the chair of the Senate Education Committee attributed rising admission requirements and costs to restructuring, arguing that the average student increasingly had no hope of going to college.

ENROLLMENT PLANNING

Legislators are concerned about affordability. Presidents argue that access and capacity are the real underlying issues. In fall 2005, New Jersey's three public state colleges and six comprehensive state universities enrolled almost 75,000 undergraduates (70% attending full time) and over 14,000 graduate students. The nine institutions conferred about 44 percent of the baccalaureate degrees in the state, more than any other sector. About 96 percent of the undergraduates at the traditional state colleges and universities are New Jersey residents.

In 2001, state colleges and universities proposed increasing the enrollment capacity at four-year public colleges and universities by 15,000 students. Four years later, in the fall of 2005, the institutions did not have the resources to expand, even though the expected wave of baby boom echo applications was upon them. The nine institutions received about 43,600 applications for full-time, freshman status for only about 9,800 freshman slots. The institutions project that the number of applications will approach 50,000 by the year 2009.

INFORMATION

The state colleges and universities must file the same four reports as the public research institutions regarding finances; the amount spent on government relations, public relations, and legal costs; the results of a financial audit; and the condition of the institution, including information about students, faculty, trustees, degree and certificate programs, research, public service, and major capital projects.

The New Jersey Association of State Colleges and Universities also produces an annual report that features accomplishments and highlights; an annual sourcebook, targeted at the legislature and the media, that profiles each institution and describes recent state trends in affordability and access; and information to support the state colleges and universities in policy discussions with the executive and legislative branches.

FISCAL POLICIES

Since 1995, the CHE has suggested that the state pay two-thirds and students pay one-third of the operating costs for public four-year colleges and universities (New Jersey Commission on Higher Education 2005, pp. 27, 28). For nearly twenty years, however, state support has not recognized enrollment growth or new program development, causing the senior public institutions to rely increasingly on tuition and fees. Students are now paying about half of the cost of their institution's educational and general expenses.

The state's approach to funding public four-year colleges and universities involves no formula, and increases are not related to enrollments. One sector organization representative said, "The funding is purely discretionary and administered on the basis of history. There is a process; we start with the base and come up with priority packages. However, this is simply an exercise. The actual increase will be whatever you received historically plus some percentage increase." A staff member in the Office of the Governor confirmed this assessment: "All colleges essentially receive the same percentage increase. Institutions are not currently being rewarded in return for what they are doing or for what they want to do." Funding was actually decreased in three out five fiscal years between 2002 and 2006. By the last fiscal year of this period, the average in-state tuition at the state colleges and universities was $5,745.

Like the public research institutions, the state colleges and universities may spend their resources on their institutional priorities, with little restriction from the state. Under the market-driven system that has been in place since 1994, each institution has adopted goals and objectives to fulfill its distinctive mission, and each institution's trustees and administrators—rather than officials in Trenton—direct where money is spent to achieve that mission.

Without direct state appropriations or available debt service funds, public institutions arrange their own capital funding by pledging student fees for debt service. They are now paying a steep price for relying so heavily on campus-backed bonds for capital construction. Measured by the ratio of debt to revenue, five of the state colleges and universities (the College of New Jersey, Ramapo College, Rowan University, Montclair State University, and New Jersey City University) are among the top fifteen most leveraged public institutions in the country. Of these five, all but NJCU are among the top fifteen most leveraged institutions, public and private, nationally. Two of New Jersey's state colleges and universities have the dubious distinction of leading the nation in different measures of debt. The College of New Jersey, with almost $350 million in total debt, has the highest level among colleges and universities in the country, and Ramapo College has the largest ratio of debt to resources, at 6.5 to 1 (Nelson 2006, pp. 22–26).

Despite these dangerous debt levels, the legislature is reluctant to provide more state capital funds without more oversight. A chair of the Senate Budget and Appropriations Committee told the presidents: "I could give you $5 billion, and you could do whatever you want in your institutions, and it might not open the door for one individual. That is something that we have to put in check, because that is not where we want to go."

County/Community Colleges

New Jersey has as close to an ideal arrangement for community colleges (also known as county colleges) as might be found in any state. The nineteen community colleges serving New Jersey's twenty-one counties bring all residents within reasonable commuting distance of at least one institution. The system was created in 1962, the first four county colleges began operating in 1966, and ten more opened by the end of the 1960s. Three were established during the 1970s, and the last two began in 1982.

New Jersey's county colleges enrolled over 350,000 students in credit, noncredit, and workforce training programs in 2005–6. Of those students, a total of 151,885 were degree-seeking, including 73,931 full-time students and 77,954 part-time students. Nearly 90 percent of county college students attend their home-county colleges. Students who enroll at community colleges outside of their county generally do so when they want to pursue programs not offered at their home campus.

In addition to institutional governing boards, county colleges, like their state college and university counterparts, have a professionally staffed organization with statutory status as an advocate and advisor to the governor. The New Jersey Council of County Colleges (NJCCC) has a number of statewide responsibilities, including submitting a single budget request on behalf of all the county colleges; determining by action of member presidents whether a new academic program developed by a member institution will be forwarded for consideration by the statewide Presidents' Council; and providing training programs for new trustees.

Trustees

Each county college is governed by its own eleven-member board. Two members are appointed by the governor and eight by the county's Board of Freeholders. The county superintendent of schools serves ex officio. County colleges sponsored by more than one county have two additional members who are appointed by the freeholders in each county. Trustees appoint a CEO.

Each county college board of trustees has the authority to determine how the funds it receives will be spent. New Jersey's market-driven approach allows the county colleges to achieve their missions and priorities with little oversight from the state or their home counties. Like their senior public colleagues, the county colleges are subject to an independent financial audit, which is considered a public document.

Faculty

All of New Jersey's community colleges are involved in some form of collective bargaining. The NJEA has local bargaining units representing the faculty at all but three of the county colleges. In addition to representing local units in contract negotiations, the NJEA has successfully lobbied for statutory changes benefiting the county colleges' workforce. For example, in January 2006, the governor signed an NJEA initiative requiring the boards of trustees of the county colleges to provide nonacademic support staff with adequate notice before laying them off.

Rules for County Colleges

PLANNING

The major document shaping recent planning in county colleges is the New Jersey Community College Compact, established by former governor McGreevey in 2003. Under the compact, the New Jersey Council of County Colleges identified ways in which the county colleges would support statewide education initiatives administered by the Department of Education and statewide workforce development programs administered by the Department of Labor and Workforce Development. The Department of Education's ventures included teacher education programs to address projected teacher shortages in the state, the "twelfth-grade option program" for high school students to enroll in county college courses, and career academies throughout the state. The Department of Labor's undertakings included customized training programs through the Workforce Development Partnership Program, workforce literacy programs, and the Self Employment Assistance Program.

PROGRAM INITIATIVES

Two initiatives are already underway as a result of the Community College Compact. The New Pathways to Teaching in New Jersey program, started in 2002, provides professionals changing careers with an alternate route to earning a teacher's certificate. These students start at a county college and complete the certification process with the Department of Education. The county colleges have also partnered with the Department of Labor and Workforce Development and union leaders to develop New Jersey Pathways Leading Apprentices to a College Education, which awards college credits for registered apprenticeships in the building and construction trades.

The Restructuring Act confirmed the authority of county college boards of trustees to determine an educational curriculum and college programs consistent with their institution's mission or approved by the CHE. Community colleges now offer more than 450 programs leading to Associate in Arts (AA), Associate in Science (AS), or Associate in Applied Science (AAS) degrees. According to a 2005 report by the NJCCC, business and health professions account for about one-quarter and one-fifth, respectively, of all community college graduates. County colleges also offer more than 300 certificate programs. These programs expanded rapidly after restructuring, because there was no requirement for Presidents' Council and CHE approval. This change helped community colleges move quickly on programs related to industry.

Like their colleagues in state colleges and universities, county college officials believe that restructuring has contributed to collaboration but not to mission creep. One example they cite is Brookdale's Coastal Communiversity, an alliance of two county colleges and six baccalaureate-granting institutions to offer selected degree programs in Monmouth County. Another is the Ocean County College / Kean University Alliance which enables Ocean County College (OCC) students who complete their associate's degree to obtain a Kean University bachelor's degree through courses offered on the OCC campus in such fields as criminal justice, elementary education, history, nursing, and sociology. Kean also offers master's degrees at OCC.

Not all collaborations have succeeded. Burlington County College had an arrangement with NJIT to offer programs in engineering, but NJIT eventually pulled out. Burlington's president approached several other New Jersey institutions but did not find a new partner. He eventually arranged thirteen degree-completion programs with Drexel University in Philadelphia, and this arrangement with an out-of-state university was approved by the Presidents' Council and CHE.

ENROLLMENT PLANNING

The county colleges describe themselves as the fastest growing and by far the largest provider of higher education in New Jersey. Because this growth is uneven across the state, each institution has devised its own enrollment plan to address its home county's needs and the priorities for new campus facilities.

Remediation policies differ from institution to institution. Each college decides which students need to be tested, when they are tested, the testing instruments used, and the scores for placement in remediation. As a result, it is difficult to compare remediation data across institutions, and the CHE does not aggregate this information. At the other end of the enrollment spectrum, New Jersey's county colleges can offer NJ STARS scholarships to students who graduate in the top 20 percent of their high school class. In fall 2004—

the first year of the NJ STARS program—1,157 freshmen participated, and 753 of them continued into their sophomore year. A new class of 1,731 NJ STARS freshmen started in fall 2005 (Farbman 2005).

Almost all colleges and universities in New Jersey participate in a state-wide articulation and transfer system that was developed to allow students to determine which courses will transfer for credit and to enable colleges to review transcripts electronically. Community colleges continue to complain about the participation of some senior institutions. Moreover, the two- and four-year public sectors are debating the transfer of county college credits in teaching programs. The legislature wants the issue resolved quickly to help New Jersey's low-income school districts get more teachers for preschool through grade 3, and it has threatened a statutory solution. Friction in the area of teacher education—and in transfer and articulation overall—is viewed by some policy leaders as evidence that the early sense of collaboration under restructuring has eroded and that the market-based structure of the state's higher education system may need to be constrained.

INFORMATION

The county colleges, like other public colleges and universities in New Jersey, must file reports on finances; the amount spent on government relations, public relations, and legal costs; the results of a financial audit; and the condition of the institution, including information about students, faculty, trustees, degree and certificate programs, research and public service, and major capital projects. The NJCCC coordinates government relations at the state level by providing testimony and other information to lawmakers and to the governor's staff. The organization also supports trustees by providing newsletters, directories, and legislative analysis. A County College Association for Institutional Research and Planning works with the NJCCC to collect data and present it to the CHE, the Department of the Treasury, and other state agencies.

FISCAL POLICIES

The NJCCC submits an annual budget request to the state treasurer for support for the county colleges, based on a formula that provides foundation funding for each institution plus allocations based on full-time-equivalent student enrollments. Under New Jersey law, the state is supposed to provide between 43 and 50 percent of the operating costs for these institutions. Each county has a Board of School Estimate (typically three freeholders and two trustees) that determines the overall budget for its community college after holding a public hearing. The freeholder board then collects and appropriates the necessary amount in the same manner it uses for other county purposes.

When former governor Whitman restructured higher education in 1994, she made a commitment of $12 million a year in new funds to county colleges, in exchange for limited tuition increases. Between 1995 and 2005, the average annual tuition increase was 2.8 percent. The average tuition for full-time, in-county students in 2005–6 was $2,325. State support, however, has never met its statutory level of funding, and there is often little predictability regarding increased support from one year to the next. County support varies widely across the state, with some paying more than one-third of their institution's operating expenses and others providing significantly less (Mann and Forsberg 2006, p. 22). State higher education officials have recently focused on getting county, student, and state levels to one-third each (New Jersey Commission on Higher Education 2005, p. 30). By 2005, because of state funding levels and significant enrollment growth, the state provided 28 percent of county college costs, counties provided 28 percent, and students paid 44 percent through tuition (New Jersey Council of County Colleges 2005, p. 9).

In addition to periodic state bond programs, New Jersey's county colleges have access to a debt-financed revolving fund for construction and maintenance, with debt service shared equally by the state and the county. The NJCCC recommends new construction and renovation projects to the state treasurer according to institutional priorities, but it does not undertake comprehensive planning for the sector. Upon the treasurer's approval, counties issue the bonds and the state then reimburses the counties for half of the annual debt service on the bonds.

Between 1995 and 2005, about $500 million was allocated for capital projects at the county colleges. In 2004, the legislature raised the ceiling on the total principal amount of the fund from $165 million to $265 million, an increase designed to help the county colleges expand their capacity to address growing enrollment.

For the most part, public higher education in New Jersey is a state-planned creation dating from the last half of the twentieth century. Beginning with the acquisition of previously private Rutgers University in the mid-1950s, the state developed a public system of research universities, comprehensive four-year colleges and universities, and community colleges, either by founding new institutions or converting and expanding pre-existing ones. Among the new institutions was a college-without-walls serving a statewide mission. Most of this development was guided by the firm hand of a strong Board of Higher

Education, led by a chancellor who also served as a member of the governor's cabinet. Independent institutions function as full partners in providing state higher education services.

In 1985 and again in 1994, legislation deregulated public higher education, shifting the center of influence from a strong coordinating board in Trenton to individual governing boards and presidents. To ensure coordination and encourage voluntary collaboration across sectors, the 1994 Restructuring Act created a Presidents' Council that brought together the CEOs from all institutions of higher education and required close collaboration with the Commission on Higher Education, the successor to the Board of Higher Education.

The weakened regulatory link between higher education and state government, along with the rules created by the managed market approach, have been a concern for some legislators and for independent institutions. Public colleges and universities, while enjoying increased autonomy, remain—in the minds of those who manage them and the elected leaders who fund them— attentive to state goals and priorities. The state is heavily involved in benchmarking, a process used to track system performance by comparing national and state indicators. Public institutions publish annual accountability reports. The CHE prescribes the format for these reports and publishes its own accountability report for the system.

More than two decades ago, New Jersey decoupled operating support for its public comprehensive and research universities from their student enrollments. There is no funding formula, and increases are usually determined by applying a percentage to what each institution received the previous year. Independent institutions also receive state operating dollars. Individual governing boards determine tuition levels in all four sectors, an arrangement that has allowed public colleges and universities to compete with private institutions for a larger share of student aid funding. Between 1994 and 2002, no state agency intervened in the authority of any board to set tuition. Since then, there have been annual constraints to prevent institutions from raising tuitions by more than specified amounts. There are also fairly widespread concerns that the absence of an incentive for increasing enrollments has caused some of the four-year state colleges and universities to be less sensitive to the need for additional student spaces and less responsive to students transferring from community colleges than would be optimal for the state. Deregulation and reliance on market principles to reduce state costs have been accompanied by state budget cuts and very high debt levels for many of the state's public institutions.

CHAPTER EIGHT

New Ways of Thinking about Policy and Performance

�֍

This chapter compares rules with performance and state effort across all five case study states. Here we explain the analytical procedures we used to identify influential rules that apply in all of these states, as well as report the rules that contribute to either high or low performance for the preparation, participation, and completion indicators. We then examine state effort in relation to the rules. The first two sections therefore present the results of our analysis. The third section offers a broad, comprehensive look at the combination of rules and effort that most influence performance. We also summarize the lessons learned over the course of our study by advancing a series of propositions about the relationships between rules and performance. Finally, we suggest how rules can be changed to use policy as a lever to pursue public priorities.

RELATING RULES TO PERFORMANCE

The conceptual framework from chapter 1 proposes that rules influence performance. Chapter 2 provides the major categories and subcategories of rules and the performance indicators of preparation, participation, and completion for New Mexico, California, South Dakota, New York, and New Jersey. The case studies in chapters 3–7 detail the actors and structures for each state and document examples of how rules play out in such action situations as planning, budgeting, and program development. In this final chapter, we identify which of the 58 rules (abstracted from the case studies and validated through meetings with policy leaders in each state) systematically differentiate high and low performance.

For the analysis, we used a variation of the matrix approach suggested by

Miles and Huberman (1994) to examine each of the 58 rules in relation to each of the 15 indicators of performance for preparation, participation, and completion. Relationships between rules and performance could be positive, negative, or nonexistent. A *positive* relationship was one where the rule was present in the two states ranking above the median on a specific indicator and absent in the two states ranking below the median. A *negative* relationship was one where the rule was absent in the two states ranking above the median and present in the two states ranking below the median. All other combinations were treated as the *absence* of a relationship. In this way, a rule explains either high or low performance, but never both. This method represents the most logical and restrictive approach in sorting out relationships and interpreting results. We now report linkages using the rule categories described in chapter 2.

System Design Rules

The rules associated with three of the five subthemes of system design influence performance. Coordinating boards and use of the private sector are generally positive influences on performance, while the presence of self-governing public institutions (those without statewide governance or coordination) is generally linked to lower performance on undergraduate indicators. The influence of these differing design options is reversed for enrollments of adults who are twenty-five and older, with coordinating boards and the private sectors performing less well than self-governing institutions. The design and governance rules and the performance indicators to which they are linked are shown in table 8.1.

State Leadership Rules

Three subthemes within the state leadership rules relate to differences in the performance of the case study states. The presence of state-defined goals, priorities, and accountability arrangements and the use of steering and market forces have a positive influence on most undergraduate indicators, while the use of incentives negatively corresponds to performance. Again, opposite effects occur for the enrollment of older adults. The state leadership rules and the performance indicators to which they are linked are shown in table 8.2.

Access and Achievement Rules

Five subthemes within the access and achievement rules affected performance in the case study states. Need-based student aid, a program for improving access for disadvantaged students, and measuring learning outcomes positively influence almost all associated performance indicators. Convening actors across the K–12 and higher education sectors and high-stakes high school graduation exams generally correspond to lower performance, but their effects are limited primarily to selected preparation and participation categories. The access and achievement rules and the performance indicators to which they are linked are shown in tables 8.3 and 8.4.

Fiscal Policies

Three subthemes within the fiscal policy rules are tied to differences in the performance of the case study states. State funding for private institutions positively influences a number of performance indicators, except enrollment for the twenty-five-and-older population. Enrollment funding and the extensive use of community colleges negatively correspond with completion indicators. The fiscal policy rules and the performance indicators to which they link are shown in tables 8.5.

Research and Development and Information

Two of the rule categories defined in chapter 2 did not emerge as significant predictors of performance among the five case study states: research and development and information. The indicators in our study primarily focus on undergraduate performance, and that may well explain why research and development rules yield no association with performance. The absence of any relationship between information rules and performance was somewhat surprising. We expected to find that higher-performing states would possess useful information systems and reports, since information is usually described in higher education literature as an important component in formulating policy priorities and in tracking progress in meeting them. Such data is also usually regarded as essential in establishing accountability. Our results may well be one of the artifacts of our choice of states and the relative development of their information-gathering and -reporting capabilities at the time of our study. Higher-performing New Jersey and lower-performing New

TABLE 8.1
System Design Rules and Performance

	Rules				
	Statewide coordination		Self-governing	Private sector	
Performance	Regulatory authority	Program approval	Individual boards	Independents have formal role	19% or more independent enrollment
High school completion	+	+		+	+
K–12 achievement*	+ (4)**	+ (4)	– (4)	+ (4)	+ (4)
Chance for college	+	+		+	+
Low-income participation				+	+
18–24 enrollment					
25–49 enrollment	–	–		–	–
2-yr. retention	+	+		+	+
4-yr. retention					
3-yr. graduation					+
6-yr. graduation				+	
Bachelor's per 100 undergraduates	+	+	–		
2-yr. credentials	+	+	–		

* K–12 achievement indicators include: 8th graders scoring at or above "proficient" on the national assessment exam in math; low-income 8th graders scoring at or above "proficient" on the national assessment exam in math; 8th graders scoring at or above "proficient" on the national assessment exam in reading; and 7th to 12th graders taught by teachers with a major in their subject.

** The number in parentheses indicates the number of K–12 achievement indicators that were positively or negatively related to the rule.

Mexico possessed the two most comprehensive data systems among our five states. The case studies indicate that New Jersey generated information that was employed at state and institutional levels. Although data exists in New Mexico, it was not used in a manner that informed decision making or consistently tracked performance for improvement purposes. Higher-performing New York and lower-performing California also had comparable information systems that were strong at the segmental levels, but weak at the state level. South Dakota was somewhere in the middle, with strong system coordination of a database largely compiled and maintained at the institutional level. Interestingly, by the end of our study both New York and California had made sig-

TABLE 8.2
State Leadership

	Rules				
	Defined goals and priorities			Use of market forces	Incentives
Performance	Goals explicitly identified	Executive policy agenda	Leaders work together on priorities	Use market forces intentionally	Incentives to pay attention to goals
High school completion	+	+	+	+	
K–12 achievement*	+ (4)**	+ (4)	− (4)	+ (4)	
Chance for college	+	+	+	+	
Low-income participation	+	+	+		
18–24 enrollment					−
25–49 enrollment	−	−	−	−	
2-yr. retention	+	+	+		
4-yr. retention					
3-yr. graduation					
6-yr. graduation	+	+	+		−
Bachelor's per 100 undergraduates	+	+	+	+	
2-yr. credentials	+	+	+	+	

* K–12 achievement indicators include: 8th graders scoring at or above "proficient" on the national assessment exam in math; low-income 8th graders scoring at or above "proficient" on the national assessment exam in math; 8th graders scoring at or above "proficient" on the national assessment exam in reading; and 7th to 12th graders taught by teachers with a major in their subject.
** The number in parentheses indicates the number of K–12 achievement indicators that were positively or negatively related to the rule.

nificant progress toward developing student unit information systems at the statewide level. We are left with the conclusion that states increasingly view comprehensive statewide data systems as essential, but that such systems did not emerge as a distinguishing variable in our study.

The connection between rules and performance that this analysis produced also makes it clear that only 23 rules have links to performance (either high or low) for the five case study states and that not all of the rules assigned to a subtheme were influential. In addition, some of the rules that did emerge impacted differentially on indicators within a performance subcategory. For

TABLE 8.3
Access and Achievement

| | Rules | | | |
| | Need-based aid | | | State-coordinated access programs |
Performance	State grants provide tuition	State grants can be used at private IHEs	Aid for non-traditional students	Program for disad-vantaged residents
High school completion	+	+	+	+
K–12 achievement*	+ (4)**	+ (4)	+ (4)	+ (1)
Chance for college				
Low-income participation				+
18–24 enrollment	+	+	+	
25–49 enrollment				−
2-yr. retention	+	+	+	+
4-yr. retention				
3-yr. graduation				
6-yr. graduation	+	+	+	+
Bachelor's per 100 undergraduates	+	+	+	
2-yr. credentials	+	+	+	

* K–12 achievement indicators include: 8th graders scoring at or above "proficient" on the national assessment exam in math; low-income 8th graders scoring at or above "proficient" on the national assessment exam in math; 8th graders scoring at or above "proficient" on the national assessment exam in reading; and 7th to 12th graders taught by teachers with a major in their subject.
** The number in parentheses indicates the number of K–12 achievement indicators that were positively or negatively related to the rule.

example, rules that help to explain baccalaureate completion rates for tradi-tionally aged students do not influence completion rates for community col-lege students, many of whom fall into the older age bracket. And states which emphasize rules to increase participation and completion rates for younger students may actually experience lower performance with their adult, part-time populations.

STATE EFFORT AND PERFORMANCE

We examined the relationships between rules and state effort—as measured by appropriations either per $1,000 of personal income or per capita—to ex-

TABLE 8.4
Access and Achievement

| | Rules | | |
| | Measured learning | Convening K–12 sectors | High school graduation exam |
Performance	Some standardized methods for measuring learning	Formal arrangements for convening actors	Individual boards
High school completion			–
K–12 achievement*	+ (1)**	– (1)	– (2)
Chance for college			–
Low-income participation		–	
18–24 enrollment			
25–49 enrollment		+	
2-yr. retention		–	
4-yr. retention			
3-yr. graduation			
6-yr. graduation		–	
Bachelor's per 100 undergraduates	+		
2-yr. credentials	+		

* K–12 achievement indicators include: 8th graders scoring at or above "proficient" on the national assessment exam in math; low-income 8th graders scoring at or above "proficient" on the national assessment exam in math; 8th graders scoring at or above "proficient" on the national assessment exam in reading; and 7th to 12th graders taught by teachers with a major in their subject.
** The number in parentheses indicates the number of K–12 achievement indicators that were positively or negatively related to the rule.

plore the question of whether the performance outcomes we observed could be attributed to the level of state investment. We used a similar approach to the one previously described for linking rules and performance. For the effort analysis, we used only the 23 rules identified earlier as being positively or negatively linked to performance. The relationship between rules and effort was characterized as *high* where rules from that subtheme were present in both of the states ranking above the median on effort and absent in both of the states ranking below the median. We classified the relationship as *low* if the rules from that subtheme were present in both of the states ranking below the median on effort and absent in both states ranking above the median. Table 8.6 reports subthemes linked to performance, where one or more rules within a subtheme were associated with either high or low state effort. As in

TABLE 8.5
Fiscal Policies

	Rules				
	Support for private colleges		Enrollment-based	Use of low-tuition 2-year colleges	
Performance	Receive operating support	Receive capital project support***	Operating support for 4-yr. colleges based on enrollments	2-yr. colleges submit requests directly	2-yr. tuition less than half that of 4-yr.
High school completion	+	+	–		
K–12 achievement*	+ (4)**	+ (4)	– (4)	– (1)	– (1)
Chance for college	+	+	–		
Low-income participation	+	+			
18–24 enrollment					
25–49 enrollment	–	–	+		
2-yr. retention	+	+	–		
4-yr. retention					
3-yr. graduation					
6-yr. graduation	+	+			
Bachelor's per 100 undergraduates	+	+	–	–	–
2-yr. credentials	+	+	–	–	–

* K–12 achievement indicators include: 8th graders scoring at or above "proficient" on the national assessment exam in math; low-income 8th graders scoring at or above "proficient" on the national assessment exam in math; 8th graders scoring at or above "proficient" on the national assessment exam in reading; and 7th to 12th graders taught by teachers with a major in their subject.
** The number in parentheses indicates the number of K–12 achievement indicators that were positively or negatively related to the rule.
*** Included in this column is the rule "private universities are eligible to receive state funds for research facilities," although it is not listed separately on the table.

our previous analysis, there were no subthemes in which one rule was linked with high effort while another rule within the same subtheme was tied to low effort.

Eight of the subthemes in table 8.6 associated with lower state effort include one or more rules that also corresponded to higher performance on preparation, participation, or completion indicators. States that achieved higher performance in our study with lower state effort had the following rules:

TABLE 8.6

Rules Associated with Higher or Lower State Appropriations per $1,000 in Personal Income or Per Capita

Rules	State Effort
System Design	
Statewide coordination and regulation	Low
Self-governing public IHEs	High
Use of the private sector	Low
State Leadership	
Defined goals and priorities	Low
Use of steering and market forces	Low
Access and Achievement	
Need-based student aid	Low
State-coordinated access programs	Low
Measuring learning outcomes	Low
Fiscal	
State fiscal support for private colleges	Low
Enrollment-based state appropriations	High
Extensive use of low-tuition two-year colleges	High

- an agency of the state has regulatory authority for all public higher education, including—at a minimum—the authority to approve or reject new academic programs when a change in institutional mission could be a concern
- a significant private sector has a defined role in state planning to meet higher education needs
- elected officials and educational leaders work together to craft a policy agenda for higher education in a process where state goals are explicitly identified and periodically reviewed
- the state uses market forces as an intentional strategy to encourage responsiveness and efficiency
- state grants that are based on need and designed to cover most, if not all, tuition in the public sector are awarded to students attending both public and private institutions
- the state has coordinated programs for improving access to higher education for residents who are facing economic or educational disadvantages
- the state uses standardized methods for measuring learning outcomes in at least some subjects
- private institutions receive both operating and capital appropriations from the state

All three of the subthemes in table 8.6 linked with higher state effort included at least one rule associated with lower performance on several performance indicators. States with lower performance despite higher effort have the following rules:

- each public institution has its own governing board which operates without significant state oversight
- operating appropriations for four-year public institutions are based primarily on enrollments
- tuition and fees for two-year colleges are less than half those for the lowest-cost four-year institution

COMBINATION OF RULES AND STATE EFFORT ON PERFORMANCE

No single rule accounts for the total result for any one performance indicator. Our results suggest that the influence of rules, across categories, combines with state effort to exert a cumulative and interacting dynamic on performance. The analysis is informed, however, by examining each category of rules in tandem with state effort to create reasonable insights into the rules-and-performance connection. In this section, we more directly draw on the case study results to show how the system design, state leadership, access and achievement, and fiscal policy rules shown in table 8.6 combine with state effort and influence performance.

System Design and Performance

States need a coordinating entity with appropriate authority to set reasonable boundaries within which universities with their own governing boards are encouraged to balance institutional or segmental priorities against those of other stakeholders. States also need excellent public and private institutions, including research universities, comprehensive colleges and universities, and community colleges and technical institutes. The tension between the preferences of committed professionals serving within a particular type of institution and the needs and priorities of a broader range of stakeholders has been documented in an extensive set of literature stretching back for more than forty years (see, for example, Glenny, Lyman, Dalglish 1973; Millett 1984; Schick et al. 1992; and MacTaggert 1998). For a state to achieve sustained performance on a range of indicators over time, institutions must work together as a system as well as pursue individual excellence. There is considerable evidence that often-competing requirements are best balanced when the mix of higher education actors includes advocates for the public interest. States with a higher rating on the undergraduate performance indicators used in our study had a state-level entity with the authority to require institutions to address statewide goals and priorities and work together to coordinate programs and services.

The inclusion of private institutions as an integral part of system design for meeting state higher education needs has a positive relationship to both effort and performance. State effort for the five study states was inversely related to the size of their private sectors and the extent to which the rules integrated that sector as part of a strategy for meeting state higher education needs. New York and New Jersey have the largest proportion of students enrolled in the private sector, while California and New Mexico have the lowest. New York and New Jersey also fully integrate their private institutions into their state planning. Using private colleges and universities to help meet overall higher education needs achieves better performance with less state effort, particularly when states also intentionally use market forces to encourage responsiveness and efficiency. Among the five case study states and in the larger national arena, state coordinating boards have a better track record for integrating public and private higher education than unified governing boards do, in part because the latter have an institutional advocacy role while the former are structured to advocate the public interest.

The relationship between system design rules and performance did indicate a tradeoff between rules and performance for traditional-age college students versus students twenty-five and older. System design rules related to coordination and use of the private sector enhanced participation and completion indicators for younger college students but negatively influenced indicators for older students.

The tradeoffs inherent in the choices states make also surfaced as tensions between undergraduate and graduate education in some of the case studies. Constitutionally autonomous research universities operating without effective state oversight—as in New Mexico and California—achieve gains in research, but require more state effort and record lower performance on a number of indicators of undergraduate performance. One of the reasons for this relationship is evident in the data comparing research expenditures in public universities (Kelly and Jones 2005) with effort and performance infor-

TABLE 8.7

A Comparison of Effort, Performance, and Research Expenditures

	California	New Jersey	New Mexico	New York	South Dakota	National Median
Effort per $1,000 personal income	7.30	5.26	13.42	5.54	7.16	6.89
Bachelor's degrees awarded per 100 undergraduates	6.1	9.7	6.6	11.9	10.5	10.0
Research expenditures per full-time faculty ($)	195,107	119,094	103,703	70,541	39,942	74,774

Sources: Effort and Bachelor's degrees: National Information Center for Higher Education Policymaking and Analysis 2002;
Research expenditures: Kelly and Jones 2005.

mation from our study. Table 8.7 compares effort, bachelor's degrees awarded per 100 undergraduates, and research expenditures in public research universities per full-time faculty member. States that place a high priority on maintaining distinguished public research universities tend to spend more on such institutions than states where undergraduate education receives equal or greater emphasis, and these expenditures show up in the effort column. Indeed, states make choices about preferred goals along an entire range of possible outcomes, or these choices are made by default through the political process in states where agencies that represent the public interest are weak or nonexistent.

State-level coordination is much stronger in New York, New Jersey, and South Dakota, and these states generally experience higher performance on undergraduate indicators with less state effort. However, New York's spending on research in its public universities is also low for an industrial state with significant dependence on research for economic competitiveness. Significantly, a recent preliminary report by a commission appointed by former governor Spitzer concludes that New York's national research standings have suffered because public research universities have been underfunded (New York State Commission on Higher Education 2007). Three of the remaining states (California, New Jersey, and South Dakota) seem to achieve a reasonable balance between effort and research expenditures. California, which has the weakest coordinating arrangements among this set of three states and spends considerably more than any of the other four states, does least well on this indicator of baccalaureate completion. New Mexico is the significant outlier, requiring much higher effort to sustain its research expenditures and experiencing generally low performance on undergraduate indicators.

The case study states with autonomous research universities operating in the absence of effective state coordination (California and New Mexico) tend to pursue research prominence as a priority. Those same states also spend the most tax dollars on their higher education systems and perform less well on undergraduate indicators. Where the division of state resources is left primarily to the political process, undergraduate education seems likely to be short-changed, simply because research universities are typically more influential with legislators and governors. There appears to be no simple solution for simultaneously achieving excellence in both research and undergraduate education. States may focus their efforts on research, but only California is an undisputed model of research excellence among our study states. New Mexico is clearly allocating a sizeable amount of funds toward research prominence, yet states such as New Jersey appear to invest lower amounts for better results in undergraduate education and at least equal if not better results in research. What is clear from the system design rules is that coordination and the use of the private sector increases efficiency in the entire state system and improves undergraduate performance.

State Leadership and Performance

In the higher-performing states, a particular entity organized a process to convene policymakers and higher education leaders to define and review priorities. That entity was often a higher education agency, even though its form differed across states. The commonality was that state-level policy leaders were actively engaged in identifying goals and setting priorities, and they possessed the authority for adopting rules or processes that influenced institutions to consider these items and adopt strategic responses to them. New Jersey has well-defined priorities for its higher education system, which are translated into the actions needed from colleges and universities by the efforts of the New Jersey Commission on Higher Education and the Council of Presidents. While goals and priorities are spelled out in a state planning document, each institution chooses its own strategies for response. New York defines priorities at the level of its two large, geographically distinct, comprehensive public systems. Such an arrangement seems dictated by an opaque political process and the profound differences between the needs of the populations served by the City University of New York and the State University of New York. Concurrently, however, a strong coordinating board oversees a planning process that helps to ensure that the plans developed by public and private institutions respond to state priorities and that changes in programs and related policies are consistent with approved institutional plans. In South Dakota, elected political leaders and higher education representatives sit around a common table to decide joint goals and priorities. They are significantly helped in this process by the state's small size.

In California, there is some sense that the goals of the University of California segment were the de facto goals of the state. The California State University segment gets generally better marks for including state concerns and priorities in its planning processes, but there is little communication across segments. The governor does what he can to influence the priorities of these two four-year segments through one-on-one negotiations focused on the annual budget. Few expect consistent behavior from the districts for the highly independent California Community Colleges, even though the state's Board of Governors (essentially a coordinating board for community colleges) does what it can to encourage institutional attention to state concerns. In New Mexico, state higher education goals have been the sum of whatever the institutions decide to provide, as long as it includes plenty of access. Dissatisfaction with the ability of a weak coordinating board to achieve better outcomes was one of the factors leading to New Mexico's decision to disband its board in favor of a secretary of higher education serving as a member of the governor's staff.

In addition to having statewide agencies with the regulatory authority to plan, set priorities, and encourage institutions to respond, higher-performing states make use of market forces to steer institutions toward actions consistent with state priorities. During our study, New Jersey made the strongest intentional effort to use market forces, allowing each four-year institution to establish its own tuition charges and severing linkages between state appropriations and enrollments. The New Jersey experience was, however, not entirely reassuring for market advocates. The state addressed the response of many four-year institutions to limit enrollments by subsidizing community colleges to keep tuition increases in check. By the end of our study, New Jersey had also decided to place caps on the allowable increases. In addition, the state achieved the distinction of having some of the most heavily indebted public colleges in the nation. New York, like New Jersey, has decoupled state appropriations for four-year institutions from enrollments and has deregulated many aspects of public institutional activities. However, the state has never relaxed its firm control over tuition, nor has it made any explicit commitment to a market model. Both New York and New Jersey have policies that integrate public and private institutions in meeting state priorities, an arrangement that helps to encourage competition.

The unified Board of Regents in South Dakota works with state policymakers to provide explicit policy priorities for its institutions, but it has increasingly limited competition between those institutions as it urges each to differentiate its mission from the others. The California Master Plan was designed to lessen the degree to which the public segments vie against each other by specifying missions and enrollment pools. However, the plan also reduces attention to statewide issues and the probability of collaboration across the segments. Overall, California lacks authoritative mechanisms for regulating or steering the entire system. We have already noted that during our study, New Mexico had no statewide goals and priorities for higher education beyond that of access, and the state displayed no evidence of using market forces to influence the behaviors of institutional actors.

Access and Achievement and Performance

States use need-based student aid, state-coordinated access programs, and the measurement of at least some learning outcomes to achieve higher performance with lower effort. New York treated its largest-in-the-country, need-based student aid program as an entitlement, coordinating tuition increases with changes in maximum grants so that students with scant resources received state grants equal to the tuition at public institutions. Students attending private institutions are also eligible for grants equal in dollar amount to those with similar needs attending public institutions. The state handles its large federal GEAR UP program through its student aid agency, while the statewide coordinating board has responsibility for most other access programs, although the two agencies work closely together. New York has also been a national leader in the measurement of learning outcomes. New Jersey offers extensive need-based student aid but, unlike New York, it does not commit to meeting the needs of all of the state's eligible students. A special equal opportunity fund, with its own governing board, operates under the general oversight of the New Jersey Commission on Higher Education to manage the state's special access programs in both public and private institutions. California also provides extensive need-based assistance to students at both public and private institutions but, like New Jersey, does not appropriate enough funds to meet the needs of all eligible students. Access programs in California are coordinated in some instances by segmental offices, in others by individual institutions. This state's GEAR UP program was coordinated by a voluntary agency established specifically for that purpose.

Although merit-based programs were not associated with enhanced performance on preparation, participation, or completion, two of the case study states use merit aid as a policy tool. South Dakota's merit-based student assistance program is of recent origin. Even though they are eligible, tribal colleges do not participate, in part because few of their students would meet the test score requirements. Access programs are the responsibility of the individual institutions. New Mexico's profile is very much like South Dakota's, with one important difference. While merit aid is the dominant form in both states, New Mexico distributes proportionately almost as much student aid as New Jersey. Also like South Dakota, access programs in New Mexico are institution-based.

Fiscal Policy and Performance

Fiscal policies also distinguish higher-performing, lower-effort states from their counterparts. Lower-performing, higher-effort New Mexico and California place the most emphasis on enrollments when funding four-year institutions. The other three case study states decouple state appropriations from enrollments for public four-year institutions. New Jersey and New York provide operating funds to private institutions based on the number of state residents they either enroll or graduate. California and New Mexico both enroll more students at very low-cost community colleges than at public four-year institutions, with the ratio in California in particular being more than two to one. South Dakota really does not have any comprehensive community colleges, and New Jersey and New York enroll significantly fewer students in community colleges, where tuitions are more than double those charged in California and New Mexico.

Intersection between State and Federal Rules

Federal rules interact with state rules as part of the overall equation. Rules that create a level playing field for public and private higher education sectors, combined with need-based federal student aid, help to create environments that are well designed for steering strategies that use market forces. More recent federal access programs like GEAR UP have requirements for collaboration across segments and sectors, affording a clear advantage to states such as New Jersey, New York, and South Dakota that have effective interface agencies already in place to guide this type of project. In contrast, New Mexico and California must rely on some combination of institutional, segmental, or voluntary agencies to provide the necessary leadership and coordination.

The most influential federal rules may well be those that guide the distribution of competitive grants and contracts for research. New Mexico, with its relatively small population and two major research universities, as well as California, with its incomparable University of California system, spend large amounts of state funds on infrastructure and attracting star researchers. In order to afford this investment, both states make extensive use of low-tuition community colleges that, according to most accounts, are underfunded for the tasks they are asked to assume. Not surprisingly, states that focus their efforts on research enterprises also perform least well on the undergraduate indicators.

Finally, federal rules on reporting and dissemination significantly reduce the discrepancies across states in terms of the information available to policymakers. Despite the limitations on data available from the Board of Regents in New York, state policymakers in the governor's office routinely relied on federal data and the *Chronicle of Higher Education* (which also uses federal databases) to check the information they received from institutions.

State Ability to Change Rules

A state's ability to change rules in areas that influence institutional behaviors is essential to achieving performance consistent with effort and priorities. States that do not define priorities or structure their systems to maximize collaboration and integrate market parameters have a limited capacity to influence institutional responsiveness to changing public needs. Of course, public priorities and professional values are not always at odds, nor is it valid to assume that segmental or institutional governing boards ignore the public interest. On the basis of the five case study states, however, the public interest and professional values do conflict on important issues, and systems with less ability to change rules will require more state effort and show lower performance on the indicators used in our study.

New Jersey demonstrated the greatest capacity to change rules to align with priorities and to structure its system to maximize collaboration and integrate market parameters. New Jersey also altered its system design, replacing a very powerful Department of Higher Education with a much weaker commission and a statutory President's Council. Even with this change, the state still maintained state-level entities with the responsibility to structure and steer the system while working toward defined state priorities. South Dakota, through its consolidated governing board, was able to implement priorities, accountability measures, and collaboration for all four-year colleges and universities, but the state lacked the ability to coordinate rule changes for the four-year sector with those for technical institutes. New York established statewide priorities, but left accountability and collaboration for public higher education to the oversight of its two segmental governing boards. Priorities, accountability, and collaboration in California were almost exclusively segmental concerns, although voluntary councils—augmented by a statewide coordinating council—provided for some collaboration on issues that served mutual institutional interests. In New Mexico, decisions about system behaviors were made almost entirely at the institutional level. Dissatisfaction with this arrangement contributed in part to the decision to replace a coordinating board with a secretary of education who is directly responsible to the governor. This is only the latest in a series of changes aimed at strengthening the state's capacity to influence the actions of its higher education system. In the past, changes in the definition of the central agency's authority were accompanied by changes in the behaviors of legislators and institutional representatives who, in each instance, continued to find ways to undermine and circumvent the agency's effectiveness. The jury is still out on whether the latest change will alter the informal norms for conducting higher education business in New Mexico.

Rules changed, to some degree, in all of the states during the course of our study. The most important difference, from our perspective, involves where the rule changes were determined and the degree to which the interest of the entire range of public stakeholders was represented in this process. Statewide rule changes in New Jersey, New York and South Dakota clearly altered the behaviors and leadership of higher education professionals. Aided by the absence of constitutional constraints and favorable system designs, elected officials seemed able to achieve a reasonable balance between the preferences and values of higher education professionals and those of other stakeholders. By contrast, rule changes in California and New Mexico occurred at the segmental or institutional level, with little apparent influence from elected state officials other than through the budget process.

In chapter 1, we proposed that state higher education performance is the outcome of efforts by institutional actors who seek to achieve preferred goals within a playing field that is defined by rules. Rules arise from state and federal constitutions, statutes, court decisions, agency regulations, and budget appropriations. These rules also emerge from the norms of informal practices over time by those who are involved in the game. Rules are in a constant state of dynamic tension as the shifting interests of coalition groups seek changes that advance their values and preferences. Some rules are easier to change than others. It may also not be feasible to implement various rules because of the way a system is designed. In such instances, changing the system may be an important first step toward improving performance. It is the responsibility of state government to be sure that, in the aggregate, the rules balance the public interest of all stakeholders against the interests and expertise of the professionals who work within state higher education systems.

Based on the information from our case studies and on national data-reporting performance, we reached several conclusions:

- Actors' perceptions about rules do predict performance. States that are dissatisfied with the performance of their higher education systems should change the rules that influence relevant behaviors.
- States that lack some type of an effective interface agency operating between higher education and state government are at a significant disadvantage in achieving high performance on undergraduate indicators, regardless of effort.
- States can improve performance by deciding on a small number of public priorities for higher education and then pursuing them though intentional steering strategies that use market forces and accountability for learning outcomes to encourage institutional responsiveness and efficiency.
- Private institutions should be included in strategies for attaining public priorities.
- A state's need-based student assistance should offset tuition charges in public institutions for the neediest students.
- Access and student success strategies should be planned and coordinated by a statewide agency to ensure that competition for the best students does

not overshadow concern for those who have the potential to become competent and productive citizens if they are provided with adequate support.

- Resource allocation strategies should target desired performance outcomes
  and include the private sector whenever possible.
- Aspirations for research excellence should not be funded through strategies that place most undergraduates in low-cost institutions that lack the
  resources to respond effectively to these students.

We do not mean to suggest that rules are the only—or even the most important—variables that influence performance. Higher education literature
confirms that other factors, such as wealth and state characteristics, have a
major impact as well. But rules do define the arenas in which behaviors produce outcomes. They therefore offer an important and accessible mechanism
through which policymakers can influence performance over time.

A state's ability to change rules in ways that increase the probability of
achieving outcomes consistent with the public interest depends upon where
the authority for establishing new rules resides. Policymakers and higher education leaders are most effective if they can instigate changes that support the
development of goals and priorities at the state level. The capacity to make
state-level change is essential for state leaders, because some rules of the game
must transcend the interests and missions of individual institutions, segments, or sectors. States enhance performance and efficiency by adopting rules
in ways that balance the influence of both professional and public interests
and that provide for meaningful input from a wide range of stakeholders.

Appendix

Rules Observed, Including Those Not Associated with Differences in Performance

---

RULES IN USE

Design and Governance

Statewide Planning

The overall structure of higher education in the state was intentionally designed
through a process involving a broad and representative group of stakeholders.
The state has a process intended to ensure that any new institution will respond to
demographic or programmatic needs.

Statewide Coordination and Regulation

An agency of the state has planning and coordinating authority for all public higher
education.
An agency of the state has regulatory authority for all public higher education.
An agency of the state has the authority to approve new academic programs when
cost or duplication could be a concern.
An agency of the state has the authority to approve new academic programs when a
change in institutional mission could be a concern.
Less-selective public institutions are subject to greater regulatory authority.
Most two- and four-year public IHEs, either statewide or in regional groupings,
share a common governing board.
The state has a coordinated approach to providing distance education.

Self-Governing Public IHEs

Each IHE has its own governing board with responsibility to appoint a CEO.
The legal status of some IHEs constrains the policy options of elected and appointed
officials.

Use of the Private Sector

Independent IHEs have a formally defined role in serving the state's higher education
needs.
Independent IHEs enroll 19% or more of the state's total enrollment.

Extensive Two-Year Colleges

Most geographic regions of the state have an IHE within commuting distance.
Half or more of all undergraduates are enrolled in two-year colleges.

State Leadership

Defined Goals and Priorities

State goals for higher education are explicitly identified and periodically reviewed.
The executive branch (e.g., governor or staff, secretary of education or staff, state
coordinating agency) sets forth a policy agenda for higher education.
Elected policy officials and educational leaders work together to plan and establish
priorities for higher education.
Leaders from business and industry are routinely involved in setting or influencing
state priorities.
IHEs must have a strategic plan in place as a condition for receiving state funding.

Use of Market Forces and Accountability

The state has used market forces as an intentional strategy to encourage responsiveness and efficiency.
IHEs are publicly accountable for their performance in relation to state goals and
priorities, according to some established format.

Incentives, Deregulation, and Operational Flexibility

The state has used deregulation as an intentional strategy to encourage responsiveness and efficiency.
Colleges and universities have incentives for paying attention to state goals and
priorities.

Information

Data Gathering

One or more state-managed databases contain the information necessary for planning and evaluating higher education services.
Data definitions are standardized across the state, so that IHE data and state agency
data are consistent.
The database(s) include a student unit record system that enables users to track
enrollments and completions.
A statewide board or agency is the primary provider of higher education information
to state officials and lawmakers.

Data for Decision Making

A statewide board or agency is assigned the responsibility of analyzing data and making recommendations to the executive and legislative branches of government.

There is an established procedure or forum to bring major stakeholders together to review information on IHE performance.

Access and Achievement

Open-Access Community Colleges

A system of locally responsive community colleges provides open access to state residents.

Community colleges work closely with the public schools to help students make the transition to college.

Transfer between two- and four-year IHEs is governed primarily by statewide policies that enforce common standards.

Need-Based Student Aid

State grants are awarded on the basis of need to provide eligible students with most, if not all, of the tuition and/or fees at a public institution.

State grants are awarded on the basis of need to provide eligible students with tuition assistance at private institutions.

Non-traditional-age IHE students are eligible for student aid comparable to their traditional-age counterparts.

Merit-Based Rewards and Assistance

State policies reward student achievement.

Non-need-based awards pay most, if not all, tuition charges at public institutions for students who meet prescribed academic achievement standards.

State-Coordinated Access Programs

The state has a coordinated program for improving access to higher education for residents facing economic or educational disadvantages.

High School Graduation Exam

The state uses a standardized examination to determine whether a student graduates from high school.

Measuring College Learning Outcomes

The state uses standardized methods for measuring college student learning outcomes in at least some subjects.

Convening K–16 Actors

There are formal, functioning arrangements for convening the entire range of K–16 actors to encourage collaboration on such student success issues as teacher education, college readiness, and student transition.

Fiscal Policies

State Budget Submission Procedures

A statewide higher education board or agency reviews and/or consolidates IHE budget requests and provides advice to the governor and the legislature.

Public four-year institutions submit individual or segmental budget requests directly to a central agency of state government.

Public two-year institutions submit individual or segmental budget requests directly to a central agency of state government.

State Fiscal Support for Private Colleges

Independent colleges receive direct state operating support.

Private IHEs are eligible to receive public funds for capital improvements.

Authority to Set Tuition and Fees

Tuition and fee levels are essentially determined through negotiations between policy officials and higher education leaders.

All four-year IHE governing boards have the authority to raise tuition or fees.

Basis for Determining State Appropriations

Operating appropriations for four-year public institutions are based primarily on enrollment levels.

State operating appropriations are essentially determined through negotiations between policy officials and higher education leaders.

Formal state-level fiscal regulation is focused more on how funds are expended than on what outcomes are accomplished.

Performance on specified indicators related to state goals is one criterion used to determine state funding for institutions.

Reliance on Low-Tuition Two-Year Colleges

Two-year college tuition and/or fees are less than half that of the lowest-cost four-year IHE.

Research and Development

State Incentive Grants for Research and Labor Force Training

State incentive grants are offered to improve labor force training.

State incentive grants are offered to improve university research in selected areas.

State Funds for Research Facilities in Private Institutions

Private universities are eligible to receive state funds for improving their research facilities.

Public Institution Endowment and Development Boards

Public institutions are authorized to create endowment and development boards separate from the trustees and to invest private funds according to the best judgment of such boards.

UNUSED RULES IN EXISTING CATEGORIES AND SUBTHEMES

IHEs have the operational freedom to design their own strategies for responding to state goals and priorities.

State plans and strategies can influence actual system design.

IHEs determine the performance information that is publicly available.

There are attempts to tie funding to programs that are considered important to economic development.

There is state-level coordination of IHEs and other agencies (e.g., workforce and labor agencies) with regard to state economic development policy.

There is a statewide plan for aligning academic research and development with industry needs.

There is a statewide plan for aligning degree and certificate production with industry needs.

References

Achieve. 2006. *Closing the expectations gap 2006: An annual 50-state progress report on the alignment of high school policies with the demands of college and work* (February). Washington, DC: Achieve.

Alexander, K. 2006. The states' failure to support higher education. *Chronicle of Higher Education* 53 (43): B16.

Beardsley, M. 2006. NJ Commission on Higher Education appoints new executive director and adds two new members. News release, February 24. Commission on Higher Education, Trenton, NJ.

Berdahl, R. O. 1971. *Statewide coordination of higher education.* Washington, DC: American Council on Education.

Bowes, S. G. 1997. New Mexico's 2-year colleges: A diverse enterprise. *Community College Journal of Research and Practice* 21:103–19.

Burke, J. C. 2005. The many faces of accountability. In *Achieving accountability in higher education: Balancing public, academic, and market demand,* ed. J. C. Burke, 1–24. San Francisco: Jossey-Bass.

Burke, J. C. and associates. 2002. *Funding public colleges and universities for performance: Popularity, problems, and prospects.* Albany, NY: Rockefeller Institute Press.

Burke, J. C., and S. Modarresi. 2000. To keep or not to keep performance funding: Signals from stockholders. *Journal of Higher Education* 71 (4): 432–53.

California Community Colleges. 2004. *An aspiration for excellence: A review of the System Office for the California Community Colleges* (review report). Sacramento: California Community Colleges.

California Postsecondary Education Commission. 2004. *University eligibility study for the class of 2003.* Sacramento: California Postsecondary Education Commission.

———. 2006. *Keeping college affordable in California: Draft report of the special panel on affordability* (December). Sacramento: California Postsecondary Education Commission.

Callan, P. M., and J. E. Finney, eds. 1997. *Public and private financing of higher education: Shaping public policy for the future.* Phoenix: American Council on Education / Oryx Press.

Chronicle of Higher Education Almanac. 2002. Special issue, *Chronicle of Higher Education* 47 (1).

Citizens Committee for Higher Education in New Jersey. 1966. *A call to action.* Princeton: Citizens Committee for Higher Education in New Jersey.

City University of New York. 2000. *Master plan 2000–2004.* New York: City University of New York.

———. 2004. *Master plan 2004–2008.* New York: City University of New York.

———. 2006. *2007–2008 budget request.* New York: City University of New York.

Clark, B. R. 1983. *The higher education system: Academic organization in cross-national perspective.* Berkeley: University of California Press.

Clark, B. S. 1998. *Political economy: A comparative approach.* 2nd ed. Westport, CT: Praeger.

Cohen, M. D., J. G. March, and J. P. Olsen. 1972. A garbage can model of organizational choice. *Administrative Science Quarterly* 17:1–25.

Coleman, H. A., J. W. Hughes, and D. Kehler. 2001. *Fiscal responsibility.* New Brunswick: Fund for New Jersey.

College Board. 2005. *Trends in college pricing: 2005.* Washington, DC: College Board.

Commission on Independent Colleges and Universities. 2004. *Master plan independent higher education in New York State 2004–2012.* Albany, NY: Commission on Independent Colleges and Universities.

Corzine, J. S. 2006. *Fiscal year 2007 budget in brief.* Trenton, NJ: Office of Management and Budget, New Jersey Department of the Treasury.

Dill, D. D. 1997. Higher education markets and public policy. *Higher Education Policy* 10 (3/4): 167–85.

Easton, D. 1953. *The political system: An inquiry into the state of political science.* New York: Alfred A. Knopf.

Farbman, J. C. 2005. NJ STARS: Freshmen enrollment jumps 50 percent statewide. News release, December 1. New Jersey Council of County Colleges, Trenton.

Fineman, E. 2006. Commission announces funding to help establish nanotech facility at Rutgers University. News release, May 19. Commission on Science and Technology, Trenton, NJ.

Glenny, L.A. 1959. *Autonomy of public colleges: The challenge of coordination.* New York: McGraw-Hill.

Glenny, L. A., and T. Dalglish. 1973. *Public universities, state agencies and the law: Constitutional autonomy in decline.* Berkeley: Univerity of California Center For Research and Development in Higher Education.

Grindle, M. S. 1996. *Challenging the state: Crisis and innovation in Latin America and Africa.* New York: Cambridge University Press.

Hauptman, A. M. 1997. Financing American higher education in the 1990s. In *ASHE reader on finance in higher education,* ed. J. L. Yeager, G. M. Nelson, E. A. Potter, J. C. Weidman, and T. G. Zullo. 2nd ed. Boston: Pearson Custom Publishing.

Hayward, G. C., D. P. Jones, A. C. J. McGuinness, A. Timar, and N. Shulock. 2004. *Ensuring access with quality to California's community colleges.* National Center Report No. 04–3. San Jose, CA: National Center for Public Policy and Higher Education.

Hearn, J. C., and C. P. Griswold. 1994. State-level centralization and policy innovation in U.S. postsecondary education. *Educational Evaluation and Policy Analysis* 16 (2): 161–90.

Hearn, J. C., C. P. Griswold, and G. Marine. 1996. Region, resources, and reason: A contextual analysis of state tuition and student aid policies. *Research in Higher Education* 37 (1): 241–78.

Heck, R. H. 2004. *Studying educational and social policy: Theoretical concepts and research methods.* Mahwah, NJ: Lawrence Erlbaum Associates.

Heller, D. 1999. The effects of tuition and state financial aid on public college enrollment. *Review of Higher Education* 23 (1): 65–89.

Higher Education Restructuring Act of 1994, Public Law 1994, c. 48. *New Jersey statutes annotated* § 18A:3B-1 et seq.

Hossler, D., J. P. Lund, J. Ramin, S. Westfall, and S. Irish. 1997. State funding for higher education. *Journal of Higher Education* 69 (2): 173.

Hughes, J. W., and J. J. Seneca. 2005. *An economy at risk: The imperatives for a science and technology policy for New Jersey.* Report prepared for the New Jersey Commission on Science and Technology. http://policy.rutgers.edu/reports/other/SciTech_Report.pdf (accessed May 7, 2006).

Johnson, M. 2005. *Remarks to the New Jersey Commission on Higher Education.* State of New Jersey Commision on Higher Education. www.state.nj.us/higher education/GEARUPRemarksMJohnson.htm (accessed June 6, 2006).

Joint Committee to Develop a Master Plan for Education. 2002. *The California master plan for education.* Sacramento: California Legislature Joint Committee.

Jones, D. 2006. *Remaining competitive in a global economy: An outsider's perspective on the higher education issues facing California.* Sacramento, CA: National Center For Higher Education Management Systems.

Kelly, P. J., and D. P. Jones. 2005. *A new look at the institutional component of higher education finance: A guide for evaluating performance relative to financial resources.* Boulder, CO: National Center for Higher Education Management Systems.

Kent, R., ed. 2009. *Las políticas de educación superior en México durante la modernización: Un análisis regional.* Mexico City: ANUIES.

Kingdon, J. W. 1984. *Agendas, alternatives, and public policies.* Glenview, IL: Scott, Foresman.

Legislative Analyst's Office. 2003. *CPEC: A review of its mission and responsibilities* (January). Sacramento, CA: Legislative Analyst's Office.

———. 2005. *A primer: Funding higher education.* Sacramento, CA: Legislative Analyst's Office.

Lowry, R. C. 2001. Governmental structure, trustee selection, and public university prices and spending. *American Journal of Political Science* 45 (4): 845–61.

MacTaggert, T. J. 1998. *Seeking excellence through independence: Liberating colleges and universities from excessive regulation.* San Francisco: Jossey-Bass.

Mann, A. R., and M. E. Forsberg. 2006. *Flunking out: New Jersey's support for higher education falls short.* Trenton: New Jersey Policy Perspective.

Marcus, L. R. 1997. Restructuring state higher education governance patterns. *Review of Higher Education* 20 (4): 399–418.

Martinez, M. 2004. *Postsecondary participation and state policy: Meeting the future demand.* Herndon, VA: Stylus Publishing.

Martinez, M., J. Farias, and E. Arellano. 2002. State higher education report cards: What's in a grade? *Review of Higher Education* 26 (1): 1–18.

Mayor's Advisory Task Force on the City University of New York. 1999. *The City University of New York: An institution adrift* (June). New York: Office of the Mayor.

McGuinness, A. C., R. M. Epper, and S. Arrendondo. 1994. *State postsecondary education structures handbook.* Denver: Education Commission of the States.

McLendon, M. K. 2003. State governance reform of higher education. In *Higher education: Handbook of theory and research,* vol. 18, ed. J. C. Smart and W. G. Tierney, 57–143. Dordrecht, Netherlands: Kluwer Academic Publishers.

McLendon, M. K., D. Heller, and S. Young. 2001. State postsecondary policy innovation: Politics, competition, and interstate migration of policy ideas. Paper presented at the annual meeting of the Midwest Political Science Association, Illinois.

McNichol, D. 2006. Bond debt in N.J. grows: At $33B owed, state solidifies no. 3 rank. *Trenton Times,* May 9, A1.

Miles, M. B., and A. M. Huberman. 1994. *Qualitative data analysis: An expanded sourcebook.* Thousand Oaks, CA: Sage Publications.

Millet. J. D. 1984. *Conflict in higher education: State government coordination versus institutional independence.* San Francisco: Jossey-Bass.

Moos, M. C., and F. E. Rourke. 1959. *The campus and the state.* Baltimore: John Hopkins University Press.

Mortenson, T. 1999. *The paradox of higher education opportunity in New Mexico.* Submitted to the New Mexico Legislative Finance Committee, Santa Fe, NM.

National Association of State Student Grant and Aid Programs. 2005. *36th annual survey report on state-sponsored student financial aid: 2004–2005 academic year.* National Association of State Student Grant and Aid Programs. www.nass gap.org/viewrepository.aspx?categoryID=228#document_422 (accessed June 7, 2006).

National Center for Higher Education Management Systems (NCHEMS). 1999a. *An assessment of the New Mexico Commission on Higher Education* (December). Boulder, CO: National Center for Higher Education Management Systems.

———. 1999b. *An assessment of New Mexico higher education* (November). Boulder, CO: National Center for Higher Education Management Systems.

National Center for Public Policy and Higher Education (NCPPHE). 2000a. College opportunity varies greatly by state: New report card grades states on higher education performance. News release, November 30. http://measuringup.highereducation.org/newsroom/nationalpressdir.cfm?myyear=2000.

———. 2000b. *Measuring up 2000: The state-by-state report card for higher education.* San Jose, CA: National Center for Public Policy and Higher Education.

————. 2002. *Measuring up 2002: The state-by-state report card for higher education.* San Jose, CA: National Center for Public Policy and Higher Education.

————. 2003. *Purposes, policies, performance: Higher education and the fulfillment of a state's public agenda.* San Jose, CA: National Center for Public Policy and Higher Education.

————. 2004. *Measuring up 2004: The state-by-state report card for higher education.* San Jose, CA: National Center for Public Policy and Higher Education.

————. 2006a. *Measuring up 2006: The state-by-state report card for higher education.* San Jose, CA: National Center for Public Policy and Higher Education. Also available online at http://measuringup.highereducation.org/.

————. 2006b. *Measuring up 2006: The state report card on higher education–New Jersey.* San Jose, CA: National Center for Public Policy and Higher Education.

Nelson, J. 2006. Credit trends in higher education: U.S. and New Jersey. Paper presented at the meeting of the New Jersey Educational Facilities Authority, New Jersey.

New Jersey Commission on Higher Education. 2004. *New Jersey's colleges and universities' 7th annual systemwide accountability report.* Trenton: New Jersey Commission on Higher Education.

————. 2005. *Update 2005: A blueprint for excellence; New Jersey's long-range plan for higher education.* Trenton: New Jersey Commission on Higher Education.

New Jersey Commission on Higher Education and New Jersey Presidents' Council. 1999. *The five-year assessment of higher education restructuring* (July). Trenton: New Jersey Commission on Higher Education.

New Jersey Commission on Science and Technology. 2006. *Mission statement.* New Jersey Commission on Science and Technology. www.state.nj.us/scitech/about/ (accessed July 10, 2006).

New Jersey Council of County Colleges. 2005. *Welcome to the board: A manual for community college trustees.* Trenton: New Jersey Council of County Colleges.

New Jersey Educational Facilities Authority. 2005. *Financial statements and supplemental financial information* (December 31). Princeton: New Jersey Educational Facilities Authority.

New Jersey Higher Education Student Assistance Authority. 2005. *2004 Annual report.* Trenton: New Jersey Higher Education Student Assistance Authority.

New Jersey Institute of Technology Act of 1995. *New Jersey statutes annotated* §§ 18A:64E-12 to 18A:64E-32.

New Jersey Student Tuition Assistance Reward Scholarship II (NJ STARS II) Program Act. *New Jersey statutes annotated* §§ 18A:71B-86.1 to 18A:71B-86.7.

New Mexico Commission on Higher Education (NMCHE). 1999a. *The condition of higher education in New Mexico.* Santa Fe: New Mexico Commission on Higher Education.

————. 1999b. *The roles and responsibilities of the New Mexico Commission on Higher Education: A report by the NMCHE* (June). Santa Fe: New Mexico Commission on Higher Education.

———. 2000. *The condition of higher education in New Mexico*. Santa Fe: New Mexico Commission on Higher Education.

———. 2001. *The condition of higher education in New Mexico*. Santa Fe: New Mexico Commission on Higher Education.

———. 2002. *The condition of higher education in New Mexico*. Santa Fe: New Mexico Commission on Higher Education.

———. 2003. *The condition of higher education in New Mexico*. Santa Fe: New Mexico Commission on Higher Education.

———. 2004. *The condition of higher education in New Mexico*. Santa Fe: New Mexico Commission on Higher Education.

———. 2005. *The condition of higher education in New Mexico*. Santa Fe: New Mexico Commission on Higher Education.

New Mexico Commission on Higher Education and New Mexico Public Education Department (NMCHE & NMPED). 2000. *Teacher supply and demand* (September). Santa Fe: New Mexico Commission on Higher Education and New Mexico State Department of Education.

New Mexico Higher Education Department (NMHED). 2006a. *The condition of higher education in New Mexico*. Santa Fe: New Mexico Higher Education Department.

———. 2006b. *Lottery program projections*. Santa Fe: New Mexico Higher Education Department.

———. 2006c. *Update on higher education facilities index*. Santa Fe: New Mexico Higher Education Department.

New York State Commission on Higher Education. 2007. *A preliminary report of findings and recommendations: Executive summary* (December). www.hecommission.state.ny.us.

New York State Education Department. 2007. Liberty Partnerships Program. www.highered.nysed.gov/kiap/PCPPU/lpp/home1.htm.

New York State Higher Education Services Corporation. 2006. *Surpassing Boundaries: 2005–2006 Annual Report*. Albany, NY: Higher Education Services Corporation.

North, D. C. 1990. *Institutions, institutional change, and economic performance*. New York: Cambridge University Press.

Ostrom, E. 1999. Institutional rational choice: An assessment of the institutional analysis and development framework. In Sabatier 1999, 35–78.

Ostrom, E., R. Gardner, and J. Walker. 1994. *Rules, games, and common pool resources*. Ann Arbor: Univeresity of Michigan Press.

Palmer, J. C., ed. 2005. Grapevine. www.grapevine.ilstu.edu/ (accessed January 4, 2005).

Poughkeepsie Journal. 2007. Change at top key for SUNY. March 20.

QSR International. 2002. N6 (NUD*IST 6). Doncaster, Victoria, Australia: QSR International.

QuickFacts. http://quickfacts.census.gov/qfd/index.html (for South Dakota, accessed 2004; for New Mexico, accessed 2007).

Richardson, R. C., K. Reeves-Bracco, P. M. Callan, and J. E. Finney. 1999. *Designing state higher education systems for a new century*. Phoenix, AZ: American Council on Education / Oryx Press.

Robst, J. 2001. Cost efficiency in public higher educational institutions. *Journal of Higher Education* 72 (6): 730–51.

Sabatier, P. A. 1999. *Theories of the policy process*. Boulder, CO: Westview Press.

Schick, E. B., R. I. Novak, J. A. Norton, and H. G. Elam. 1992. *Shared visions of public higher education governance: Structures and leadership that work*. Washington, DC: American Association of State Colleges and Universities.

Schlager, E. 1995. Policymaking and collective action: Defining coalitions within the ACF. *Policy Sciences* 28:243–70.

Shulock, N. 2002. *California community colleges' leadership challenge: A view from the field*. Sacramento: Institute for Higher Education Leadership and Policy, California State University.

Shulock, N., and C. Moore. 2002. *An accountability framework for California higher education: Informing public policy and improving outcomes* (policy issue report). Sacramento: California State University–Sacramento.

———. 2004. *Diminishing access to the baccalaureate through transfer: The impact of state policies and implications for California* (policy issue report). Sacramento: California State University–Sacramento.

Smalling, T. R. 2006. Inextricably linked: Institutional decision-making and rules; Shared governance at a multi-campus state higher education system. PhD diss., New York University.

South Dakota Board of Regents. www.sdbor.edu. Annual fact books from 1995 to the present available online.

———. 2003. *Opportunities for South Dakota* (June). Pierre: South Dakota Board of Regents.

———. 2004. *Performance funding: Allocation for FY '05 update* (May). Pierre: South Dakota Board of Regents.

———. 2005a. *Accountability report*. Pierre: South Dakota Board of Regents.

———. 2005b. *Management report: SDSU*. Pierre: South Dakota Board of Regents.

———. 2005c. *Resource compact: Annual adjustment and performance funding, FY06*. Pierre: South Dakota Board of Regents.

St. John, E. P., G. D. Musoba, and A. B. Simmons. 2003. Keeping the promise: The impact of Indiana's Twenty-first Century Scholars Program. *Review of Higher Education* 27 (1): 103–23.

State University of New York. 1995. *Rethinking SUNY*. Albany: State University of New York.

———. 2004a. *Master Plan 2004–2008*. Albany: State University of New York.

———. 2004b. *Mission Review*. www.suny.edu/provost/missionreview.cfm (accessed October 18, 2004).

Stonecash, J. M., ed. 2001. *Governing New York State*. 4th ed. Albany: State University of New York Press.

Tax Foundation. 2006. *State and local property tax collections per capita by state, fiscal year 2004.* www.taxfoundation.org/taxdata/show/251.html (accessed May 20, 2006).

University of California Office of the President. 2006. *2007–2008 budget for state capital improvements* (November). Oakland: University of California.

University of Medicine and Dentistry of New Jersey. 2005. *Self-study report: Submitted to the Middles States Commission on Higher Education* (February). Newark: University of Medicine and Dentistry of New Jersey.

University of the State of New York. 2005. *The Board of Regents statewide plan for higher education.* Albany: Office of Higher Education, New York State Education Department.

U.S. Census Bureau. 1990. *General population and housing characteristics: 1990, New Jersey.* http://factfinder.census.gov/servlet/QTTable?_bm=n&_lang=en&qr _name=DEC_1990_STF1_DP1&ds_name=DEC_1990_STF1_&geo_id=04000 US34 (accessed May 14, 2006).

———. 2005. *2005 American community survey: New Jersey.* http://factfinder. census.gov/servlet/ACSSAFFFacts?_event=Search&_lang=en&_sse=on&geo _id=04000US34&_state=04000US34 (accessed May 14, 2006).

Volkwein, J. F. 1989. Changes in quality among public universities. *Journal of Higher Education* 60 (2): 136–51.

Western Interstate Commission for Higher Education (WICHE). 2003. *Knocking at the college door: Projections of high school graduates by state and race/ethnicity, 1988–2018.* Boulder, CO: Western Interstate Commission for Higher Education.

Williams, G. L. 1995. The marketization of higher education reforms and potential reforms in higher education finance. In *Emerging patterns of social demand and university reform: Through a glass darkly,* ed. D.D. Dill and B. Sporn, 170–71. Tarrytown, NY: Elsevier Science.

Yovnello, N., and J. Erickson. 2006. *Statement to Assembly Higher Education Committee.* Edison: Council of New Jersey State College Locals, AFT, AFL-CIO.

Zahariadis, N. 1999. Garbage can model. In Sabatier 1999, 73–93.

Index